PRO SE PRISONER:
GUIDE TO BUILD WEALTH

Credit & Investing

C.A. Knuckles

Freebird Publishers

Box 541, North Dighton, MA 02764

Info@FreebirdPublishers.com

www.FreebirdPublishers.com

All Freebird Publishers titles, imprints, and distributed lines are available at special quantity discounts for bulk purchases for sales promotions, premiums, fundraising, educational, or institutional use.

ISBN: 978-1-952159-45-9

Printed in the United States of America

DEDICATION

To those lost in the cycle of poverty, incarceration, and poverty-stricken ghettos. Behind me is a strong woman who has pushed me to do great things. I will never forget the role you played in my success. I love you, and thank you!

ACKNOWLEDGEMENT

Thanks to Freebird Publishers for their support. I want to extend my appreciation to all the people who helped with research for this book series. I am grateful to all the prisoners who became pro se prisoners by purchasing my books in the Pro Se Prisoners: Guide to Build Wealth series. I sincerely thank you for your continued support, and I will keep providing knowledge.

Thank you. The Forgotten Voices!

CONTENTS

CREDIT FUNDAMENTALS TO BUILD WEALTH

INVESTING FOR WEALTH BUILDING

UNCHAINED MIND:
The Case for Financial Literacy for Prisoners

Can I ask a question? If 65% of Americans have under $1000 in savings, 67% of sports players go broke, and 57% of marriage problems are because of financial problems, how can we expect society to help prisoners transition back into society if society can't even manage their own finances? Take a moment and think. You will soon see that the prison system's problems start and end with finances. Prison promised me rehabilitation, but what does that mean if we don't teach prisoners financial literacy? The greatest threat to the safety of society is releasing a financially illiterate prisoner! 85% chance of re-entering prison in 1-3 years upon release. Knowing this and being in prison since I was 15 years old (32 years old now). I took this to heart and set out to change this.

My goal is to teach every prisoner how to build wealth using financial literacy tools. Prison didn't offer business classes, wealth building, credit courses, real estate investing, stock investing, or even the bare minimum of managing money in your prison account. Why is this? I figured out that it's financially counterproductive for DOC to teach you about financial literacy if their business model is to make money from you coming back and forth to prison.

You must understand how the prison system works – as a business, first change it as best you can. DOC underestimates prisoners: they look at us as incapable of seeing this. Financial literacy is needed in prison because it teaches prisoners tools that are transferable to society upon release and while they are still in prison. Money is a complex subject that's not taught in the prison system in America. Some of our only experience with it is in the streets selling drugs. Our lack of financial knowledge is deeply linked to our environment.

Look around any prison, and you will see all types of people lost, others conducting business, others reading the newspaper. As I sit in prison, I see an opportunity, with the added bonus of time to prepare, study, and take action. My case for financial literacy led me to my passion, helping and creating opportunities for prisoners, through my "Pro se Prisoner" books, articles, workbooks, and entrepreneur classes, which teach prisoners about financial literacy, which is the ability to understand and effectively use various financial skills, including personal financial management, budgeting, and investing. This gives prisoners a mental plan for financial success, which I call "self-help business." Prison is a paradox: Amid cruel punishment, there is also self-rehabilitation by prisoners determined to change. As a prisoner, you come to prison with nothing; my goal is to show DOC that prisoners shouldn't leave prison the same way they came in. If the protection of public safety is the goal, then financial literacy should be the plan to achieve that goal. Prisoners should know that you were kept in your cells to stop their thinking, so you must instead use it to expand it. What you don't understand, you should confront. Create financial knowledge by confronting the fact that you don't know anything about it. One book can open a door that's encased in a closed mind. Mentally restricted from pursuing proper education, we allow our minds to be blocked off from financial literacy.

Our fight for justice in courts and educational freedom is also held up because of constant struggles to be treated fairly. So instead of complaining, I chose to do something about it that not only helps me see my purpose but also helps others like me who sit in prison closed off from the real world who also have no clue how to provide for their families other than sell drugs, rob, or kill. As I'm writing this, it's nine people in the dayroom, and it's 8:55 am; that means 80% of my tier is asleep in their cells, the other 15% at a prison-related job. My goal is to show that 95% of what the value of our time here is—not distracted by the bills, housing, and food that most people fight to obtain in the real world. My choice to speak for prisoners is my choice because, for too long, others have spoken for us. My goal is to help 1 of 3 Americans who have criminal records. If you think that just locking everybody up for long periods of time, then the USA should be the safest country in the world! Prisons haven't kept America safe. It has made certain communities that were already deprived of financial means worse. As prisoners, we must not let our story end with coming to prison but rather let it start now so we can "Unchain" our minds to pursue real knowledge about wealth and financial literacy before it's too late.

More of us need to write to prison officials and try to get financial literacy classes in our prisons. The case for it outweighs any other reason or justification they have for not having it. For public safety purposes, financially literate prisoners coming back into society is better for public safety than releasing a financially illiterate prisoner back into society. Because one way or another, prisoners return to the outside community. This book gives you the open door to financial knowledge; take it and use it to take action in your lives. But most importantly, allow it to "Unchain Your Mind."

"Plot, Plan & Execute"
Pro se Prisoner

C.A. Knuckles

CREDIT FUNDAMENTALS TO BUILD WEALTH

BASIC UNDERSTANDING

Most people's understanding of credit is wrong. Credit is nothing more than the intent to pay back the money later. If you don't pay back the agreed-upon amount when it's due, you lose credibility with lenders, affecting your credit score. Building wealth is the goal; a good credit score will allow you to borrow money to finance your future.

Let's understand your score before we get into building credit for wealth. We are putting you in control of your credit before it controls your life.

Credit Score Chart

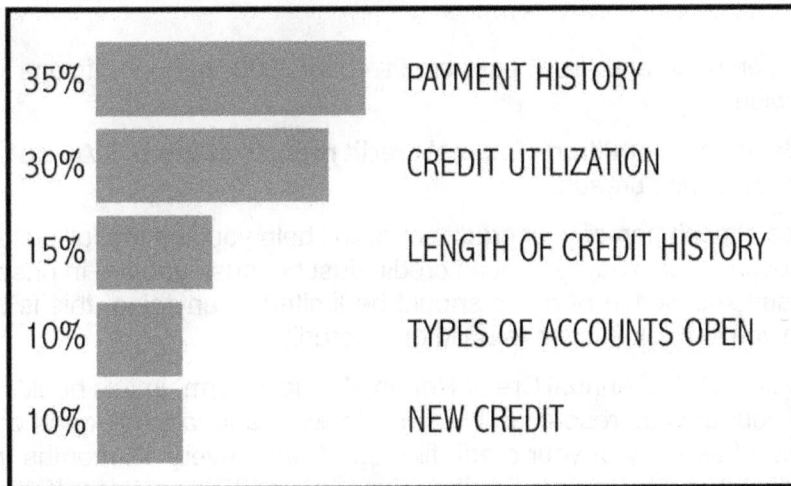

Percentage	Category
35%	PAYMENT HISTORY
30%	CREDIT UTILIZATION
15%	LENGTH OF CREDIT HISTORY
10%	TYPES OF ACCOUNTS OPEN
10%	NEW CREDIT

35% PAYMENT HISTORY: Basically, it means paying your bills. This accounts for the majority of your credit score.

30% UTILIZATION: The amount borrowed vs. the available amount you can borrow.

15% AGE OF ACCOUNTS: Every bureau averages the age of your account. The older the account, the more credibility you will have on file. Never close accounts in good standing. This can affect your utilization rate because it lowers the amount of credit available, raising it.

10% CREDIT MIX: These include the three types of accounts the credit bureau uses to calculate your score. 1 Open accounts. 2 Revolving accounts. 3 Installment Accounts. Open accounts mean accounts that need to be paid off in full at the end of each month. Revolving accounts are accounts with no set payment, and you can borrow against them. Installment accounts have set monthly payments.

10% NEW CREDIT AND INQUIRIES: Never have excessive inquiries in a short period because this will show banks you are desperate. These inquiries only affect your credit score for 24 months or two years, so limit the number of lines of credit you apply for.

These (%) above show you the full definition of each credit area important to your overall credit health.

Credit card companies, including banks, report to three (3) credit bureaus.

1. Experian
2. Equifax
3. TransUnion

Under Federal law, all three (3) credit bureaus must give you one free credit report a year. Remember – these are just data sources. Their job is only to provide data; they make money by selling your information to any and all creditors.

Experian: Keeps personal and business credit on file. Over 240 million citizens' files are held with Experian.

Equifax: Keeps personal and business credit—over 800 million citizens and 93 million businesses worldwide.

TransUnion holds up to 200 million citizens' credit reports in the U.S.A., but it is the smallest of the major three (3) credit bureaus.

Knowing the basics of each part of your credit score will help you see the full picture of your credit profile along with every possible way to build credit. Just because you are in prison doesn't mean you understand, and knowledge of credit should be limited. If anything, this is the time to seek this knowledge so you can take action to build great credit.

The first step is to submit the "Annual Credit Report Request Form" in this book's "Index" section. You can also get your outside resources by going to www.annualcreditreport.com. By law, you have a right to get a free copy of your credit file report once every 12 months from each of the three main credit reporting companies: Equifax, Experion, and TransUnion. If you can't, by some chance, copy the form from the book, put all the required information on a blank sheet of paper, and send it to:

Annual Credit Report Service
P.O. Box 105281
Atlanta, GA 30348-5281

Make sure you start with this to check your history!

Although those are the three (3) major credit bureaus, there are other third-party credit bureaus that you should also be aware of.

Lexis Nexus: If you're in prison, you know these people personally because this is how you do legal research for your case. But it's a private entity with one of the world's largest databases of private information. They sell your data and verify it for other credit agencies.

Innovis: Their focus is on fraud protection and prevention. Check records once a year, plus it's free.

Sage Stream is another credit reporting agency that provides consumer reports and scores, usually for people between 18 and 34.

Chex System: Any information relating to bad checks written, this company keeps this information, which can last for up to 5 years.

Therefore, these companies together help credit bureaus verify negative accounts. Unfortunately, these companies hold your data and sell it to others. Okay, now the part where you can get control of your data from these companies. Lexis Nexis allows you to opt out and freeze your report. To do so, go to http://www.lexisnexus.com/oo.jsp, login, and opt-out. Make sure to give it at least 30 days to make sure it's frozen. The same thing can be done with Sage Stream, but you must send them a letter to freeze your report. Make sure to include the following necessary information:

1. First and Last Name
2. Social Security Number (copy of card)
3. Date of Birth
4. Primary Phone Number
5. Address Including Zip Code
6. Two Forms of Identification (Driver's License or State Issued Identification Card, recent cable or phone statement with address)
7. Copy of Birth Certificate

Sage Stream
Phone: 888-395-0277
Web: www.sagestreamllc.com
Address: Sage Stream, LLC Consumer Office
P.O. Box 503793
San Diego, CA 92150
Fax: 959-312-6275

The same rules apply to all others that hold your date.

Innovis Consumer Assistance
P.O. Box 26
Pittsburg, PA 15230-0026

Many companies sell your data to third parties, so the basic idea is to understand your rights so you can stop them. We aim to build wealth, and regaining credit control is the first step in that process. To see the full list, check out www.stopdatamoving.me. Also, use the above addresses to ask for a copy of your file from them. (Check the resource section for more information and forms.)

Credit bureaus don't expect the average consumer to know the laws they must obey. These include the Fair Credit Reporting Act (FCRA): This law gives you the power to get items removed from your report if it's inaccurate, incomplete, or unverifiable. See the "Resource Section" to get a list of sources on how to get your free credit report from all three credit bureaus. Lastly, the only scores or ratings that matter are FICO® scores because these are the most widely used scores that the Fair Isaac Corporation created. This is your basic understanding of credit; now, let's move on to finding and building credit so you can start utilizing it to buy assets and get out of debt.

BUILDING PERSONAL CREDIT

Many in your position and mine (prison) think that we can't build credit, get credit cards, loans, or a 720-credit score. Building credit from prison is easy and will open doors that have never opened in your life. How can you get ahead upon release if you have no credit? Having no credit is like having bad credit. I'm not going to fill your head with all the basic bull crap about this is good; this is bad. We will start our journey fast and keep moving fast.

First, let's get to the 8 easy steps behind building credit for yourself.

1. Get your free credit report (If you have credit)
2. Check for errors
3. Dispute Errors (If you have credit)
4. Pay late or past due accounts (If you have credit)
5. Increase credit limits (If you have credit cards)
6. Pay off high-interest accounts first (If you have credit cards)
7. Open a new credit card (If you have credit)
8. Pay balances on time (If you have credit)

Everybody doesn't have credit in prison, but if you do, follow these steps first and then move on to this point. One of the best places to start building credit on a monthly basis is SELF.inc; this app and website allow you to choose a credit-builder account for as low as $25. Get your outside resources to open this account today. Choose a monthly amount of $25, $35, $48, and $150. Start by paying a $9 administrative fee. Next month, pay the monthly plan that you chose. If you choose $35 per month for 24 months, for example, Each month, you build a credit history with all three credit bureaus. After 24 months, you've established a credit history, and you get $724 back refunded at the end of the 24 months. Self gets $116; you get back $724; you get 24 months of credit history and on-time payment history. Remember, payment history accounts for 35% of your credit score. (www.Self.inc) Self allows you to pay small amounts each month for a year for a loan, which shows up on your credit report if payments are made on time. Get your outside support, someone you trust, to download the app or log into the website (www.self.inc), fill out the application with your first and last name, social security number, date of birth, and address on the street you will use to establish personal credit (Don't use prison address). Within three months, you will be able to get a credit SELF CREDIT CARD that will allow you to get a credit limit. Six (6) months in the program, your credit would be in the 600s.

Another app to get your outside support to download is Sable, which gives you a debit card and credit card; each on-time payment allows you to build your credit score. Sable debit allows you to upload money; Sable One is Sable's credit card, which allows you to build credit based on the monthly sum you upload to Sable. Again, it is easy to set up, the same as before with Self. Inc, no identification card is needed, and it is easy for people who are incarcerated. Also, check out Cred.ai; it is just like Sable.

Next is a promising new credit builder app called Kikoff. They report to Equifax, Experion, and TransUnion. It starts off as an installment credit line (Revolving); you must purchase $10 books or something from their platform; in return, they allow you to pay it back at a rate of $2 a month for a $10-20 item. You can buy as many things as possible. You get a positive report from the above three credit agencies for every on-time payment. Kikoff will then offer a credit builder loan with reporting to TransUnion. After 12 months of paying $10-12 a month, you will get $120 back on a $10 monthly loan. Basically, you pay a fee to Kikoff (a small fee), and they build credit and give you 95% of your money back after the loan is paid off. The same is set up; it requires no personal identification; get your outside support to download it, fill out an application in your name with all the correct info, and you will be approved.

Building personal credit isn't hard; the same formula applies and has been used over and over again by those who invest in knowledge and get the process understood. Knowing that your credit score is one of the most important factors in your personal financial well-being is the start of building true wealth. As they say, "numbers don't lie." It's true with credit: the better the score (number), the better doors open up for loans, higher credit limits, etc. Build your credit because having a thin credit file shows you don't have enough credit history to generate a score.

Other ways to build credit easy and affordable while sitting in your prison cell are through:

1. Credit Builder Loans

Credit builder loans are loans specifically for people who need to build credit and have a low or no credit history. There is an easy approval process and straightforward steps to obtain these accounts. First, the money that's borrowed is put into a savings account. Second, you make monthly payments based on your interest rate every month. Third, the lender will, in turn, report your monthly payments to the three credit bureaus. Fourth, once you have satisfied the loan amount, you'll be given your funds back in your bank account or with a check.

- Self App – Offers a form of credit-building loans
- Kikoff – Offers these for as little as $5 a month.
- Republic Bank.com – Offers 12–18-month terms
- Credit.earncheese.com
- Meetava.com – offers multiple plans

2. Apply for a Personal Loan

Many banks and lenders will offer these services to you. This is another excellent way to build credit. It's similar to credit builder loans because you make payments monthly until the loan is paid back. There will be higher APRs than other loans, but the benefits of building a credit foundation are more important. Getting a personal loan can be done at traditional banks or lending platforms that function like banks but are more flexible in who they can lend to.

3. Apply for a Secured Credit Card

Secured credit cards are one of the best ways to start your credit-building process. These cards have lower approval thresholds because you put the money upfront to establish your credit limit. Whatever you deposit = your credit. A $100 deposit gets you a $100 line of credit: your money on the line, not the credit card officer. Most importantly, before applying, make sure the credit card company reports your on-time payments to all (3) credit bureaus. The best way to do this is to pay on time for up to 4-6 months and then upgrade to an unsecured credit card. The credit card issuer now puts up the money for the credit limit. Some easy-to-apply for secure credit cards are:

- **Open Sky Secured Visa**
  - No credit check, SSN#, Address, Security Deposit
  - Set your credit limit by making a $200-$3,000 deposit
  - Reports to all (3) credit bureaus.
  - www.okenskycc.com

- **First Progress Platinum Elite Secured Mastercard**
  - No credit history required (Deposit $200)
  - No minimum credit score for approval
  - Security deposit is refundable (Annual Fee: $49)
  - www.timeforprogress.com/bills/apply

- **Discover IT Secured Card**
  - Security deposit required but refundable.
  - Also has a cash-back rewards program, which allows you to earn points when spending.
  - www.discover.com (min $200, 2% cashback)

- **Petal 1 or Petal 2**
  - 2%-10% cash back
  - $300 - $3,000 limits, no annual fee
  - www.petalcard.com

- **Capital One Quicksilver Secured Cash Rewards**
  - SSN, valid address
  - www.applynow.capitalone.com

Remember, you are in prison, so you must use different ways to show these credit card companies that you are a functional member of society. There are a few things to do when you apply or fill out these applications. They require you to use your real name, social security number (SSN), and a valid address. Make sure you use the same address on all applications for credit builder loans and cards. Don't use a prison address! For anything. When your outside support goes through the application, they ask for "employer." Of course, you're in prison, so here is the trick. In part one, I show you how to set up an LLC from prison, use your LLC as your employer, and mark that you are employed. If they ask for a position, put CEO, etc. Then, when you get to the part about your annual salary, you can put the minimum salary for a first-year CEO ($52,000). Next, they will ask for monthly rent to the address and ask your outside support how much they pay in rent or, if they own it, what the monthly payments are. These banks care more about your identity and SSN than anything else. 90% of these services only require an SSN (Social Security Number) and address to set up. Sometimes, you will run into services that require I.D. verification, but that's rare when building credit. Of course, if you do run into this form of verifying your identity, then you can use these services. None of this violates prison rules as long as you don't use the prison address, prison number, or any mail that comes from these companies, come through normal prison mail rooms. That's the point of using your family address uptown or your address where you live uptown or plan to be released to.

Don't let your lack of access to the internet or outside be why you deny yourself access to these legal credit-building services.

4. Other Options

- **BILLS**: Paying bills with credit cards also allows you to build credit. You can also make companies charge you to build credit. You can make companies charge your card to pay bills. With this, you can set up autopay and make sure you pay the full balance every month.

- **RENT**: Apps such as "Rental Kharma" and "Rent Track" will report your rent payments to credit bureaus on your behalf, which helps your credit score. You can download these apps (outside contact), and they can use your information (SSN, etc.) to pay the rent through your bank account, thus allowing you to build up your credit.

- **ALTRO**: Allows you to do this free of charge. (Report Rent Payments).

These suggestions should build up your credit in multiple ways without much effort, providing reliable strategies that work. Once you have done the above for six months or more, the next step is to start applying for unsecured credit cards from these companies.

- UNSECURED CREDIT CARDS: Starting out doing the above is important. So, continue to do that, along with starting the process of applying for unsecured credit cards. Unsecured credit has the following:

  - Not guaranteed by any asset.

  - Has higher interest rates.

  - It is more difficult to get approved by lenders.

  - Not connected to a deposit put down as collateral. So, the credit limit is determined by the credit score of the person trying to obtain a credit card.

All lines of credit are revolving loans that can be used for any purpose while also allowing you to build credit in the process.

Back when the U.S. was on the gold standard, cash was king. People loved paying by checks everywhere. Now, since money is debt (read "What is Money?"), credit cards are now king. They are accepted everywhere and are used to build wealth and credit. Remember, only use unsecured credit after using the previously mentioned credit-building tools (i.e., secured credit cards). Banks and credit card companies are in the business of making money. So that's why they give you so many rewards once they see a good credit score, which means they can trust you. This form of credit allows you to track your spending with ease. With credit cards, all this will appear on your account, even better on some websites and apps. Allow you to see your spending broken down into specific categories.

Apps such as "Mint" and "You Need a Budget" allow you to import data from your credit cards, which will show these breakdowns as you spend. This data about unsecured credit use will help you cut back or spend more effectively. Other advantages included building credit this way, allowing you to find a house more easily, establishing your business credit (P.G. Loan Options), and helping with renting an apartment when the landlord wants to check your credit. Some of the most used types of credit cards are:

- **CASH BACK CREDIT CARDS:** These are a form of rewards card that offers cash back for each dollar you spend. You can use these to earn simple rewards on spending without worrying about what's the best out there.

- **REWARDS CREDIT CARDS:** These are generally any credit cards that offer rewards on spending. Rewards can be cash back, points that can be redeemed for statement credits, gift cards, travel merchandise, and more.

- **RETAIL STORE CARDS:** There are two types of these cards. 1) Closed Loop Store Cards can only be used at the associated store or member stores approved by the retail store, and 2) Open Loop Store Cards can be used anywhere but usually offer the best rewards at associate and partner stores. Best of all, retail store cards are really good for you because they're a great way to start building credit for the first time. Let your family shop at the stores to get perks from stores and discounts while you build your credit in the process.

- **0% Intro APR & Low-Interest Credit Card:** Credit cards that offer 0% APR on new purchases help you save on many big expenses you want to pay off over time. These 0% APR credit cards tend to also have high variable rates after initial offers end. They are best for when you make a purchase and pay down over time. One other thing is to pay the balance in full at the end of each period.

Pro se Tip: CREDIT SCORE RANGE	
800+	Excellent
740-799	Very Good
670-739	Good
580-669	Fair
<580	Poor

Here are some credit cards and apps that should help you continue to build wealth with credit cards.

- Capital One Platinum
  - No annual fee
  - 580-669 (Fair credit)
  - Purchase Rate: 22.9% APR
  - www.capitalone.com
- Capital One Quicksilver One
  - 1.5% cash back on every purchase
  - Annual Fee: $39
  - Purchase Rate: 22.99 APR
  - Credit Level: 580-669 (Fair Credit)
  - www.capitalone.com
- Chime Credit Card
  - $100 sign-up bonus
  - Setup chime account first with the app
  - No credit checks
  - No annual fees
  - No deposit
- Extra Debit Card
  - Builds credit on all purchases
  - No credit checks
  - Mobile app
  - Rewards Points

BEST CREDIT CARDS PER SECTOR

- Chase Freedom Unlimited Card
    - Best cashback credit card (www.chase.com)
- American Express Gold Card
    - Best rewards card (www.americanexpress.com)
- Chase Sapphire Preferred Card
    - Best credit card welcome bonus (www.chase.com)
- Citi Double Cash Card
    - Best no annual fee credit card (citicards.citi.com)
- Discover it Miles
    - Best no-annual fee travel credit card (www.discover.com)
- Citi Simplicity Card – No late fees ever
    - Best balance transfer card (citicards.citi.com)
- Titanium Rewards Visa Signature Card from Andrews Federal Credit Union
    - Best low-interest credit card (www.andrewsFCU.com)
- Discover It Secured Credit Card
    - Best secure credit card (www.discover.com)
- Petal 2 Cash Back, No Fees Visa Credit Card
    - Best for building credit (www.petalcard.com)
- Discover It Student Cash Back
    - Best for college students (www.discover.com)
- Chase Sapphire Reserve
    - Best dining rewards credit card (www.chase.com)
- Pen Fed Platinum Rewards Visa
    - Signature Card (www.PenFed.com)
- Blue Cash Preferred Card from American Express
    - Best grocery rewards credit card (www.americanexpress.com)
- Capital One Savor Cash
    - Best entertainment rewards card (www.capitalone.com)
- Petal 2 Cash Back, No Fees, Visa Credit Card
    - Best for average credit (www.petalcards.com)

- Capital One Venture Rewards Credit Card
  - Best credit card for Global Entry and/or TSA Precheck credit (www.capitalone.com)

All the above credit cards will require different types of credit scores. In the beginning, it will take a while to get here, but once you get your score for seven straight months up into ten months with on-time payments, you will be offered all types of stuff. Start with secure credit cards for six months and constantly build up that score while you sit in that cell, thinking of the businesses and wealth you want to build. Another form of credit card is "Retail Credit Cards." after 4 months with the secure and credit builder apps, start building with these. Here are just a few that offer the best rewards, minus the fees:

- Amazon Prime Rewards Visa Signature Card
  - Fee: $0 (Apply at: www.amazon.com)
  - 5% cash back at Amazon.com and Whole Foods Market
- Walmart Credit Card
  - Fee: $0
  - 1% -5% cashback
  - www.walmart.com
- Amazon.com Store Card
  - 5% cashback
  - Fee: $0
  - www.amazon.com
- Costco Anywhere Visa Card by Citi
  - Fee: $0
  - 1%-4% cashback
  - www.citicards.citi.com
- Paypal.com Card
  - Fee: $0
  - Earn unlimited cashback on all credit card purchases with PayPal
  - www.paypal.com
- Lowes Advantage Card
  - Fee: $0
  - 650-699 (fair credit score)
  - 5% off Lowes purchases
  - www.lowes.com

- Target RedCard
    - Fee: $0
    - 5% discount at register, free shipping
    - www.target.com
- My Walgreens Credit Card
    - $25 cash rewards
    - 10% cash rewards on Walgreens branded purchases
    - 5% cash rewards on other brands. Redeem rewards at checkout
    - Pharmacy perks and discounts
    - 3% on grocery and health purchases
    - No Fee: $0
    - Free credit monitoring
    - www.walgreens.com or use the app

One way to get the best use out of these cards is to think of them in the context of what I call "pattern Pairing Credit Cards," which I describe as mixing and using multiple cards for everyday expenses. For instance, if you get 1.5%-5% of every dollar, you spend either cash or points that you can redeem. If you spend ($1,000 a month, you can earn $180 to $240 a year without any special effort but mixing different cashback and reward cards. The chart below will bring this to light by using different rewards %'s for everyday spending needs you might use credit for.

PATTERN PAIRING CREDIT CARDS CHART			
Groceries	$400/month	6% Rewards Rate	$288 a year
Restaurant	$130/month	5% Rewards Rate	$81 a year
Gas	$100/month	5% for 6 months, 3% after	$48 a year
Amazon.com	$100/month	5% Rewards Rate	$42 a year
Streaming Media	$50/month	6% Rewards Rate	$36 a year
Travel	$50/month	6% Rewards Rate	$50 a year
		TOTAL	$545 Annual

Everyday needs can be obtained by using credit cards; since you reach this level of credit, more doors can be built financially. Credit is the beginning of your financial journey. Obtaining loans based on your personal and business credit to purchase assets is the key to building wealth. But what's important is the fact that you learn in prison how to build credit and pay bills. So, upon release, you have this concept under control. Obtaining this knowledge now allows you to be ahead of 85% of the prisoners who get released every year with no financial education, no credit, no work ethic, or money saved to build or start their lives over on a good foot. We can continue to blame the system or develop our own system to teach and learn from each other, but I chose the latter.

Pro Se Tip

While the above is really hard work, I have a trick that could help you get that business idea or investment in your plans off the ground. It's called the "CASH OFF CREDIT CARD TRICK."

For example, later on, you will learn about business formation, investing, etc. Some of those things require money upfront to set up. One way to pay for it is to remove cash from your credit card. MoneyGram app or website allows you to use your credit card to send money anywhere. They will send a check to whomever you want to send it to. Once you send it using the credit card, you give the confirmation number to the person picking it up from the MoneyGram location. That person can then deposit those funds into your bank account for you to use at your discretion. Don't do this unless you have a solid business plan and idea. Pay off the full amount of the credit card at the end of each month. (I prefer the 145 of each month) Then, pay again at the end so that you can record the payment history for one monthly payment cycle. Another way is to use a credit card to purchase a "Visa Vanilla Gift Card," say a $300 gift card; then you take that gift card and get a money order, use that money order to put the money in your bank account. Anybody in your circle can do this for you. Usually, the gift card doesn't require your name, but the money order will. Most banks allow you to take a picture of it and deposit it into your account so that you can put your name on the money order. Later, we will get into the checking account in another part. This journey we are going on will help you and your family learn to build wealth. We can't keep complaining without solutions or ideas to build wealth for ourselves; there is too much information at our disposal not to take advantage of this moment in time. Do it now and live better upon release; wait until you get home and fall victim to all the criminal justice system cracks in the floor that awaits. When that parole agent is on you to get a job or return to prison, tell them, "I own a business; as a CEO, I have a job, one that I created for myself"! Watch how the mood changes and how they look at you. Always produce what is unexpected; don't do what's expected. Moving along!

BUILDING BUSINESS CREDIT

Welcome to your introduction to building wealth through business credit. If you read my previous book, *Pro se Prisoner: How to Buy Stocks and Bitcoin,* there was a bonus book in the back called *Pro se Prisoner: The Ph. D Manual (Poor, hungry & Driven to Success)* which showed you how to start an LLC in your state for the lowest cost possible. You must first have a formed entity (i.e., LLC) to build business credit. See the Resource Section for websites for your Secretary of State to get paperwork to form an LLC.

Just as a general overview of business credit, it is obtained in the name of your business' EIN/Tax ID number. (Note that this is different than your SSN for personal credit). Business credit is largely based on the company's ability to repay its creditors/obligations. Business credit scores will be built with three major credit agencies. As noted above, getting started must start with setting up your business; first, it must be the name of your business. Make sure that your name isn't already taken. Never start a business using D.B.A. (Doing Business As). Always check social media to see if your chosen name is taken. Next, visit www.godaddy.com to see if your company's domain name has already been taken. Get your name selected, decide on it, and move on to the next step. Deciding on a business address should be next in this process. This is important because it should be the same on all documents. Never use a UPS Store mailbox or post office box because they will be flagged as high risk. Lenders look for physical addresses, and the best choice if you're just starting out is a "Virtual Address," you can check out companies such as www.regus.com or www.alliancevirtualoffice.com, put your state in there and get a low-cost address to make your company legit to lenders. Choosing a business entity is next. This includes LLCs, C-Corps, or S-Corps.

C-corps are the most popular form of business entity. C-Corps have shareholders, and there are no limits on the number of shareholders. C-Corps are double taxed on the corporate and individual levels (More on this in Part 3: Taxes).

S-Corps are used by many small business owners, plus unlike C-Corps, they're not double taxed. S-corps are not taxed at the corporate level. However, S-Corps is limited to only 100 shareholders, unlike the unlimited number of C-Corps shareholders. Lenders love S-Corps because they look more professional to them.

LLCs are unique. They don't have shareholders like C-Corps and S-Corps. The owners are "members" and are not taxed at the corporate level (no double taxation). Members are not personally liable for the company's liabilities and debts. Individuals, corporations, or other LLCs can own LLCs.

It's completely up to you to decide what structure you want to start. Just starting out, you should take advantage of the LLC entity. When forming any of the above structures, do your research with your Secretary of State to figure out the cost. But there are websites that will do everything for you, such as www.legalzoom.com and www.incfile.com. You can have them file all the paperwork and bank information for a couple of hundred dollars to get you started.

Once we establish the structure, you must apply for an Employer Identification Number (EIN), which identifies taxpayers required to pay business taxes. When you apply for this 9-digit number, you must do so in either of the four (4) ways: 1) online, 2) via Fax, 3) by mail, or 4) calling over the phone. Make sure your virtual business address is the same on all forms. Starting out, you can use a home address, but some lenders will know it's a home address. Keep this in mind!

When applying online for your EIN number, fill out an application and print out an EIN confirmation to save your documents. The number to apply by fax is 855-641-6935. You must still obtain IRS Form SS-4. You will get it via fax within four business days. Applying by mail taxes the most time – 4 weeks or more. Obtain Form SS-4 and fill it out and return it to:

Internal Revenue Service
Attn: EIN Operation
Cincinnati, OH 45999

Lastly, the phone is the fastest way to get your EIN number. Call the IRS at (800) 829-1040, select English, and choose number 3 for business taxes. Once you answer the desired questions, you will receive the EIN number during this phone call.

Getting your company logo is the next step to building wealth through credit. Many talented prisoners in prison can draw a logo. For you, that might be the cheapest and fastest way to get your logo. As a matter of fact, my LLC did this; my company, The Attic Group, LLC, paid one of my friends to draw the first logo. Also, my Pro se Prisoner, LLC did the same for my logo, all for under $250 for both logos. If you want to do it on the outside, you can check out freelance websites like Fiverr.com and find someone worldwide to design your logo. Once you design it, make sure to get your business name and logo trademarked, if not in the beginning, at some point in the future, to protect your brand.

Buying a domain name in your company name should be followed by the logo design. Check godaddy.com for free to see if your name was taken. First, try your company name in its original form; if it is unavailable that way, shorten or abbreviate it. As a rule, don't go over the top with design or website. Keep it short and simple, but you must include the following pages:

1. Home Page

2. About Us

3. Contact Us

Your website should also include a professional email account (yourname@yourbusiness.com). Most, if not all, companies that sell the domain will include this. I know this seems like a lot, but we must get out of the habit of trying to take the shortcut through everything we do. As I sit in prison writing this, I'm reminded of all the mistakes I made doing it myself from a maximum-security prison cell. Everything I write about to you I've tried before writing about it. My experiences are laid out in these pages. I start an investment group and publishing group while sitting in a cell, using my family member's address on all the paperwork. My concept now is to get it done correctly the first time because I don't want to repeat and waste time doing something incorrectly. I had to remember that this isn't the streets; it's a legitimate business that will help build wealth if treated properly. Time to me is important – I don't like to waste it. The Pro se Prisoner motto: "Plot, Plan & Execute". If it goes against that, I move away from it. Just give me some time with you, and I will teach you how to apply for credit, use it to buy assets, and avoid paying taxes like the (0.01%). Just my opinion! Let's get back to the next step to building business credit.

Today, social media is the most effective way to reach a group of people at a minimum cost. Create your presence on the below social media sites:

Facebook	www.facebook.com
LinkedIn	www.linkedin.com
Google	www.plus.google.com
Tumblr	www.tumblr.com
Twitter	www.twitter.com
Instagram	www.instagram.com
Snapchat	www.snapchat.com
Pinterest	www.pintrest.com

Your credibility as a business will grow now because you have put your company and brand on the internet. Take a breath; you are the CEO of your own company or brand; how for you to take it is up to you. But hold up; the work isn't done yet. Now, let's move on to obtaining a business bank account. Upon opening a business bank account, the majority of banks will want "Articles of Incorporation" and "IRS EIN Number Document" from the IRS. While some allow opening a small business checking account over the phone, it varies, so ask questions. Options to consider are:

- Navy Federal Credit Union (Business Checking)
- PayPal Business (Download App, Fill Out Application)
- NorthOne (Business Checking)
- Novo (banknovo.com)
- NBKC (www.nbkc.com/business)
- Bluevine (www.bluevine.com/checking)

Picking one that fits your needs is a must for your LLC. If you use www.incfile.com and pay for them to set up your bank account when they file your LLC paperwork, you won't have to do anything because they will contact Bank of America and get you a business checking account. All this is included in their fee.

PayPal business should be set up even if you use Incfile; they offer one-of-a-kind business tools for your business. Now that we have that out of the way let's build wealth by building up your business credit. Business reporting agencies that report business credit are:

- Dun & Bradstreet
- Experian Business
- Equifax Business

Briefly, let's review these (3) three business credit agents. Dun & Bradstreet is the biggest of the three (3) and is used by most vendors who give out business credit. A little thing to be aware of is that most landlords use them to check business credit when applying for a lease for office space. Also, you must obtain your [DUNS number]. This starts the process of building business credit. This number will enable your business to borrow without a PG (Personal Guarantee). These numbers are free from fedgov.dnb.com/webform/pages/CCRSearch.jsp. Once on the site, request the "Free DUNS" number, then fill out the form. After you obtain your DUN number, it will give you access to (iUpdate) to view your profile. Dun and Bradstreet use a (Paydex Score) to determine creditworthiness. It measures how on time you are with your payments in a 24-month period.

Experian Business Credit assigns your business a business information number (BIN Number). To obtain a credit report from Experian, you must have a vendor report and a tradeline to Experian. Lenders and banks mostly use Equifax Business Credit. While very few lenders report to Equifax, it's also good to remember that it's the least used by reporting agencies. You can obtain an Equifax business credit report by going to the following website: www.equifac.com/business/business_credit_reports_small_business/

While the above three credit bureaus are the main ones your business will report to, some businesses just don't have the qualifications to report to them; that's why we have the third-party credit bureaus below.

- ChexSystems (www.chexsystems.com)
- FD Insight (www.factualdata.com)
- Credit.net
- Cortera (www.cortera.com)
- PayNet (www.paynet.com)
- Accurint Business (www.accurit.com)

We will explore this topic further and request your information from these agencies at least 60-90 days after building up vendor accounts.

VENDOR ACCOUNTS

Now that we have all the paperwork out of the way, let's get on to the real essence of building business credit. Although you sit in prison, don't allow your current situation to hinder your quest to build a business with good credit.

Vendor Accounts are lines of credit extended to your business by a company that wants to be paid back in 30, 60, or 90 days. They will give you an approved limit and a timeframe for repayment. One of the most important things to remember is that each vendor selected must report to one of the (3) main credit agencies. The formula to build strong business credit is as follows.

- (5) Vendor Accounts
- (3) Revolving Accounts
- (1) Bank Loan

Vendors accounts can take up to 30-90 days to start building up a solid credit score. These accounts can take sometimes 4-6 months. You can set up your business bank account to pay (Net 15), which means the 15 days of each month. The quicker you pay them, the better your credit score will be because you will be deemed reliable in the vendor's eyes. Make each minimum purchase from each of the (5) vendor accounts: $50.00.

Pro se Tip: (!)

Up your approval odds by listing (5) employees if your LLC is only run by you or a manager. Now, if you are starting off with more than (5) employees list it correctly.

Round 1 Accounts

- ULINE (www.uline.com)

  Net 30/ Reports to D&B and Experian

  Apply Online

  Create an account, sign in, place an order, and at check out, choose Bill Me (Net 30)

- Quill (www.quill.com)

  Net 30/ Reports to D&B and Experian

  Apply Online

  Register for a new account, place an order, and at checkout, select "invoice my account."

- Grainger (www.grainger.com) See an enclosed example of Net 30

  Net 30

  Reports to D&B

  Apply Online

  Register for a new account, place an order, and at check out, select "open account" as your payment method.

As you need a minimum of (5) five (Round 1 Vendor Accounts), the above is the best selection to get you started. With anything in life, the amount of time and effort you put into "Revolving Accounts" are lines of credit where you can pay a minimum amount due every month. Most importantly, these accounts are unlike "Vendor Accounts". The entire balance isn't due in a specified term (i.e., Net 30, 60, or 90). While these types of accounts report to Experian, they will report to Equifax and Dun and Bradstreet on certain occasions.

GRAINGER.

PAGE 1

5862 HARRISON AVE.
ROCKFORD, IL 61108-8127
www.grainger.com

ORIGINAL INVOICE

GRAINGER ACCOUNT NUMBER	800001166
INVOICE NUMBER	9198830003
INVOICE DATE	12/04/2013
DUE DATE	01/03/2014
AMOUNT DUE	$1,698.86

SHIP TO
ATTN: ATTENTION
SAMPLE COMPANY
123 ADDRESS CT
KINGSTON IL 60145-0000

PO NUMBER:	123456
PO RELEASE:	333
DEPARTMENT:	7777777
PROJECT/JOB:	4444
REQUISITIONER:	REQUIST NAME
CALLER:	SHARON CARPENTE
CUSTOMER PHONE:	555-555-5555
ORDER NUMBER:	1188465007
INCO TERMS:	FOB ORIGIN

BILL TO
SAMPLE COMPANY
123 ADDRESS CT
KINGSTON IL 60145-0000

THANK YOU!

FEI NUMBER 36-1150280
FOR QUESTIONS ABOUT THIS INVOICE OR ACCOUNT CALL *1-800-472-4643*

PO LINE #	ITEM #	DESCRIPTION	QUANTITY	UNIT PRICE	TOTAL
50	1AJC4	IMPACT WRENCH CARE KIT,W/4Z623 MANUFACTURER # 212-TK2	9	48.70	438.30
		Delivery #6234391114 Date Shipped:12/04/2013 Carrier: UPS GROUND TEST No:of Pkgs:2 Wt: 0.990 Trk #:TRACKING123456789012			
20	1AJC4	IMPACT WRENCH CARE KIT,W/4Z623 MANUFACTURER # 212-TK2	6	48.70	292.20
30	2WZU3	COTTER PIN,18-8,1/4X1 1/2 L,PK 50 MANUFACTURER # 03-250-1500	7	27.95	195.65
40	2YJ17	WEB SLING SHACKLE,ROUND PIN,10800 LB. MANUFACTURER # M704	8	48.65	389.20
		Delivery #6234391115 Date Shipped:12/04/2013 Carrier: UPS GROUND TEST No:of Pkgs:1 Wt: 34.090 Trk #:TRACKING234567890123			
10	2YJ17	WEB SLING SHACKLE,ROUND PIN,10800 LB. MANUFACTURER # M704	5	48.65	243.25
		Delivery #6234391116 Date Shipped:12/04/2013 Carrier: UPS GROUND TEST No:of Pkgs:5 Wt: 14.900 Trk #:TRACKING345678901234			

INVOICE SUB TOTAL	1,558.60
TAX	140.26

These items are sold for domestic consumption in the United States. If exported, purchaser assumes full responsibility for compliance with US export controls.

PAYMENT TERMS Net 30 days - PAY THIS INVOICE NO STATEMENT SENT PAYABLE IN U.S. DOLLARS.	**AMOUNT DUE**	**$1,698.86**

▲ **PLEASE DETACH THIS PORTION AND RETURN WITH YOUR PAYMENT** ▲

BILL TO:

SAMPLE COMPANY
123 ADDRESS CT
KINGSTON IL 60145-0000
UNITED STATES OF AMERICA

REMIT TO:
GRAINGER
DEPT. 800001166
PALATINE, IL 60038-0001

800001166919883000310001698861001402610000000100000014010366

X	ACCOUNT NUMBER	DATE	INVOICE NUMBER	AMOUNT DUE
	800001166	12/04/2013	9198830003	$1,698.86

PAGE 2

GRAINGER STANDARD TERMS AND CONDITIONS

A. SALES POLICY

1. Wholesale Only.
W.W. Grainger, Inc. ("Grainger") sells products for business use to customers with proper business identification, which is required from all customers prior to purchase.

2. Prices.
Prices listed are wholesale, do not include freight, handling fees, taxes, and/or duties, and are subject to correction or change without notice. Market sensitive commodity products will be priced according to current market conditions. Customer should contact the local Grainger branch or check online at www.grainger.com for current pricing. Export orders may be subject to other special pricing. Grainger reserves the right to accept or reject any order.

3. Sales Tax.
Customers are responsible for payment of all applicable state and local taxes, or for providing a valid sales tax exemption certificate. When placing an order, customer shall indicate which products are tax exempt.

4. Payment and Credit Terms.
Grainger accepts cash, checks, money orders, Visa, MasterCard, and American Express. For customers with established Grainger credit, payment terms are net thirty (30) days from the date of shipment or pick-up. All credit extended by Grainger to customer, and the limits of such credit, is at Grainger's sole discretion, and may be reduced or revoked by Grainger at any time, for any reason. Grainger reserves the right to charge a convenience fee for late payments. Grainger further reserves the right to charge customer a late payment fee at the rate of one and one-half percent (1-1/2%) of the amount due for each month or portion thereof that the amount due remains unpaid, or such amount as may be permitted under applicable law. Anticipation and cash discounts are not allowed. Export orders are subject to special export payment terms and conditions. All payments must be made in U.S. dollars. Grainger shall have the right of set-off and deduction for any sums owed by customer to Grainger. If customer fails to make payment within thirty (30) days of shipment or pick-up, or fails to comply with Grainger's credit terms, or fails to supply adequate assurance of full performance to Grainger within a reasonable time after requested by Grainger (such time as specified in Grainger's request), Grainger may defer shipments until such payment or compliance is made, require cash in advance for any further shipments, demand immediate payment of all amounts then owed, elect to pursue collection action (including without limitation, attorneys' fees and any and all other associated costs of collection), and/or may, at its option, cancel all or any part of an unshipped order.

Customer agrees to assume responsibility for, and customer hereby unconditionally guarantees payment of, as provided herein, all purchases made by customer, its subsidiaries and affiliates. Each of customer's subsidiaries and affiliates purchasing from Grainger will be jointly and severally liable for purchases with customer, and customer is also acting as agent for such subsidiaries and affiliates.

5. Credit Balance.
Customer agrees that any credit balance(s) issued by Grainger will be applied to customer's account within one (1) year of its issuance. IF CUSTOMER HAS NOT REQUESTED THE CREDIT BALANCE WITHIN ONE (1) YEAR, ANY REMAINING CREDIT BALANCE WILL BE CANCELLED, AND GRAINGER SHALL HAVE NO FURTHER LIABILITY.

B. FREIGHT POLICY
Prices stated are F.O.B. origin, freight prepaid to destination specified in the order. Grainger charges a shipping and handling fee (which includes internal handling and related costs) on each order which is applied at time of order and reflected on customer's invoice. Receipts for shipping and handling charges will not be furnished. Grainger covers shipping and handling for standard ground delivery for orders over US $1500 before tax and freight (including any back orders). C.O.D. shipments are not permitted. Other terms and conditions may apply for other than standard delivery ("Other Freight Services"), including without limitation, expedited same day delivery, air freight, freight collect, export orders, hazardous materials, customer's carrier, shipments outside the contiguous U.S., or other special handling by the carrier. Any charges incurred for Other Freight Services must be paid by customer. Fuel surcharges may be applied. Title and risk of loss pass to customer upon tender of shipment to the carrier. If the product is damaged in transit, customer's only recourse is to file a claim with the carrier.

C. WARRANTY POLICY

1. LIMITED WARRANTY.
ALL PRODUCTS SOLD ARE WARRANTED BY GRAINGER ONLY TO CUSTOMERS FOR: (I) RESALE; OR (II) USE IN BUSINESS, GOVERNMENT, OR ORIGINAL EQUIPMENT MANUFACTURE. GRAINGER WARRANTS PRODUCTS AGAINST DEFECTS IN MATERIALS AND WORKMANSHIP UNDER NORMAL USE FOR A PERIOD OF ONE (1) YEAR AFTER THE DATE OF PURCHASE FROM GRAINGER, UNLESS OTHERWISE STATED. PROVIDED THAT GRAINGER ACCEPTS THE PRODUCT FOR RETURN DURING THE LIMITED WARRANTY PERIOD, GRAINGER MAY, AT ITS OPTION: (I) REPAIR; (II) REPLACE; OR (III) REFUND THE AMOUNT PAID BY CUSTOMER. CUSTOMER MUST RETURN THE PRODUCT TO THE APPROPRIATE GRAINGER BRANCH OR AUTHORIZED SERVICE LOCATION, AS DESIGNATED BY GRAINGER, SHIPPING COSTS PREPAID. GRAINGER'S REPAIR, REPLACEMENT, OR REFUND OF AMOUNTS PAID BY CUSTOMER FOR THE PRODUCT, SHALL BE CUSTOMER'S SOLE AND EXCLUSIVE REMEDY.

2. WARRANTY DISCLAIMER.
a. NO WARRANTY OR AFFIRMATION OF FACT, EXPRESS OR IMPLIED, OTHER THAN AS SET FORTH IN THE LIMITED WARRANTY STATEMENT ABOVE, IS MADE OR AUTHORIZED BY GRAINGER. GRAINGER DISCLAIMS ANY LIABILITY FOR CLAIMS ARISING OUT OF PRODUCT MISUSE, IMPROPER PRODUCT SELECTION, IMPROPER INSTALLATION, PRODUCT MODIFICATION, MISREPAIR OR MISAPPLICATION. GRAINGER EXPRESSLY DISCLAIMS ANY WARRANTY THAT THE PRODUCTS: (I) ARE MERCHANTABLE; (II) FIT FOR A PARTICULAR PURPOSE; OR (III) DO NOT AND WILL NOT INFRINGE UPON OTHER'S INTELLECTUAL PROPERTY RIGHTS.
b. GRAINGER MAKES NO WARRANTIES TO THOSE DEFINED AS CONSUMERS IN THE MAGNUSON-MOSS WARRANTY-FEDERAL TRADE COMMISSION IMPROVEMENT ACT.

3. LIMITATION OF LIABILITY.
GRAINGER EXPRESSLY DISCLAIMS ANY LIABILITY FOR CONSEQUENTIAL, INCIDENTAL, SPECIAL, EXEMPLARY, OR PUNITIVE DAMAGES. GRAINGER'S LIABILITY IN ALL CIRCUMSTANCES IS LIMITED TO, AND SHALL NOT EXCEED, THE PURCHASE PRICE PAID FOR THE PRODUCT THAT GIVES RISE TO ANY LIABILITY.

4. Warranty Product Return.
Before returning any product, customer shall: (I) write or call the local Grainger branch from which the product was purchased; (ii) in the case of an internet order, contact www.grainger.com and provide the date, the original invoice number, the stock number, anc a description of the defect; or (iii) call Customer Care at 1-888-361-8649, and provide the date, the original invoice number, the stock number, and a description of the defect. Proof c purchase is required in all cases.

5. Manufacturer's Warrranty.
For information on a specific manufacturer's warranty, please contact the local Grainger branch or call Customer Care at 1-888-361-8649.

6. Product Compliance and Suitabilty.
Jurisdictions have varying laws, codes and regulations governing construction, installation, and/or use of products for a particular purpose. Certain products may not be available for sale in all areas. Grainger does not guarantee compliance or suitability of the products it sells with any laws, codes or regulations, nor does Grainger accept responsibility for construction, installation and/or use of a product. It is customer's responsibility to review the product application and all applicable laws, codes and regulations for each relevant jurisdiction to be sure that the construction, installation, and/or use involving the products ar compliant.

D. PRODUCT INFORMATION

1. Catalog/Website Information.
Grainger reserves the right to correct publishing errors in its catalogs or any of its websites. Product depictions in the catalog or websites are for illustrative purposes only. Possession of, or access to, any Grainger catalog, literature or websites does not constitute the right to purchase products.

2. Product Substitution.
Products and/or country of origin may be substituted and may not be identical to description and/or images in the catalog or on the website.

3. Occupational Safety and Health Administration ("OSHA") Hazardous Substance.
Material Safety Data Sheets ("MSDS") for OSHA defined hazardous substances are prepared and supplied by the manufacturers. GRAINGER MAKES NO WARRANTIES ANC EXPRESSLY DISCLAIMS ALL LIABILITY TO ANY CUSTOMER OR USER WITH RESPECT TO THE ACCURACY OF THE INFORMATION OR THE SUITABILITY OF THE RECOMMENDATIONS IN ANY MSDS. CUSTOMER IS SOLELY RESPONSIBLE FOR ANY RELIANCE ON OR USE OF ANY INFORMATION, AND FOR USE OR APPLICATIO OF ANY PRODUCT.

4. MSDS and Proposition 65 Product Requests.
MSDS and a list of Proposition 65 products are available: (i) at the local Grainger branch; (ii) by contacting Grainger, Dept. B1.L57, Attn: Environmental Health and Safety Dept., 100 Grainger Parkway, Lake Forest, IL 60045-5201 U.S.; (iii) by calling Grainger's MSDS Request Line at 1-877-286-9860; or (iv) by logging on to www.grainger.com and clicking on the "Resources" tab at the top of the page.

5. Important Notice to Federal Customers Re: Country Of Origin.
While all products listed on GSA Advantage!® meet the requirements of the Trade Agreements Act ("TAA"), as implemented by Federal Acquisition Regulations Part 25, other products sold by Grainger may not meet the requirements. At the time of purchase, Grainger will advise customers with proper identification as an authorized schedule customer whether or not a product is "TAA-compliant." Any federal customer purchasing a non-TAA item will be making an "open market" purchase that is not covered by any contract. Federal customers are advised that the open market purchases are NOT GSA schedule purchases. By purchasing any product on the open market, the customer represents that it has authority to make such purchase and has complied with all applicable procurement regulations.

6. ARRA Orders.
It is the customer's responsibility to advise Grainger whether this order is funded in any part by funds from or related to the American Reinvestment and Recovery Act ("ARRA") (Pub. L. No. 111-5) (i.e., Stimulus Funds). Upon request, Grainger will provide country of origin information so that customer may determine compliance with any applicable requirements under ARRA Section 1605 or any other applicable regulations.

E. GENERAL TERMS

1. Force Majeure.
Grainger shall not be liable for any delay in, or impairment of, performance resulting in whole or in part from any force majeure event, including but not limited to acts of God, labor disruptions, acts of war, acts of terrorism (whether actual or threatened), governmental decrees or controls, insurrections, epidemics, quarantines, shortages, communication or power failures, fire, accident, explosion, inability to procure or ship product or obtain permits and licenses, inability to procure supplies or raw materials, severe weather conditions, catastrophic events, or any other circumstance or cause beyond the reasonable control of Grainger in the conduct of its business.

2. Grainger's Performance of Services.
Customer will hold harmless and indemnify Grainger, its officers, directors, employees, agents, subcontractors or representatives from and against any and all claims, including bodily injury, death, or damage to personal property, and all other losses, liabilities, obligations, demands, actions and expenses, whether direct or indirect, known or unknown, absolute or contingent, incurred by Grainger related to the performance of services for customer (including without limitation, settlement costs, attorneys' fees, and any and all other expenses for defending any actions or threatened actions) arising out of, in whole or in part, any act or omission of customer, its employees, agents, subcontractors or representatives.

3. Cancellation.
All product order cancellations must be approved by Grainger, and may be subject to restocking fees and other charges.

4. Product Return.
Product returns must be made within one (1) year from date of purchase, unless otherwise indicated. Customer should call the local Grainger branch, or go to www.grainger.com, for instructions. Returned product must be in original packaging, unused, undamaged, and in saleable condition. Proof of purchase is required in all cases.

F. EXPORT SALES
Orders for export sales are subject to the terms conditions found at www.grainger.com and can be accessed by clicking on the "Terms of Sale" link.

A FULL STATEMENT OF GRAINGER'S TERMS AND CONDITIONS IS AVAILABLE ON WWW.GRAINGER.COM AND IS

Pro se Tip: (!)

Do not apply for a revolving account unless you have at least (5) five vendor accounts reporting at a minimum of two or three months of payments.

Some of the first round of revolving accounts should be these:

- FedEx Office

  Net 30

  Apply Online

  You will need your EIN & DUNS No.

- Staples

  Net 30

  Apply online or Fax application.

  I will check all three credit bureaus' credit reports; if there is no credit, they use the 411 directories and EIN. These accounts might be Personal Guarantee (P.G.)

- Fuelman Fleet Card

  Net 30

  Apply Online

  You must list at least 5 employees; if you do, it will require a Personal Guarantee (P.G.)

- UPS

  Net 30

  Apply Online (To get a billing account, you have to specify the daily pickup time.

- Aramark

  Net 30

  Apply Online

  We will need a Duns No., two trade references, and a bank reference.

- 4 Imprint

  Net 30

  Fax or Email Application

  I will check D&B, so use your Duns no. when filling out your application.

There are many more "Revolving lines of credit" offered by many other companies. Check the list below and get all the information you need to make the best decision for yourself.

REVOLVING ACCOUNTS LIST

- Lowes Hardware
- Auto Zone
- UPS
- McBee
- Exxon Mobile Business Fleet
- Conoco Fleet
- Budget Corporate Account
- Crownofficesupplies.com
- Shirtsy.com
- Officedepot.com

- Macy's
- 1-800-FLOWERS
- Dell
- Amazon
- Sherwin Williams
- Global Fleet
- Conoco Fleet
- Nav.com
- Quill.com
- Tryjeeves.com

It will take several months to build good business credit. A formula is outlined below to get an idea of the process.

> #1: Month 1-2 (Vendor Credit)
>
> #2: Month 3-4 (Retail Credit)
>
> #3 Month: 5-6 (Cash Cards)

After six months, you'll be able to get business loans and lines of credit for your business. Using other people's money to start and build your business is key. You don't need money to make money. Wealthy people build businesses up off of credit and debt. Business credit is the difference between building a successful business and a failing one; it's really up to you.

Being a visionary in prison is the exception to the rule. Gaining financial information is hard to come by in prison, and obtaining financial wealth is even harder. You must be willing to do things others don't want to, like reading about and learning financial literacy while in prison, so you step back into the world (10) "ten" steps ahead of any competition. Learning about Business Credit is one of the steps in the process of gaining a proper financial education. Leverage this knowledge to develop your business so that it's successful. These are your fundamentals of building a business; get started now!

Separate Sources of Funding

If you build up your personal credit, you can also use it as a last resort for funding. Use the list below to apply for these separate sources of funding.

- Vendor and Revolving Accounts (P.G. required)

- Account Receivables Financing
- SBA Loans
- Revenue Credit Lines
- Private Funds Financing
- Real Estate Financing
- Revenue Lending
- Merchant Advances
- Crowd Funding
- Leasing Equipment
- Collateral Financing
- Equipment Financing

All these separate sources of financing must be obtained through a Personal Guarantee (P.G.), which means that you will have to use your personal credit to obtain these. But only use these sources to finance your business as a last option. Following the above steps in the first section should be your priority. Please don't sit in that seat you're in, surrounded by thoughtless people, and allow yourself to be swallowed up by self-doubt or that "I can't build a business from prison" naysayers. Yes, you can! I did it, and my brother has done it from a maximum-security prison cell. In your quest to build your business credit, always know there is a difference between making and keeping money; owning a business is your straightforward path to building wealth. Securing financing and funding is the most important aspect of owning and building your business. There are many more options than the ones listed above.

Naturally, your bank is the first place for you as a business owner. But the downside to that is you have to have good credit and financials for approval. Get your quick checklist log by getting your outside support to Google "SBA Loan Approval Checklist." You're looking mainly for this page, although there are probably others (www.sba.gov/content/business-loan-checklist). Having this list will help you apply for these bank loans.

While banks are still a good place to start, the majority of financing comes from Alternative lenders. Many banks focus on credit and financials. These alternative lenders focus mainly on one aspect of your business. These may be three (3) categories: Credit, Collateral, and Cash Flow. Some use one or the following: credit. Others use cash flow or collateral.

If the collateral is used – asset-based, they will still let you get financing even with bad credit or no reporting at this stage of your business. All that is required for lending is the business's acceptable collateral (assets). Examples include:

- 401(K) Accounts
- Stocks
- Inventory
- Equipment

- Real Estate
- Car Lot Inventory
- Purchase Orders
- Account Receivables

Once you use this form of lending, if you default, the lender takes the collateral (asset) you used to get the financing. It's less of a risk to these lenders because assets are put up front if things go wrong within your business.

Cash flow lending is probably the easiest and quickest way to obtain money. No collateral or bad credit will stop you from getting it. All that is needed is monthly deposits of $10,000, with at least (6) six monthly transactions. Between 10%-12% of your annual revenues can be advanced to you. Rates range from 7-50%, which usually depends on risk. Starting out, you will get approved for a 6–18-month payback window. Pay back the first one, and your terms get better and better.

Other sources include Credit Lines. I will touch briefly on these because they're the hardest, and you will need to have 2-3 years of tax returns to apply. Financials are everything for this form of funding because that's the case. Starting out, you must wait to apply these tips but still need to know about them. Knowledge is power! As I said above, you will need 2-3 years of tax returns and to give your P&L Statement (Profit & Loss Statement), a business plan, along with bank statements. Multiple things will only be accumulated over several years. When calculating your approval amounts for credit lines, these lenders look at profits on your tax returns, which should always show an increase in profit yearly. Personal and business credit will be looked at.

Last but not least, another funding source can come from a common practice known as Merchant and Revenue Advances. It is much easier to obtain than regular loans and credit lines. No financials are needed, not even tax returns. Plan out your pathway to funding using the Alternative Sources provided above.

The SBA offers other lines of credit called "CAPLines." This refers to the SBA's multiple programs to help business owners with short-term capital needs. Remember, these are loans, so all of the usually listed qualifications apply. While you sit in prison, wondering how you can do this? As a Pro Se Prisoner, we adjust and do it ourselves; my goal is to provide all the wealth-building strategies employed by 0.01%. Using the S.B.A. as a source of capital for your company fits into our motto of: "Plot, Plan, & Execute" on any given knowledge because we don't use excuses!

Some of these SBA CAPLines include:

- **Seasonal Line:** Advances against anticipated inventory and accounts receivables. It can be a loan or revolving account.
- **Builders Line:** For general contractors or builders that are contrasting or renovating commercial residential buildings. Mainly used for direct labor and material costs, this will also make the building project serve as collateral for this type of financing.
- **Contract Line:** Finance material and labor costs for assignable contracts.
- **Working Capital Line:** Borrowers must use the loan proceeds for short-term working capital/operating needs.

- **SBA Express:** This program, run by the SBA, offers credit lines to qualified borrowers. Up to $350,000. 6.5% base rate. For over $25,000, you will be required to put up some form of collateral. Good personal and business cred. Also, it requires at least $10,000 in your bank account over the last 90 days.

In 2022, it's not enough to have an idea—you have to take action on it. Plus, don't limit yourself to conventional ways of obtaining financing; go outside the box and look around at all the opportunities out there. From your list, go after these Alternative sources for financing.

Business Credit Cards

At this point in building that all-important business credit, you should have a very good credit score. The next step to building up your business credit is obtaining business credit cards. Below is a list of potential cards you should try to apply for:

- Capital One Sparks 1% Classic
  - Unlimited 1% cashback
  - No minimum purchase
  - No expiration dates
  - 5% cashback on hotels, rental cars, book through Capital One Travel
  - Fee: $0
  - Credit Score: Fair
  - www.capitalone.com
- American Express Blue Business Cash Card
  - Fee: $0
  - 0% Intro APR
  - 2% cashback for the first $50,000
  - www.americanexpress.com
- U.S. Bank Business Platinum
  - Fee: $0
  - 0% Intro APR
  - Balance Transfers 0% for 20 billing cycles
  - Pay for overtime by splitting eligible purchases of $100 into equal monthly payments
  - www.bizcards.usbank.com
- Ramp Corporate Card
  - Unlimited 1.5% cashback
  - No fee: $0 of any kind

- No ACH fees: $0
- No minimum income: $0
- Credit score: N/A
- No P.G. (Personal Guarantee)
- www.ramp.com

- Divvy
  - No fee: $0
  - Unlimited virtual card creation
  - Cashback rewards
  - www.getdivvy.com

- Brex
  - No P.G. (Personal Guarantee)
  - 8x for using ridesharing apps (rewards)
  - 5x for travel (rewards)
  - 4x for restaurant use (rewards)
  - 3x for software purchases (rewards)
  - www.brex.com

- Stripe Corporate Card
  - No APR
  - Fees: $0
  - Unlimited cashback
  - No P.G. (Personal Guarantee)
  - 1.5% cashback

- Capital One Spark Cash Plus
  - Fee $150 Annual
  - Cashback 2%-5%
  - Bonus Offer: $1,000
  - Credit: Good
  - www.capitalone.com

- Ink Business Preferred Credit Card
  - Fee $95 Annual
  - 1%-3% points/$1

- o Bonus offer: 100,000 points
- o Credit: Good
- Capital One Spark Miles for Business
  - o Travel Rewards
  - o Fee: $0 Intro for 1st year, $95 after
  - o Bonus Offer: 50,000 miles
  - o Credit: Good, 1-7 points/$1
  - o www.capitalone.com

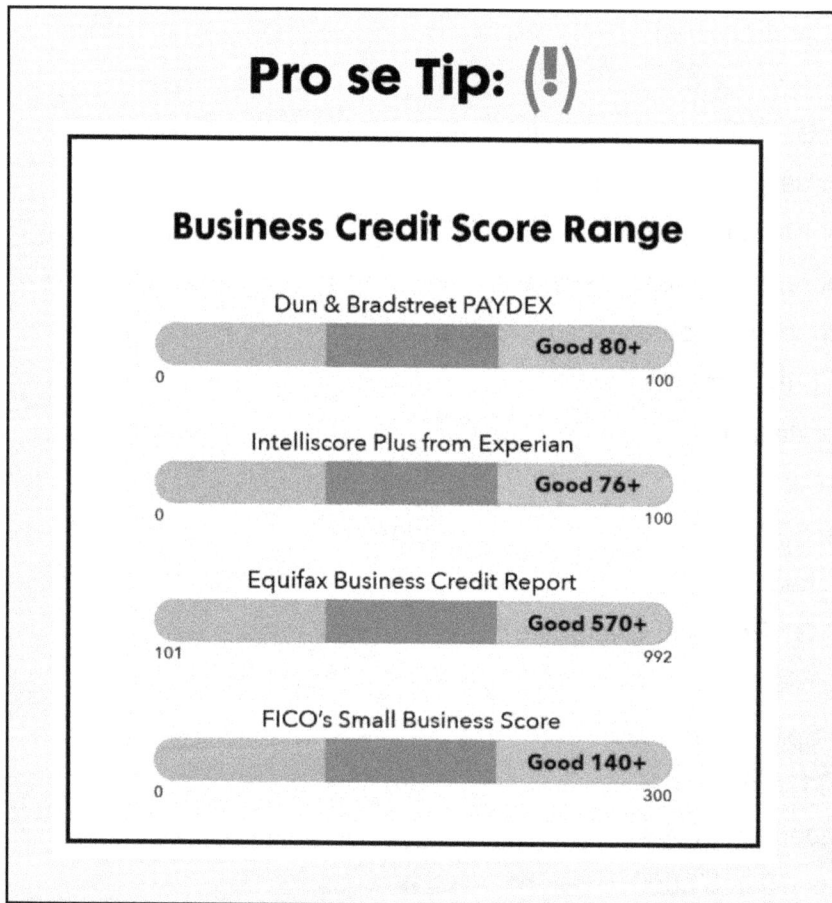

Pro se Tip: (!)

Business Credit Score Range

Dun & Bradstreet PAYDEX

Good 80+

0   100

Intelliscore Plus from Experian

Good 76+

0   100

Equifax Business Credit Report

Good 570+

101   992

FICO's Small Business Score

Good 140+

0   300

Other Credit Opportunities

- Credit STRONG Business: Best Credit Builder Loan
  - o Once you sign up, your loan is put into a savings account as collateral
  - o Monthly payments, with part going towards the principal amount and part of them going

to interest.

- o Reports payments as a Financial tradeline to Equifax, PayNet, and SBFE (Report to D&B and Experian)
- o Won't check your business or personal credit score when you apply
- o Must have three months in business to qualify, plus EIN

- Navi: Best Vendor Business Tradelines

  - o www.nav.com
  - o Offer the only business credit subscription service that lets you access your business credit score and reports from D&B
  - o Promises never to report negative business credit
  - o Price: $39.99 per month

- Credit Suite: Best Credit Builder Program

  - o www.creditsuite.com
  - o Helps you get 411 listings and establish a business bank account.
  - o Get initial business credit
  - o Shows you how to get initial vendor tradelines
  - o Get your business revolving credit
  - o Price: $3,000

- Divvy: The Best Business Credit Builder Card

  - o www.getdivvy.com
  - o Business credit card and credit lines
  - o Comes with budgeting software and rewards
  - o Plus, it is FREE $$$
  - o Not much credit? You get a secured line of credit, which you pre-funded before spending.
  - o No Fees
  - o Rewards: on restaurant, hotel spending, and reoccurring software subscriptions.

- Tillful

  - o www.tillful.com
  - o No credit check, nor will you have to sign a personal guarantee to qualify
  - o Must have LLC, EIN, and Tillful credit account
  - o Also, can't do business in restricted industries
  - o 1.5% cashback on your purchases with a Tillful card.

- Wells Fargo Business Secured Credit Card
    - www.wellsfargo.com
    - Traditional secured card
    - You must deposit $500 to $25,000 to qualify; eventually, you will graduate to an unsecured business line.
    - 1.5% cashback, 1 point for every dollar spent
    - 1,000 bonus points each time you spend more than $1,000 in a billing cycle.
    - Reports to SBFE

Net 60 Accounts (Business)

Once you have established Net 30 accounts with on-time payments for at least 90 days, it's time to move on to Net 60 accounts. Some that you should try out are:

- Amazon Net 55
    - Amazon business account allows you to buy anything your business needs
    - 55 days to pay off the balance on the account
- Supplied
    - www.supplied.co
    - Must apply through "Rumbleship"
    - No credit checks
    - Can apply at checkout on the website also
- Faire
    - www.faire.com
    - Sells products to small businesses
    - Net 60
    - Pay history and sales are considered
    - No interest, no fees, or penalties as long as you pay online
- Plume Card from American Express
    - Not a vendor per say
    - Corporate card with net terms
    - Helps better manage cash flow by extending payment terms
    - Net 60: pay before Net 60 is up, and you get benefits
    - Unlimited 1.5% cashback on purchases that are paid for within ten days of your statement closing date

- o www.americanexpress.com
- Abound
  - o www.helloabound.com
  - o Some min., as low as $30
  - o Free shipping for the first 72 hours, then 15% of the total order

Check the index section for a full list of Net 30 – 60 vendors.

Tier 2 (Advance Trade Credit)

Tier 2 is also known as advance trade credit. These tradelines in this tier are harder to get than those associated with Tier 1 (Net 30-60) vendors. They require credit checks, but the benefits are that they have better terms, higher credit limits, and longer payment terms. Usually, these Tier 2 accounts should only be obtained once you have been in business and building your business credit with a positive payment history for up to 2 years. A few of these Tier 2 advance trade credit is:

- Advanced Auto Parts
  - o Sells replacement and performance parts and accessories
  - o Reports credit: D&B
  - o Requirements: Must have five tradelines and do business as a legal entity, like an LLC or a corporation.
  - o Website: www.ebill.advancecommercial.com
- Office Depot and OfficeMax
  - o Sells office supplies
  - o Reports credit: D&B
  - o Requirements: Must have been in business for 3 years and have multiple trade lines with a positive payment history.
  - o Website: www.business.officedepot.com
- Home Depot
  - o Sells home improvement products
  - o Reporting Credit: D&B, Equifax Business, Experian Business
  - o Requirements: Must have reasonably established business with multiple Tier 1 tradelines
  - o Website: www.homedepot.com
- Lowes
  - o Sells home improvement products

- o Reports Credit: D&B
- o Requirement: Established Teir 1 tradelines and positive payment history
- o Website: www.businessapply.syf.com
- BP Fuel Credit Card
  - o Allows you to build business credit while getting cheap gas
  - o Report Credit: D&B
  - o Requirement: Must have reasonably established business credit with multiple Tier 1 tradelines.
  - o Website: www.bpbusinesssolutions.com
- Valero Fleet Card
  - o Allows you to build business credit and get cheap gas.
  - o Report Credit: D&B
  - o Requirements: Established Tier 1 tradelines and positive payment history
  - o Website: www.valerofleetcards.com

While this isn't a full list of Tier 2 companies, you can see what some of the latest in this industry of Tier 2 companies require. So, you can know what to expect in 2 to 3 years of building up Tier 1 credit. Maybe it will take you a year to accomplish excellent credit for your business. Tier 2 will be there and available to you sooner. To see a full list of Tier 2 companies, check out the "Index" section at the back of this book.

The $500 Business Credit Building Strategy

For a quick cheat code on how to spend $500 to build $100K worth of business credit in a couple of months, check this step-by-step out.

1. Purchase LLC
2. Obtain EIN & DUNS Numbers
3. Open a Business Bank Account and Write Yourself a Loan
4. Get a Tradeline with, www.nav.com
5. Open vendor accounts with ULINE, QUILL
6. Payback 5 Days Early, Rinse and Repeat
7. Do #6 until you have 3-5 payment experiences.
8. Once #7 is completed, move on to tier 2, where you will get a line of credit for up to $100k. Make sure you complete the above steps in #5-#6 for 90 days before going to tier 2. Some companies will accept your great payment history, and others may not. But the process allows you to use $500 to obtain a $100k line of credit in 90 days.
9. When you apply for vendor accounts using your business EIN number, freeze your personal credit file with the three major credit bureaus. To do this, use the website links

below:

Before You Apply For These Business Vendors, Freeze Your Personal Credit File.

- Experian: www.experian.com/freeze/center.html
- Equifax: www.equifax.com/personal/credit-report-services/credit-freeze/
- Transunion: www.transunion.com/credit-freeze

Credit Flips Wholesale

Another secret of the credit world is credit flips, which allow you to combine the different features of one card with another company's similar cards and use their combined power to benefit from flipping credit.

1. Obtain an Amex Amazon Business card from Amazon and get Net 45 terms that will double to Net 90 when combined with an Amazon Business Prime account: longer terms, better payment history, and bigger lines of credit.

2. Obtain the Sam's Club Business Mastercard. It only offers Net 30, but you can get 5% back in Sam's cash for gasoline purchases and 3% on restaurants and anything you buy from Sam's Club!

Everything that has been provided to you in this section will propel you to excellent business credit. We often have visions and ideas of what we want to accomplish, but the one person we think we need to help us never shows up. My goal has always been to provide you with information you otherwise wouldn't get in prison. So, you can better prepare financially for your freedom and be able to choose starting a business with ownership over employment. It's up to you now to use this business credit information to take action in your life. I have a purpose as I wake up in the same type of cell you are in. I own a company and have been here for 17 years (since I was 15). What I know or accomplished has been done during this incarceration. Use the knowledge, take action, and build your business using this section's credit tips. Remember, reinvent yourself to build a better future for you and your family.

Pro se Tip: (!)

Generational poverty is about mindset, not money! Intelligence is evenly distributed. Stop low-level thinking, that you pass from generation to generation. Each generation always accept the lower level. One of the greatest things that happen to me was coming to prison. Sit down and mature in there. Prison has allowed me to play offense, and not victim [defense]. Knowledge is the learning process!

Credit Fundamentals Definitions

- **Adverse Action:** An unfavorable action, such as the denial of credit, insurance, or employment, taken by a creditor or other entity affecting a consumer.

- **Annual Fees:** The yearly fee a lender charges to maintain an account.

- **Annual Percentage Rate [APR]:** The cost of credit at a yearly rate

- **Balance:** The amount of money you owe to a particular lender.

- **Bank Card:** A credit card issued through a bank.

- **Charge Card**: A credit card that requires full payment of the bill each month; no interest is charged.

- **Charge Off:** A loan or credit card debt written off as uncollectible from the borrower. The debt, however, remains valid and subject to collection.

- **Collection:** When a borrower falls behind, the lender contacts them in an effort to bring the loan current. The loan goes to collection.

- **Consumer:** Defined as an individual.

- **Credit:** A trust or promise to buy now and pay later under designated terms for goods or services.

- **Credit Card:** A card that allows a consumer to pay a portion or all of the outstanding amount each month and has a credit limit.

- **Credit Check:** An inquiry to confirm a consumer's credit payment history.

- **Credit Dispute:** To request an investigation of the accuracy of information on a credit report.

- **Credit File:** The collection of information each credit reporting agency maintains in their databases.

- **Credit History:** The record of a consumer's credit accounts and manner of payment. Credit history includes high credit, current balance, credit limit, and 24 months or more of payment history.

- **Credit Limit:** The maximum amount you are allowed to borrow from a lender under the terms of your agreement for an account.

- **Creditor:** Person or business to whom a debt is owed.

- **Dispute:** If you have reviewed your credit report and found some data to be inaccurate, you can dispute it by contacting the companies involved to start the process.

- **FICO Score:** A credit score produced from models developed by Fair Isaac Corporation. The score measures a consumer's creditworthiness and risk and is in use worldwide. Scores range from 300-850.

- **Finance Charges:** The amount you are charged to use credit.
- **Fixed-Rate Mortgage:** A mortgage where the loan's interest rate remains the same over the life of the loan.
- **Cross Monthly Income:** What you earn before taxes are deducted.
- **Interest:** The cost of borrowing or lending money, usually a percentage of the amount borrowed or loaned.
- **Interest Rate:** A % of money a lender charges for borrowing money.
- **Late Payment:** A delinquent payment is a failure to deliver a loan or debt payment on or before the time agreed.
- **Line of Credit:** Credit limit established by a creditor.

HOW TO DISPUTE
CREDIT REPORT (EXPANDED)

Any action you take to dispute your credit report must first be based on understanding a specific set of laws buried among hundreds of pages of laws and regulations passed by Congress and the IRS.

The Fair Debt Collection Practices Act [FDCPA] explains the laws that all collection agencies must follow. Another Fair Credit Collection agency must follow. Another Fair Credit Reporting Act [FCRA] explains the rules and laws that credit bureaus and creditors/banks must abide by. At the same time, the Fair Credit Billing Act [FCBA] is for disputes about "billing errors," such as charges that list the wrong date or amount, failure to post payments and other credits, etc. Others include the" Metro 2 Compliance," which standardizes the information reported to all 3 credit bureaus so that furnishers of credit information to bureaus must use the proper formatting in a form that contains 67 fields.

You can dispute inquiries on your credit report; new credit inquiries account for about 10% of your credit score. Hard inquiries will damage your credit score temporarily. If inquiries reach 2 years old, they are supposed to be automatically removed and don't affect your credit score. Once they are at least 6 months old, one-half of the effect on your score is that compared to recent inquiries. Soft inquiry (soft pull) does not damage your credit score. Once you have requested your credit report, send the below dispute unauthorized inquiries letter to remove them. These are for Experian and Equifax.

experian.

Dispute Form

Use this form for any disputes you wish to submit by mail. You can submit additional dispute forms if have several disputes. Complete all of the following information and submit by mail. Once we receive your dispute, it make take up to 30 days to process your dispute. We will then notify you of the results. You may also submit a dispute by mail using your own format.

Would you like to receive your dispute results more quickly? Enter your email address, and we will notify you as soon as your results are ready to be viewed online. _____

Be advised that written information or documents you provide with respect to your disputes may be shared with any and all creditors with which you are disputing.

Your current identification information

Name:	Middle Initial:	Generation:
Social Security number:		Date of Birth:
Mailing Address:		

Is any of the information below incorrect on your report?
- Spouse's name   ☐ Employer (Which one is incorrect?) _____
- Date of Birth (Fill in your correct date of birth) __ / __ / __   ☐ Address (Which one is incorrect?) _____
- Telephone number (Which one is incorrect?) __ / __ / __   ☐ Name (Which one is incorrect?) _____
- Social Security number (Which one is incorrect?) _____

Dispute

Company name:	Your partial account number:

I believe this item is incorrect because (Choose only one):
- ☐ Payment never late
- ☐ Account closed
- ☐ Paid in full – On what date? _____ / _____
- ☐ Account included in bankruptcy – Chapter: _____   Filing date: ___ / ___
- ☐ Not my account – Who does it belong to? _____
- ☐ Other – Must explain: _____

Dispute

Company name:	Your partial account number:

I believe this item is incorrect because (Choose only one):
- ☐ Payment never late
- ☐ Account closed
- ☐ Paid in full – On what date? _____ / _____
- ☐ Account included in bankruptcy – Chapter: _____   Filing date: ___ / ___
- ☐ Not my account – Who does it belong to? _____
- ☐ Other – Must explain: _____

Dispute

Company name:	Your partial account number:

I believe this item is incorrect because (Choose only one):
- ☐ Payment never late
- ☐ Account closed
- ☐ Paid in full – On what date? _____ / _____
- ☐ Account included in bankruptcy – Chapter: _____   Filing date: ___ / ___
- ☐ Not my account – Who does it belong to? _____
- ☐ Other – Must explain: _____

Dispute

Company name:	Your partial account number:

I believe this item is incorrect because (Choose only one):
- ☐ Payment never late
- ☐ Account closed
- ☐ Paid in full – On what date? _____ / _____
- ☐ Account included in bankruptcy – Chapter: _____   Filing date: ___ / ___
- ☐ Not my account – Who does it belong to? _____
- ☐ Other – Must explain: _____

EQUIFAX®

DISPUTE REQUEST FORM

To dispute any inaccuracies on your Equifax credit report, please send – via U.S. Mail - this form along with copies of the items below in order to verify your information and address. To ensure that your request is processed accurately, please enlarge copies of any items that contain small print (i.e. driver's license, W2 Forms, etc.). Copies that are not legible or contain highlighting may cause us to request that you resubmit your request for clarity. You can also submit disputes online at myequifax.com.

Identification Information

First Name	Last Name		Middle Initial	Suffix

Current Address	City		State	Zip

Former Address	City		State	Zip

SSN	Date of Birth
	M M D D Y Y Y Y

Proof of Identity
(check box for and include a copy of one of the following)

- Social Security Card
- Pay stub with Social Security Number
- W2 or 1099 Form

The item you select must contain your SSN

Proof of Address
(check box for and include a copy of one of the following)

- Driver's license or state identification card
- Rental lease agreement/house deed
- Pay stub with address
- Utility or phone bill (gas, electric, water, cable, mobile)

The item you select must contain your current mailing address

If your identity information differs from the information listed on your credit report, please provide a copy of your driver's license, social security card, or recent utility bill that reflects the correct information.

Complete, Print, and send (via U.S. mail) this form along with the requested documents to the following address:

Equifax Information Services LLC
P.O. Box 740241
Atlanta, GA 30374

FRAUD/IDENTITY THEFT VICTIM

Please check this box if you are disputing items on your credit report that you suspect to be fraudulent or a result of identity theft.

If you have a Police Report, FTC Identity Theft Report, or Affidavit of Fraud documenting fraud/identity theft, please include a copy with this request.

Dispute Personal Information (Is any of the information below incorrect on your credit report? If not, leave blank.)

Date of Birth (Which is incorrect)

Phone Number (Which is incorrect?)

Social Security Number (Which is incorrect?)
M M   D D   Y Y Y Y

Employers (Which are incorrect?)

Names (Which are incorrect?)

Addresses (Which are incorrect?)

EQUIFAX®

DISPUTE REQUEST FORM

Credit Account Information

Enter the information for accounts or inquiries on your credit report with any inaccuracies. Include correct information (e.g. Balance, payment date) and attach supporting documentation (e.g. account statement, payment confirmation) if applicable. Any documentation provided will be shared with the companies with which the dispute is being made as part of the dispute process.

Company Name   Account Number/Inquiry Date

DISPUTE 1

Reason for Dispute(select the most appropriate option):

Account Not Mine	Account Closed	Current/Previous Payment Status Incorrect	Fraud
Account Paid in Full	Inquiry Removal	Last payment date/Closed Date Incorrect	
Mixed with Another Person	Not Liable	Date of Last Activity Incorrect	

Other (please explain)

Dispute Details

Company Name   Account Number/Inquiry Date

DISPUTE 2

Reason for Dispute(select the most appropriate option):

Account Not Mine	Account Closed	Current/Previous Payment Status Incorrect	Fraud
Account Paid in Full	Inquiry Removal	Last payment date/Closed Date Incorrect	
Mixed with Another Person	Not Liable	Date of Last Activity Incorrect	

Other (please explain)

Dispute Details

Company Name   Account Number/Inquiry Date

DISPUTE 3

Reason for Dispute(select the most appropriate option):

Account Not Mine	Account Closed	Current/Previous Payment Status Incorrect	Fraud
Account Paid in Full	Inquiry Removal	Last payment date/Closed Date Incorrect	
Mixed with Another Person	Not Liable	Date of Last Activity Incorrect	

Other (please explain)

Dispute Details

EQUIFAX®   *DISPUTE REQUEST FORM*

Company Name   Account Number/Inquiry Date
DISPUTE 4

Reason for Dispute(select the most appropriate option):
    Account Not Mine   Account Closed   Current/Previous Payment Status Incorrect   Fraud
    Account Paid in Full   Inquiry Removal   Last payment date/Closed Date Incorrect
    Mixed with Another Person Not Liable   Date of Last Activity Incorrect
Other (please explain)

Dispute Details

Company Name   Account Number/Inquiry Date
DISPUTE 5

Reason for Dispute(select the most appropriate option):
    Account Not Mine   Account Closed   Current/Previous Payment Status Incorrect   Fraud
    Account Paid in Full   Inquiry Removal   Last payment date/Closed Date Incorrect
    Mixed with Another Person Not Liable   Date of Last Activity Incorrect
Other (please explain)

Dispute Details

Company Name   Account Number/Inquiry Date
DISPUTE 6

Reason for Dispute(select the most appropriate option):
    Account Not Mine   Account Closed   Current/Previous Payment Status Incorrect   Fraud
    Account Paid in Full   Inquiry Removal   Last payment date/Closed Date Incorrect
    Mixed with Another Person Not Liable   Date of Last Activity Incorrect
Other (please explain)

Dispute Details

EQUIFAX®

DISPUTE REQUEST FORM

DISPUTE 7

Company Name

Account Number/Inquiry Date

Reason for Dispute(select the most appropriate option):

Account Not Mine	Account Closed	Current/Previous Payment Status Incorrect	Fraud
Account Paid in Full	Inquiry Removal	Last payment date/Closed Date Incorrect	
Mixed with Another Person	Not Liable	Date of Last Activity Incorrect	

Other (please explain)

Dispute Details

DISPUTE 8

Company Name

Account Number/Inquiry Date

Reason for Dispute(select the most appropriate option):

Account Not Mine	Account Closed	Current/Previous Payment Status Incorrect	Fraud
Account Paid in Full	Inquiry Removal	Last payment date/Closed Date Incorrect	
Mixed with Another Person	Not Liable	Date of Last Activity Incorrect	

Other (please explain)

Dispute Details

DISPUTE 9

Company Name

Account Number/Inquiry Date

Reason for Dispute(select the most appropriate option):

Account Not Mine	Account Closed	Current/Previous Payment Status Incorrect	Fraud
Account Paid in Full	Inquiry Removal	Last payment date/Closed Date Incorrect	
Mixed with Another Person	Not Liable	Date of Last Activity Incorrect	

Other (please explain)

Dispute Details

EQUIFAX ®   *DISPUTE REQUEST FORM*

                    Company Name   Account Number/Inquiry Date
DISPUTE 10

Reason for Dispute(select the most appropriate option):
    Account Not Mine   Account Closed   Current/Previous Payment Status Incorrect   Fraud
    Account Paid in Full   Inquiry Removal   Last payment date/Closed Date Incorrect
    Mixed with Another Person   Not Liable   Date of Last Activity Incorrect
Other (please explain)

Dispute Details

                    Company Name   Account Number/Inquiry Date
DISPUTE 11

Reason for Dispute(select the most appropriate option):
    Account Not Mine   Account Closed   Current/Previous Payment Status Incorrect   Fraud
    Account Paid in Full   Inquiry Removal   Last payment date/Closed Date Incorrect
    Mixed with Another Person   Not Liable   Date of Last Activity Incorrect
Other (please explain)

Dispute Details

                    Company Name   Account Number/Inquiry Date
DISPUTE 12

Reason for Dispute(select the most appropriate option):
    Account Not Mine   Account Closed   Current/Previous Payment Status Incorrect   Fraud
    Account Paid in Full   Inquiry Removal   Last payment date/Closed Date Incorrect
    Mixed with Another Person   Not Liable   Date of Last Activity Incorrect
Other (please explain)

Dispute Details

When sending letters to creditors and collection agencies is a two-step process. One deals with creditors and collection agencies, and the other deals with credit bureaus. Okay! These letters must be sent by Certified Mail, with a return receipt requested. This allows you to ensure delivery within a documented timeframe from when it was received by the credit bureaus, creditors, and collection agencies. Never dispute anything online or over the phone. Under existing law, when you do it that way, you waive the right to see the method of verification received by the bureaus from the creditors. This way of using Certified Mail proves that credit bureaus and collection agencies failed to investigate properly. [It's your evidence] in the 30-day timeframe required under the law. After the 30th day or exactly 31 days after they have signed your letter, you will need to print out a new credit report to see if the collection agencies or creditors marked them with "disputed," as the law requires. If they haven't after 30 days, they have violated the "FRCA" and "FDCPA." You are able to challenge any item that you believe is unverifiable or inaccurate. These laws are filled with loopholes for disputing things, so everything is black and white. Let's say the item you claim is yours, and you still want it removed from your credit report. You can challenge it by asserting these potential errors occurred: incorrect balance, missing information, incorrect credit limit, high balance is lower than owed balance, "status" or any other field blank, "status" incorrect, incorrect high balance, late pay after an account was closed; account number inaccurate [includes x's or asterisks instead of full numbers], account type inaccurate, and invalid furnisher, etc. Oh yeah, some of the most common potential errors are the date of the last update being incorrect, the date reported inaccurate, the collection account listed with a limit, but a collection cannot have a limit, and the charge off listed as "open" or collection. Letter #1 should be sent directly to the banks or agencies that report inaccurate or unverifiable derogatory or collection items to the credit bureaus. See the Credit Index for the form at the end of this section.

Next, once you receive a letter back from a creditor/collection agency in reply to **Letter #1** saying your account was verified as accurate reporting, you should send **Letter #2** to them, but only if they respond to your **Letter #1** and say it's "verified as accurate." If they don't respond, don't send **Letter #2**. See Credit Index for Sample **Letter #2**. If you don't get a response from Letter #1 from the creditor/collection agency, you should send **Letter #2** [No Response]. See sample in Credit Index.

Just imagine you are disputing collection accounts on your report, and the collection agency doesn't answer you, but the original creditor does. This can't happen by law, so if the original creditor responded to you, send them **Letter #2 – No response/Creditor Response**. See sample in Credit Index. Under certain circumstances, the creditor/collection agency will respond with proof of original signature. On the 31st day from the date you received your first letter, check your credit report to make sure they have not marked the item "disputed." If it's not marked "disputed" in the "comment section," send **Letter #3**. See sample in Credit Index Section. If they did mark it as "disputed," send the next document, **Letter #4**. See sample in Credit Index. That simple credit repair is simple; we just have to know the process, and it's very straightforward. Remember, Letter #4 is for when you have made up your mind that you want to take legal action in small claims court. If you choose to take another route, as is your right, then you need to proceed to deal with the credit bureaus directly. No matter what you do, unless you have reason to dispute student loans or Public Records, never start disputing with the credit bureaus first. There is a "process" to this disputing game. First, you have to dispute the inaccurate, unverifiable, or unfair items, per FCRA [Section 611(a)(1)(A)], if you receive a response to your challenge dispute from the reporting agency: "saying the disputed item was verified." You have a right under existing law to ask for "Method of Verification" under FCRA, Section 611(a)(6) and (7). You must be given this method within 15 days. The trick is that most of these reporting/creditors/agencies can't do this because they never speak to anyone to get verification. These big agencies and companies use automation to do simple tasks to save money. These systems mess up what real humans would usually spot, but because they don't want to pay salaries to real humans, they contract out and computer automate this work. Hence, there are problems. Their mess-up is your gain! Once they automate the "verification," it becomes insufficient. That's why you request evidence such as the name, address, and telephone number of anyone from the original creditor they contacted.

Pro se Tip: (!)

Identity IQ is a service that allows you to check all three of your credit reports, plus offer Identity Protection. Credit Karma is another that checks your scores and credit report. Don't ever dispute by using Credit Karma.

Remember, we are following steps in the process of disputing what's on your credit report so we can push your credit score up based on a new set of circumstances. Combining disputing with building credit is a powerful tool that will improve your credit tenfold. All the templates enclosed at the back of this Part 1 that you can choose to copy; just put your information on and send it home to your network to make sure it's sent off using Certified Mail as proof that it was sent off. MAKE COPIES OF ALL YOUR DOCUMENTS AS A RECORD!

In addition to the normal stuff on the credit report that needs disputing, here are a few more areas to dispute so you can clear up your credit.

Vehicular Repossession

These are direct loans that will appear on your credit report because they are lending loans, which you are typically pre-approved for in advance. Repossession occurs when these aren't paid back, which hits your credit report as negative.

When the dealership is the lender, it is considered a "credit sale." More importantly, when this happens, the lender on your paperwork isn't the actual lender. What happens is that it's usually an outside company that purchased a contract or debt from the dealer. Credit bureaus inaccurately report this. When your credit report has this type of account as a loan instead of credit sales, you can dispute this easily.

Dispute Process:

- All documents related to vehicle purchase
- Repossession notices
- Original retail installment sales contract
- All documents from dealer and lender
- Correspondence from dealer and lender

- Documents relating to all car repairs.
- Inspection documents; and
- All payments on the car loan

Now, once your car is repossessed, the lender must provide 2 notices to you:

#1: First Notice: Redemption

This notice must be provided to the car's owner and all co-buyers or co-signers. The lender must send it to you at least 10 days before the proposed sale of the car.

Pro se Tip: (!)

Filing for bankruptcy can prevent repossession. While bankruptcy is pending you can even catch up on past-due payments or pay off the car in that timeframe.

#2 Second Notice: Deficiency

Once your car has been sold and you have received your first notice of redemption, Lenders are required to send out a second notice stating the amount that the lender credited you from the resale, as well as a cancellation notice of the original sales contract.

All car dealers and lenders must follow these laws:

- Uniform Commercial Code
- Retail Installment Sales Act
- Truth in Lending Act
- Consumer Fraud Act

When laws are not followed, legal action usually follows. Now, let's get to the most important reason. I even included this in this book. I was getting the repo off your credit report by disputing it. The process is no different from the previously mentioned credit disputes, which I have talked about previously. Send Repo Letter #1 below to the collection agency, original creditor, and car dealerships.

Repo Letter #1

REPOSSESSION DISPUTE LETTER TO CREDIT BUREAU

> **Note:** This PDF is largely for educational purposes **because you need to edit it.**
>
> To edit it:
>
> 1. Open it in Microsoft Word, or your word processing software of choice.
> 2. It may be faster to download the Microsoft Word version of this document.
> 3. For more instructions, go to the end of this document.

[Your full name]
[Credit report number]
[Identifying information requested by company, typically including:
- Date of birth
- Address
- Telephone number]
[Return address, if different from your registered address on your credit report]
[Optional: Social Security number or driver's license number]

[Date]

[Credit bureau's address—one of the following:
    Equifax Information Services, LLC, P.O. Box 740256, Atlanta, GA 30374
    Experian, P.O. Box 4500, Allen, TX 75013
    TransUnion Consumer Solutions, P.O. Box 2000, Chester, PA 19016]

Re: Disputing a repossession on my credit report

Dear [Equifax, Experian, or TransUnion],

I am writing to request the investigation and correction of a repossession that appears on my credit report. The credit report number is **[report number]**. The repossession is listed under account number **[account number]**, and the account was opened on **[opening date]** with **[name of company or lender/creditor]**.

This repossession is **[inaccurate/incomplete/obsolete]** because **[describe which information is inaccurate or incomplete, or state that the repossession is more than seven years old]**. I am requesting that the item **[be removed or otherwise changed]** to correct the information.

I have enclosed copies of my credit report with the disputed information highlighted. I have also attached **[any other supporting documents, such as payment records and court documents]** to support my dispute.

Please reinvestigate this repossession, and **[delete/correct]** it as soon as possible. Thank you for your attention to this matter.

Sincerely,

[Your Name]

Enclosures: **[List documents you are enclosing, e.g., a copy of your credit report]**

Once that is done, wait at least 15 days or send the First Repo Letter before you send Repo Letter 2 below.

Repo Letter #2

Repossession Dispute

Sometimes when your car is repossessed the original creditor sells the car for less than the amount remaining on your loan. When this happens they can come after you for the balance, called the *deficiency*. This letter is for the purpose of disputing collection activities on a deficiency from a motor vehicle repossession. It may be used AFTER 2 years from the date of the repo sale, providing there has been no filed claim for a judgment. It should not be used if you have been sued, or if the repossession is less than 2 years ago. The following site has all the state's repo laws listed: http://www.nfa.org/Site_search.html

Send a copy to EACH of the parties (collection agency and original creditor) Certified Return Receipt Request.

Your Name
123 Your Street Address
Your City, ST 01234

Cheatem Collections
123 Fagetaboutit Ave
Chicago, IL

Date

Name of Original Creditor
Address of OC

Name of Original Seller (car dealer)
Addess of OS

Re: Acct # XXXX-XXXX-XXXX-XXXX (collection agency)
Re: Acct # XXXX-XXXX-XXXX-XXXX (original creditor)

Make of car:
Model:
VIN#

To Whom It May Concern:

I am writing in regard to the above referenced accounts and transactions.

This vehicle was repossessed by <Original Creditor> in the State of <Your State> on or about, xx/xx/xxxx, and resold on or about xx/xx/xxxx.

Under the laws of the State of <State where car was repossessed> UCC § <Your stat's UCC code, you will need to look this up> and State RISA and MVISA statutes a deficiency can not be claimed unless all of the required notices were properly and timely given, and all of the allowable redemption and cure time limits were adhered to.

Please provide copies of the legal notices and proof of the commercially reasonable manner of the resale of the subject vehicle.

If no such proof is provided within 14 days from receipt of this notice, the alleged claim of a deficiency will be considered null and void, and any continued collection activities, or continued reporting of this invalid claim on my credit reports will be considered a violation of the FDCPA and FCRA.

In addition, if you singularly or severally fail to comply with the above requests, I reserve the right to seek damages against all parties, under all available State and Federal statutes and UCC § 9 remedies .

Sincerely,

XXXX

There is no magic formula to the process of disputing inaccurate information on your credit report; vehicle reports are the same, just a different item on the list to be removed. Not everyone reading this is or has been in prison. Some of you have just gotten or never been incarcerated, so vehicle repossession might be for you. However, the information is needed to dispute old or new items on your credit report.

HIPPA and Medical Collections

Collection agencies love to harass people about medical bills and whether or not the lender has messed up. Remember, the same process applies to all disputes. If these agencies keep calling and sending letters about unpaid medical bills, send them letter #1 at the start of the section, "Inquiry Removal Letter #1", the same one you sent to the credit bureaus, and inform them that you want them to send you a copy of all medical bills that they claim to be yours. They often don't have proof of an agreement with the original creditor, which is important because, without it, they are not supposed to be harassing you about the alleged debt. Important to remember is that if they don't have a copy of a signed contract where you agreed to allegedly pay the charges, you can dispute and win. HIPPA violations are the easiest way to remove these off-credit reports quickly. Medical bills reveal personal medical information about you, so if any medical provider alludes to your condition or what you may have been treated for on these bills, they have violated HIPPA privacy provisions. All throughout this book, I have spoken of leverage in the financial sense; now, a violation of HIPPA gives you the same kind of leverage because the violation of HIPPA healthcare of leverage, because the violation of HIPPA by healthcare providers is an easy court case that can be won. Every citizen in the U.S.A., in prison or outside of prison, has to know your rights; these credit bureaus and collection agencies break the law thousands of times a day. But they don't care because if they have 100,000 clients and only 1,000 dispute the debt or unpaid bills from their credit report, it's a win because the 1,000 clients don't put a dent in their pocket. They know that the other 99,000 don't know the law, so they will get over on them and make more money off their debt, so the risk is worth it to them. Collection agencies will let you get your credit fixed and then turn to the people who don't know the law and continue to make money by going after those who don't know. LEARN YOUR RIGHTS! So, if you want to dispute medical bills, etc., send the below letter to the original health care provider.

Health Care Provider Letter

HIPAA & FCRA The Legal Basis

FORM LETTER TO ORIGINAL HEALTH CARE PROVIDER

(Your Name)

(address)

(City,State, zip)

s.s.# (social security #)

HIPAA Compliance Office

(health care provider creditor)

(address)

(date)

Dear Sir/Madam;

This letter is in reference to (account #) for services provided to (name of patient) on (date of service).

In regard to the bill on this account in the amount of ($___):

Insert correct insert here:(see inserts) (a) (b) or (c)

Please be advised that under Federal Statutes. the Fair Credit Reporting Act, (15 U.S.C. § 1681 et seq)and (name of your State)'s Consumer Credit Statutes,and subtitle D of the ARRA ,SEC. 13401. APPLICATION OF SECURITY PROVISIONS AND PENALTIES TO BUSINESS ASSOCIATES OF COVERED ENTITIES;and SEC. 13407(1) BREACH OF SECURITY.—The term "breach of security" means, with respect to unsecured PHR identifiable health information of an individual in a personal health record, acquisition of such information without the authorization of the individual. you may be held liable for the actions of (collection agency name). Please note that the effective date for commencing enforcement of penalties against you for any vicarious liability is February 17, 2009.

(a) Duty of furnishers of information to provide accurate information.

(1) Prohibition.

(A) Reporting information with actual knowledge of errors.

A person shall not furnish any information relating to a consumer to any consumer reporting agency if the person knows or consciously avoids knowing that the information is inaccurate.

In addition, the HIPAA and (name of your State)'s Medical Privacy Statutes and the penalty provisions of the ARRA section D, privacy provisions are in effect in this situation even though the health care services you provided may have been prior to enactment of HIPAA or ARRA .

The Privacy Rules prohibits a covered entity from using or disclosing an individual's protected health information ("PHI") unless specifically authorized by the individual or otherwise allowed under the Privacy Rules.

In general, PHI encompasses substantially all "individually identifiable health information" that is transmitted or maintained in any medium. "Individually identifiable health information" includes health information that is created or received by a health care provider, health plan, employer, or health care clearinghouse, and that relates to an individual's physical or mental health or condition, including information related to an individual's care or the PAYMENT for such care.

Your furnishing of my account information to (collection agency name), is not in compliance with HIPAA,or (name of your State}'s Privacy Act, and any subsequent reporting of this account on my credit reports to (credit reporting bureaus) is a clear violation of Public Law 104-191 ("HIPAA") since there can be no permissible business purpose in divulging protected health information to anyone on an account once there is no longer any payment due.

You are required under the FCRA and FACTA to accurately report the status of any account to the credit bureaus, and you are prohibited under the HIPAA and State privacy regulations from doing so on a PAID account, as there is no longer any permitted business purpose.

Therefore I am requesting you promptly rescind all such account information furnished to (collection agency) and require them to purge their records of all reference to this account, and that you insure that any and all reporting of this account is immediately deleted from my credit reports.

This simple procedure to request the deletion of ALL reference to this account from the records of (collection agency name) and to require them to have this account information deleted in its entirety from my credit reports will resolve this problem completely.

Please respond, in writing within 10 days that you are processing this request.

I am reserving the right, to take appropriate legal and civil action including reporting to any applicable regulatory authorities any lack of cooperation or compliance with this request.

I hereby waive my rights under HIPAA and any State Privacy Act for the single purpose of your transmission of this request and accompanying documentation in any required report you must make to your E &O insurance carrier.

Sincerely,

signature

(Your Name)

-

INSERTS

....

(insert a)

Enclosed please find my remittance of ($___) for payment in full of this account.

(insert this if the payment is less than billed)This payment in full is for services as per the attached fee schedule from XXXX XXXX)

Health Care Billing Charts

Please note, my remittance is payable ONLY to (hc provider) and may not be signed over or transferred to any third party collection agency, as this would constitute an additional violation of HIPAA and State Privacy Act rules .

Copies of this correspondence and a copy of the remittance check may be used for any further actions with State or Federal agencies

....

(insert b)

This account is in error.

It has either been paid, is a billing error,or was not transmitted in a timely manner to my insurance company.

It is not a valid bill and has been properly disputed, therefore I request complete deletion from all your agent (name of CA)'s records and archives.

....

(insert c)

This is not my account,

It has been billed to me in error. and has been properly disputed, therefore I request complete deletion from all your agent (name of CA)'s records and archives.

....

INSTRUCTIONS FOR FOLLOW UP TO "HIPAA" LETTER TO ORIGINAL CREDITOR HEALTH CARE PROVIDER

ALL FURTHER CORRESPONDENCE SHOULD BE SENT CMRR

1-

Make sure any money order has been deposited ,or you have received a return receipt from your letter if insert "b" or "c" were used.

2-

Send the follow up letter posted below.

3-

Send a copy of the follow up letter to the OC (legal dept) with the cover letter, (follows letter to CRA)

4-

If the CRA responds with verification from the CA or the OC, file a complaint with the HIPAA administration for the OC's violation of the privacy rules of HIPAA,and with any available State's Medical Privacy Act administration.

If they do NOT respond with any verification and the account is NOT deleted, file a civil suit against the OC and the CA for their liability for violations of the FCRA and FACTA.

5-

DO NOT under any circumstances, write or correspond with the CA regarding this matter, any correspondence or communication that YOU instigate, while not a waiver of your privacy rights under HIPAA, will impede any cause of action you might have as the non permitted "communication" would have come from YOU.

Please understand, the CA may have NO liability under HIPAA, they are NOT the health provider. They are not in any way covered under the provisions of the act for "old accounts", however, if the account is "new" they ALSO must abide by all the privacy act rules,if THEY violate, they can also be named in your filed complaints.

Letter To Cra After HIPAA Letter

Use this AFTER you have received the green card back and received verification that any money order has been deposited (if using insert "a")

To Equiexptu

Sirs;

This is a dispute of account information on my credit report, (report #)

Please re-investigate (or investigate if you have not previously disputed) the following disputed account on my credit report.

(give CA name and acct. #)

Please furnish me with verification that (CA name) is reporting this account from (OC name) for ($ amount) in my name.

I require the identification of the reporting party and the date of their verification.

Please be advised that this request is being made in accordance with the requirements of the FCRA and FACTA and the reporting privacy rules of the HIPAA and (your State)'s Medical Privacy Act.

Sincerely,

Ido N Tnow

(Send a copy to the HIPAA Compliance Dept. of the OC health provider with the following cover letter)

Cover Letter

Your Name

Address

HIPAA Compliance Office

OC Name

Address

Re: Letter of (date of orginal letter)

Account #(original account #)

Dear Sir or Madam;

Enclosed please find a copy of my letter(s) of dispute to (CRA (s)).

Please note, I am providing you with an additional opportunity to have this account removed from (CA) and deleted from my credit reports if you have not already done so.

I have no desire to cause you unnecessary difficulty,however,this entry of my private health care information,on my credit report, for an account that no longer has ANY permitted business purpose waiver since there is NO payment due, has caused injury to my credit reputation,and has left me no choice but to proceed with the following:

Upon my receipt of the FCRA and FACTA mandated reply from (CRA),if the account has NOT been deleted in its entirety,I will take appropriate action to enforce my rights under the HIPAA, FCRA and FACTA rules, ARRA and (your State)'s Consumer

Protection and Medical Privacy statutes.

Sincerely,

HIPAA COMPLAINT PROCESS

FILING A HIPAA COMPLAINT

FTC COMPLAINT AGAINST CRA

When you want to notify the agency that the debt is beyond the statute of limitations or subject to HIPPA privacy loans, send the letter to them on the next page.

PRE HIPAA MEDICAL DISPUTE LETTER TO CRA

PRE HIPAA MEDICAL DISPUTE LETTER TO CRA

You dispute medical accounts this way:

Dear CRA,

My name is xxxxx xxxxxx , my SS # is xxx xx xxxx.

I am sending this dispute certified mail # xxxx to make sure you receive it.

I have no knowledge or records of the following account(s) on my report # xxxxx.

xxxxx from xxxxxx

Please advise me as to the name(s) and address (es) of the medical provider(s), the date(s) and type(s) of service and to whom the service(s) was (were) provided, as any account(s) I might have had may be obsolete.

If you can obtain this information, I also would need the name of the person providing this data, and the manner in which it was provided in order that I may pursue additional legal remedies which may include a complaint against your agency to the OCR on HIPAA violations.

Please take notice that your Credit Reporting Agency falls within the purview of subtitle D of the ARRA , SEC. 13407(1) BREACH OF SECURITY.—The term "breach of security" means, with respect to unsecured PHR identifiable health information of an individual in a personal health record, acquisition of such information without the authorization of the individual.

You are therefore now subject to the jurisdiction of the OCR for HIPAA violation and the penalty rules of the HITECH Act as issued 11/30/2009.

Please note that your Credit Reporting Agency is now subject to Federal consumer financial laws, including, among others, the FCRA and Title X of the Dodd-Frank Act, and related regulations including a ban on "Abusive" Acts or Practices. (Section 1031 of the Dodd-Frank Act)

Very truly yours,

xxxxxx

HIPPA violations are serious but an easy way to get medical collection off your credit report, whether old or new. To do anything in business or building wealth, you must start with credit [repairing and building]; there is no shortcut to get this done. Sitting in prison lets you obtain the documents to clean your credit report. You don't need to pay a credit repair specialist when you can learn yourself with the 24 hours you have in a day. Credit repair is also a skill you can master, start a business, and charge other prisoners to dispute and repair their credit. Everything I'm teaching you is a business model you can learn and make money from. Everything you learn from me, always think: "How can I turn this into a business or make money?" Information with a plan to execute is powerful! Don't ever pay for a service or information from someone else; you can learn and monetize it for yourself. THINK OUTSIDE THE BOX!

Credit Freezing

While you are fixing your credit, as a way to make sure no other checks on your credit are done doing this process, put a freeze on your credit file. This blocks creditors and businesses from checking your credit history while you are disputing and repairing your credit report. Below is the website to the (3) major credit bureaus and the link to activate the freeze.

- Equifax Credit Freeze
  - www.Freeze.equifax.com
- TransUnion Credit Freeze
  - www.transunion.com/credit-freeze/place-credit-freeze
- Experian Credit Freeze
  - www.experian.com/freeze/center.html

INVESTING FOR WEALTH BUILDING

The opportunity to build wealth through the stock market is bigger than you think. I presented several basic ideas of stock investing in my last book: "Pro se Prisoner: How to Buy Stocks and Bitcoin," if you haven't purchased it, go get your copy from www.amazon.com or www.freebirdpublishers.com or wherever books are sold. Now, we are moving on to more advanced investing strategies that will teach you how to build wealth by investing in stocks while in your cell or home. Remember, being a Pro se Prisoner is a mindset achieved by gaining knowledge first, then setting your goals, and finally developing plans that you execute to achieve your goals based on your knowledge. Father time is undefeated, so what are you wasting time for? Wealth building using stocks requires devoted time on your part because you are starting at the bottom. We essentially are trading time for a piece of paper, which means nothing when building true wealth. Did you know that 80% of U.S. Stocks are owned by 10% of Americans? That's also one of the reasons why 76% of Americans live paycheck-to-paycheck! They are trading time for money, working for that 10% because they don't have the knowledge to build wealth. Rich people blame the citizens in poverty themselves, but one has to open their minds up and ask themselves: All these Americans trapped living paycheck-to-paycheck, you can't say it's solely their fault or even that they are stupid. These outdated thoughts have held people in poverty and never allowed them to build wealth.

Look around the prison. Are there financial literacy programs offered by your state DOC or Federal BOP? So technically, it's harder for you in prison and upon release because nothing is offered to help you financially. Citizens in society aren't getting help, so why would you think they would help you build wealth through financial literacy programs? I created Pro Se Prisoner to help prisoners build wealth, educate them on financial literacy, and never work for someone again. One of the ways to achieve the above is through investing.

DIVIDEND REINVESTMENT PLANS

DRIPs are what I call investments from the cell. You can obtain them by sending a letter to hundreds of companies offering these Dividend Reinvestment Plants. Enrolling in those DRIP stocks automatically gives you dividend payments, which you can use to purchase more shares. The most overview of these types of stocks can be found in my previous book dedicated to stocks and Bitcoin: "Pro se Prisoner: How To Buy Stocks and Bitcoin" by C.A. Knuckles.

Wealth is won and lost daily on the world's stock markets. Many people look at these types of investments as a gamble. Every day in prison, we take risks with gambling in sports pods, on NRA games, playing chess, or just a random conversation can turn into a bet, so the risk is tolerated at small levels as long as it benefits you, but playing the game on a high level of stock investments is better, with bigger rewards. Prisoners have sat in the cells of thousands of prisons, jails, and intake centers, wondering how to buy stocks in companies that we use products of every day. DRIPS allows you to sit in your cell, invest in multiple companies, and never leave your cell to accomplish this.

I am not a financial expert or a certified investor. However, I have accumulated a wealth of knowledge and experience from many failures along the way. My failures are why I can write about stock investing for prisoners and show you how you can start building wealth with as little as $25 a month.

"D.R.I.P.S." (Dividend Reinvestment Plans) allows you to do this. Once you purchase a DRIP from a company (e.g., Microsoft) and they pay you a dividend 3 to 4 times a year, Microsoft will automatically reinvest in Microsoft to purchase mere shares of that company, thus increasing your ownership of that stock.

Another interesting fact about DRIPs is "No-Fee" DRIPs that allow you to be charged $0.00 and build large positions in high-quality dividend-paying companies. Applications to buy them must be obtained from each company by writing them directly or getting your outside support to go on their websites to obtain them (15) of the best no-fee DRIPs with the highest returns are as follows:

- Ecolab Inc. (ECL)
- Abbot Laboratories (ABT)
- Illinois Tool Works (ITN)
- Sherwin Williams (SHW)
- A.O. Smith (AOS)
- Emerson Electric (EMR)

- Nucor Corporation (NVE)
- Johnson & Johnson (JNJ)
- Chubb Limited (CB)
- Aflac Incorporation (AFL)
- Hormel Foods (HRL)
- 3M Company (MMM)
- AbbVie Inc. (ABBV)
- Realty Income (O)
- Exxon Mobile (XOM)

Allow these stocks to be your starter kit, which allows you to buy DRIPs at no charge. Enrolling in DRIPs allows you also to compound your income over time. These companies are listed on the S&P 500 Index, with over 25 consecutive years of dividend increases. So, how do you obtain these shares of these companies from your prison cell? First, remember there are seven major stock exchanges:

- New York Stock Exchange (NYSE)
- NASDAQ (NASDAQ)
- Japan Exchange Group (JPX)
- London Stock Exchange (LSE)
- Shanghai Stock Exchange (SSE)
- Hong Kong Stock Exchange (SEHK)
- Euronext

Knowing this is important just so you can see the whole landscape, which also allows you to control how you choose to invest.

Making Your First Purchase

1. **Stock Picking:** When looking for potential DRIPs, find companies that offer long-term investment choices.

2. **How To Buy Stocks:** Each company has a transfer agent you can reach by phone number below. If you have no outside network help, write a letter to the company's shareholders division and ask for their application to join their DRIP Program. (The Address List is at the back of the book.)

3. **Read the Fine Print:** Different companies offer different plans, and all companies listed on the stock market offer these DRIP programs. Make sure to ask the company's shareholder services department to provide all the details of their plan so that you can make the most educated decision on whether to invest.

Name	Agent	Initial Investment
AbbVie	877-881-5970	$250
Exxon Mobil	800-252-1800	$250
Aflac	800-222-4256	$1,000
American Water Works	888-556-0423	$100
Hartford Financial	877-272-7740	$50
Westamerica Bancorp	877-558-4258	$100
Walmart Inc.	800-438-6278	$250
CVS Health	877-287-7526	$250
Dominion Resources	800-552-4034	$40
Cincinnati Financial	866-638-6433	$25
Ecolab Inc.	800-322-8325	$20
Abbot Laboratories	888-332-2268	$25
Illinois Tool Works	888-829-7424	$250
Sherwin Williams	800-401-1957	$10
A.O. Smith	414-339-4070	$0
Emerson Electric		$250
Nucor Corporation		$10
Johnson & Johnson		$25
Chubb Limited		n/a
Aflac Incorporations		$50
Hormel Foods		$0
3M Company		$10
Realty Income		$1,500

Check the index section for a more complete list!

Buying these DRIPs and others will help you accumulate additional shares at a lower cost. Since shares usually come from the company's reserve, they allow you to purchase fractional shares not offered on the stock exchanges.

Spend your time looking for stocks with high earnings and sales growth, good returns on equity, or pre-tax profit margins. Each stock should have an increase in the current quarter earnings per share when you look at last year's quarter at the same period.

Look for the Eps to be up at least 17 to 20% in this year's quarter compared to last year at the same time. More reading is required on this subject; order my last book for more of an in-depth dive into this space because that book is the starter guide to wealth building, and this book is to expand your knowledge to build wealth; obtaining that book will start you off. (Pro se Prisoner: How to Buy Stocks and Bitcoin). It can be obtained from www.amazon.com, www.freebirdpublishers.com, or wherever books are sold. Included in that book is a free book: Pro Se Prisoner: The Ph.D. Manual – Poor, Hungry, and Driven to Success. It is a mindset book to develop your own Pro se Prisoner mindset, but it also takes a deep look into the history of our problems and how this system was designed by the powers that be. However, it also shows how to use that knowledge to escape the victim's mindset.

Financial education is the best investment to make while sitting in your prison cell or couch in your home. Understanding the stock market and DRIPs is just a start in building wealth. It plays a role but not the only role you need to gain knowledge. Let's keep moving on our quest to build wealth. See the example DRIP application for Aflac.

AFL STOCK PLAN ENROLLMENT FORM

OPTIONS: ☐ Full Reinvestment ☐ Partial Reinvestment – No. of shares to be reinvested _____ ☐ Optional Cash Purchase Only
(will receive a dividend check)

☐ Current Shareholder Enrolling in Plan
☐ New Shareholder Enrolling in Plan – Enclosed is my check/money order for $_____ ($1,000 minimum) made payable to the AFL Stock Plan.
☐ Employee Enrolling in Plan – I am an employee of: ☐ Aflac Incorporated ☐ Aflac ☐ Aflac NY ☐ Communicorp ☐ AGI
$_____ to be deducted from my payroll check once each month ($50 minimum).
☐ Associate Enrolling in Plan – I am a currently contracted associate of: ☐ Aflac ☐ Aflac NY Associate Writing No._____
$_____ or _____ % to be deducted from my accounting statement once each month. ($50 minimum).

ACCOUNT REGISTRATION – Please list legal name(s) as they appear on the Social Security card or EIN form.

☐ **INDIVIDUAL/JOINT ACCOUNT**

NAME _____ SSN _____

JOINT OWNER (IF ANY) _____ SSN _____

JOINT OWNER (IF ANY) _____ SSN _____
Joint account will be presumed to be joint tenants with right of survivorship unless indicated otherwise.

☐ **TRUST ACCOUNT**

TRUSTEE NAME _____ SSN _____

TRUSTEE NAME _____ SSN _____

NAME OF TRUST _____ SSN/EIN _____

DATE OF TRUST _____

ACCOUNT ADDRESS, PHONE, AND EMAIL ADDRESS

ADDRESS _____

CITY ____ STATE ____ ZIP ____

☐ **CUSTODIAL ACCOUNT**

CUSTODIAN NAME _____ SSN _____

MINOR NAME _____ SSN _____

MINOR'S STATE OF RESIDENCE _____

☐ **OTHER**

If corporation must check one.
☐ C CORPORATION ☐ S CORPORATION

NAME _____ SSN/EIN _____

☐ **TRANSFER ON DEATH (TOD)**
(INDIVIDUAL/JOINT ACCOUNT ONLY)

NAME _____ SSN _____

NAME _____ SSN _____

MUST RETURN CERTIFICATES TO ADD TOD

DAYTIME PHONE /CELL NUMBER _____

EMAIL ADDRESS _____

By signing this form, I request enrollment, certify that I have received and read the AFL Stock Plan (the Plan) prospectus, and agree to abide by the terms and conditions of the Plan. If no reinvestment option is selected above, I understand that full reinvestment will apply to my account.

LEGAL SIGNATURE AS NAME APPEARS ABOVE (IF JOINT ACCOUNT, ALL PERSONS MUST SIGN. IF CUSTODIAL, REGISTERED CUSTODIAN MUST SIGN.)

SIGNATURE _____ SIGNATURE _____

ALL NEW ENROLLEES MUST COMPLETE THE SUBSTITUTE W-9 FURNISHED BELOW.
IF THE IRS HAS NOTIFIED YOU OF BACKUP WITHHOLDING, YOU MUST STRIKE THROUGH ON NUMBER 2 BELOW.

Substitute W-9
Under penalties of perjury, I certify that:
1. The number shown on this form is my correct taxpayer identification number (or I am waiting for a number to be issued to me), and
2. I am not subject to backup withholding because (a) I am exempt from backup withholding, or (b) I have not been notified by the Internal Revenue Service (IRS) that I am subject to backup withholding as a result of failure to report all interest or dividends, or (c) the IRS has notified me that I am no longer subject to backup withholding, and
3. I am a U.S. person (including a U.S. resident alien).

Signature _____ Date _____

Aflac Incorporated
Worldwide Headquarters
AFL Stock Plan
1932 Wynnton Road
Columbus GA 31999

Fax Number: 706.596.3488

Email: Shareholder@aflac.com

Toll Free Number: 1.800.227.4756

S-00193-E-11

AFL STOCK PLAN

OPTIONAL BANK DRAFT - AUTOMATIC AUTHORIZATION

(Your Financial Institution Must Be a Member of the Automated Clearing House (ACH) Network)

Aflac Incorporated (the Company) is authorized to initiate monthly withdrawals against the financial institution account indicated by the attached voided document, by electronic funds transfer and to apply those funds to the AFL Stock Plan account specified below, for the purchase of Aflac Incorporated common stock. The Company is authorized to initiate corrections to any amounts transferred in error and any claim against the Company or the financial institution involved is waived with respect to the operation of this service.

Once effective, funds will be drafted on the 25th day of each month (or if the 25th day is not a business day, the first business day thereafter), and such funds will be invested within seven (7) days. This authorization will remain in effect until the Company receives notice to terminate or revise it. The Company and the financial institution reserve the right to terminate this service at any time.

It is the shareholder's responsibility to notify the Company of changes in financial institution information. Changes may be made by providing the Company with a new Bank Draft Authorization form revising the original instructions. The Shareholder will allow the Company a reasonable amount of time for initiating, revising or terminating bank draft.

Please complete each item listed below for optional bank draft:

NOTE: Checks and/or deposit slips from financial institutions such as Savings & Loans, Trust Banks, Credit Unions and Federal Savings Banks, do not always contain the correct information for bank draft. Please verify with your financial institution that the bank routing number and bank account number shown on your attached voided document are the correct numbers to be used with the ACH Network. *

_____   _____
Social Security # / EIN#   Stock Account # (if known)

Checking account - attach a voided check
Savings account - attach a voided deposit slip
Monthly Deduction ($50 minimum) $_____

_____   _____
*Correct bank routing number (ABA)   *Correct bank account number (DDA)

Daytime Phone No. _____ Cell _____

_____   _____
Signature of Bank Account Holder   Signature of Bank Account Holder

Each bank account holder must sign for optional bank draft.

Correspondence should be addressed to: Questions: E-mail: shareholder@aflac.com

Aflac Incorporated   Call: 1.800.227.4756
Worldwide Headquarters   or Fax: 1.706.596.3488
AFL Stock Plan
1932 Wynnton Road
Columbus GA 31999

ENROLLMENT FORM ON OTHER SIDE

S-00193-B-11

MLPs (MASTER LIMITED PARTNERSHIPS)

Over the past 3 years, I have seen M.L.P.s pop up, but I never took the time to investigate them until about ten months ago. Funny fact: I watch the 1% so much that when I even read one of 10 of the 1% is moving money into something, I go into research crazy mode. Forbes reported that one of my 1% friends was moving $150 million into these Master Limited Partnerships, so naturally, I followed them to it and traced the trades. The company didn't stand out, but that's where I started my research. Here's what I found out for us in that quest for information.

Master Limited Partnerships are limited partnerships that are publicly traded on securities and exchanges around the world. (i.e. NYSE, NASDAQ, and NYSE MKT). They combine the tax benefits of a private partnership with the liquidity of a publicly traded company. Limited Partnership structures favor exceptional tax treatment, avoiding paying corporate income tax. Even better, taxes are paid (on a partially deferred basis) by the limited partner holder. MLPs are pass-through entities. Thus, MLPs are never subject to double taxation on dividends.

MLP ownership comes in two classes. 1) Limited Partnership investors who purchase shares ("units") and 2) General Partners: the owners who are responsible for managing the day-to-day operations of the MLP. Ownership interests are referred to as (units), which is in contrast to what you're probably used to from corporations ("shares"). Money generated by these MLPs is paid out to ("unit holders") in the form of ("distributions") instead of corporate ("dividends").

MLPs need to qualify not to be taxed as a corporation by qualifying under the requirements of Section 7704(a) of the Internal Revenue Code (I.R.S.) of 1986. Some qualification requirements include 90% of the MLPs' income from natural resource-based activities such as exploration, development, mining or production, processing, refining, transportation, storage, and marketing of any mineral or natural resource. MLPs were first organized in 1981, but it only took Congress 6 years to effectively limit their use by 1987 in the Real Estate and Natural Resources Sectors. So approximately 74% or the vast majority of MLPs are in energy-related businesses. Of that majority, most reside in the "midstream sub-industry," which gathers and processes, transports, and/or provides storage of crude oil, natural gas, natural gas liquids (NGLs), etc. Midstream encompasses the above and all types of commodities.

Other energy-related MLPs engage in 1) Upstream – which focuses on exploration, development, and acquisition of oil; 2) Pipeline MLPs – interstate or intrastate; gathering or transportation; 3) Natural Gas Processing/Fractionation – plants typically receive non-pipeline quality natural gas via a gathering system; 4) Storage/Terminals – these MLPs storage operators handle various commodities; 5) Shipping – Transport bulk commodities via tankers, barges, and dry bulk vessels; 6) Coal- these MLPs consist of coal-producing or coal royalty businesses.

Now, let's focus on Limited Partners and the "units" it purchases, as well as the benefits it entails. Remember, we are building wealth! Pay attention to the words in quotes, those bolded for tax purposes and wealth building. These things matter. Because MLPs are passed through tax structures, all profits and losses are passed through to the "Limited Partner." The MLP itself doesn't pay taxes on its revenues, as the vast majority of incorporated businesses do. Instead, the limited partners pay income taxes only on their portions of the MLPs' earnings. A little breakdown is needed: The wealthy own the MLP as a General Partner, and all revenue from that MLP is never taxed by the MLP itself but passed down to the limited partner. This is why ownership is everything! To answer my question about why a member of the 1%, is I study and watch move $150 million dollars to one of these operations, it is clear: Tax-Free Wealth that can be passed down to their heirs upon death and sold by their heirs tax-free (more on this later). As the Pro se Prisoner, I did the tracking and tracing for you, so all you must do is read and take action.

Pro se Tip: (!)

Deduction: An amount that is or may be deducted from taxable income.

Depletion: Used to allocate the cost of extracting natural resources.

Schedule K-1: Used to report the income, losses, and dividends for a business or financial entity's partners or the S Corporations shareholders.

Back to the limited partner, it doesn't mean anything because the wealthy own the MLP. The magic of wealth building is finding multiple ways to build wealth using different income vehicles. So, deductions, such as depreciation and depletion, also pass through to the limited partner. Limited Partners can use these deductions to reduce their taxable income. I didn't forget about you; this isn't just for the 1%; it's money for everybody. MLPs usually grow faster than inflation! Limited Partners (you, the investor), distributions, about 80%-90% even through pass-through to you by the MLP itself on its revenue, are often tax-deferred, which gives MLPs higher yields than most dividend yields offered by regular equities. Another bonus for the limited partner is that cumulative "cash distributions" could exceed the portion taxed of capital gains rate once units are sold.

The 2017 tax cut allows a 20% deduction and distribution from taxable income, which can reduce the tax that would otherwise be paid. But this benefit runs out in 2025. As was noted earlier, distributions are a return on capital. They are mostly tax-deferred. But upon the selling of your units, you will have to pay taxes based on the difference between your selling price and your adjusted basis (this refers to a material change to the recorded initial cost of an asset or security after it has already been owned, updating the original purchase cost by taking into account on increase or decrease to its value is primarily used to compute capital gains or loss on a sale for tax purposes.

Usually, an adjustment that somehow increases the "cost basis" will lower your tax burden. For instance, another way to look at this is to say you purchased $100,000 worth of MLP units, you receive $4,000 in distributions, and there is $3000 in unit depreciation. The only amount you would pay in taxes is the difference ($1,000). This is at the federal and state levels.

While distributions are okay, the (R.O.C.) Return of Capital lowers your cost basis to $0.00 if you had long enough. But if that occurs, just know that any future gains are considered capital gains in the year they are received, so sell at $0.00 when the (R.O.C.) lowers your cost basis to $0.00.

Pro se Tip: (!)

The Alerian MLP Index: is the leading gauge of energy infrastructure MLPs.

Estate planning with MLP units is another great way to avoid paying taxes while gifting or transferring these units to your heir or beneficiaries. The wealthy use this building wealth strategy, but you can also set it up and use it. When you, as a limited partner, gift or transfer your MLP units, both the withholder and beneficiaries avoid paying taxes during the transfer. During this transfer or gifting of the units, the cost will be readjusted based on the market price when the transfer happens because of death. The real beauty associated with this estate planning is that units pass tax-free upon death to heirs; these units pass tax-free at fair market value, which is determined to be the value as of the date of death.

Pro se Tip: (!)

Because most MLPs are partnerships, investors such as you will receive and have to use Schedule K-1 instead of the usual 1099 Form.

As noted previously, MLPs can be purchased and sold on securities exchanges just like regular (corporate) stock, ETFs, and options. Check current prices, but the list below includes most of the MLPs that trade on the securities market. In August 2022, I will start with just a few and then give you a more complete list after this.

Popular MLPs
2022

NAME	TICKER	August 2022 Price
Apollo Global Management	(APO)	$61.00
Magellan Midstream Partnership, LP	(MMP)	$51.57
Enviva Partners, LP	(EVA)	$73.85
Antero Midstream Partners, LP	(AM)	$10.40
Cedar Fair, LP	(FUN)	$44.37
Compass Diversified Holdings	(CODI)	$24.35
NuStar Energy, LP	(NS)	$14.98

3 High Yield MLPs

NAME	TICKER	August 2022 Price	Yield %
Crestwood Equity Partners, LP	(CEQP)	$26.29	8.59%
Energy Transfer, LP	(ET)	$11.58	7.18%
Enterprise Product Partners, LP	(EPD)	$27.19	

MLPs Stock List

MLP and MLP-Related Funds; MLP Indices

Note: MLPA does not guarantee that this table covers all MLP funds and indices. There may be funds and indices which are not included in this list. This list is for informational purposes only and does not constitute investment advice.

Fund Name	Ticker Symbol(s) (1)	Fund Type (2)	MLP / MLP-R (3)	Sponsor/Managing Company	Inception Date	RIC or C-Corp (5)
Open-End Funds						
Advisory Research MLP & Energy Income Fund	INFRX, INFIX, INFFX	OEF	MLP	Advisory Research	12/27/2010	RIC
Advisory Research MLP & Energy Infrastructure Fund	MLPPX	OEF	MLP	Advisory Research	9/13/2010	RIC
Advisory Research MLP & Equity Fund	INFEX, INFJX, INFKX	OEF	MLP	Advisory Research	8/31/2015	RIC
ALPS | Alerian MLP Infrastructure Index Fund	ALERX,ALRCX,ALRIX	OEF	MLP	ALPS Advisors	12/31/2012	C-Corp
BP Capital TwinLine Energy Fund	BPEAX, BPECX, BPEIX	OEF	MLP-R	BP Capital Fund Advisors, LLC	12/31/2013	RIC
BP Capital TwinLine MLP Fund	BPMAX,BPMCX, BPMIX	OEF	MLP	BP Capital Fund Advisors, LLC	12/31/2013	C-Corp
Catalyst MLP and Infrastructure Fund	MLXAX, MLXCX, MLXIX	OEF	MLP (4)	Catalyst Capital Advisors, LLC	12/22/2014	RIC
Center Coast MLP Focus Fund	CCCAX,CCCCX,CCCNX	OEF	MLP	Liberty Street Advisors (Adv.) and Center Coast Capital Advisors, LP Sub-Adv)	12/31/2010	C-Corp
Clearbridge Energy MLP and Infrastructure Fund	LCPAX,LCPCX,LCPIX,LCPSX	OEF	MLP-R	Legg Mason/ Clearbridge Advisors	LCPAX and LCPCX, 10/31/13; LCPIX and LCPSX, 8/30/2013	RIC
Cohen & Steers MLP & Energy Opportunity Fund	MLOAX,MLOCX,MLOIX, MLORX, MLOZX	OEF	MLP	Cohen & Steers	12/20/2013	RIC
Dreyfus MLP Fund	DMFAX, DMFCX, DMFIX, DMFYX	OEF	MLP	Dreyfus Corporation	4/30/15	C-Corp
Eagle MLP Strategy Fund	EGLAX, EGLCX, EGLIX	OEF	MLP	Eagle Global Advisors	EGLAX and EGLIX, 9/24/12; EGLCX,2/21/13	C-Corp
Goldman Sachs MLP Energy Infrastructure Fund	GLPAX, GLPCX, GMLPX, GLPIX, GLPRX	OEF	MLP	Goldman Sachs	3/28/2013	C-Corp
Highland Energy MLP Fund	HEFAX, HEFCX, HEFYX	OEF	MLP	Highland Capital Management, L.P.	12/1/2011	C-Corp
Invesco MLP Fund	ILPAX, ILPCX, ILPYX	OEF	MLP	Invesco	8/29/2014	C-Corp
James Alpha Yorkville MLP Fund	JAMLX, JMLPX, MLPCX	OEF	MLP	James Alpha Advisors, LLC; Yorkville Capital Management, LLC	8/31/2015	C-Corp

Fund Name	Ticker Symbol(s) (1)	Fund Type (2)	MLP / MLP-R (3)	Sponsor/Managing Company	Inception Date	RIC or C-Corp (5)
MainGate MLP Fund	AMLPX, IMLPX, MLCPX	OEF	MLP	Chickasaw Capital Management	2/18/2011	C-Corp
MainStay Cushing MLP Premier Fund	CSHAX, CSHCX, CSHZX	OEF	MLP	Cushing Asset Management (Swank Capital)	10/19/2010	C-Corp
MainStay Cushing Renaissance Advantage Fund	CRZAX, CRZCX, CRZZX	OEF	MLP-R	Cushing Asset Management (Swank Capital)	4/2/2013	C-Corp
MainStay Cushing Royalty Energy Income Fund	CURAX, CURCX, CURZX	OEF	MLP-R	Cushing Asset Management (Swank Capital)	7/2/2012	C-Corp
Oppenheimer SteelPath MLP Alpha Fund	MLPAX, MLPGX, MLPOX, OSPAX	OEF	MLP	SteelPath Capital Management LLC	3/31/2010	C-Corp
Oppenheimer SteelPath MLP Alpha Plus Fund	MLPLX, MLPMX, MLPNX, OSPPX	OEF	MLP	SteelPath Capital Management LLC	12/30/2011	C-Corp
Oppenheimer SteelPath MLP Income Fund	MLPDX, MLPRX, MLPZX, OSPMX	OEF	MLP	SteelPath Capital Management LLC	3/31/2010	C-Corp
Oppenheimer SteelPath MLP Select 40 Fund	MLPFX, MLPEX, MLPTX, MLPYX, OSPSX	OEF	MLP	SteelPath Capital Management LLC	3/31/2010	C-Corp
Prudential Jennison MLP Fund	PRPAX, PRPCX, PRPZX	OEF	MLP	Prudential Investments	12/18/2013	C-Corp
Salient MLP & Energy Infrastructure Fund	SMAPX, SMFPX, SMLPX,SMRPX	OEF	MLP	Salient Capital Advisors, LLC	SMAPX,12/20/12; SMFPX, 1/7/13; SMLPX 9/19/12, SMRPX 11//4/16	RIC
Tortoise MLP and Pipeline Fund	TORCX, TORIX, TORTX	OEF	MLP	Tortoise Capital Advisors, LLC	6/1/2011	RIC
Tortoise North American Energy Independence Fund	TNPTX, TNPCX, TNPIX	OEF	MLP-R	Tortoise Capital Advisors, LLC	4/1/2013	RIC
Transamerica MLP & Energy Income	TMLAX, TMCLX, TMLPX, TAMLX, TMLTX	OEF	MLP	Kayne Anderson Capital Advisors, L.P.	4/30/2013	RIC
Closed-End Funds						
Center Coast MLP and Infrastructure Fund	CEN	CEF	MLP	Center Coast Capital	9/26/2013	C-Corp
ClearBridge American Energy MLP Fund Inc.	CBA	CEF	MLP	Legg Mason/Clearbridge Advisors	6/26/2013	C-Corp
ClearBridge Energy MLP Fund Inc.	CEM	CEF	MLP	Legg Mason/Clearbridge Advisors	6/25/2010	C-Corp
ClearBridge Energy MLP Opportunity Fund Inc.	EMO	CEF	MLP	Legg Mason/Clearbridge Advisors	6/10/2011	C-Corp
ClearBridge Energy MLP Total Return Fund Inc.	CTR	CEF	MLP	Legg Mason/Clearbridge Advisors	6/27/2012	C-Corp
Cohen & Steers MLP Income and Energy Opportunity Fund	MIE	CEF	MLP	Cohen & Steers	3/28/2013	C-Corp
Cushing MLP Total Return Fund	SRV	CEF	MLP	Cushing Asset Management (Swank Capital)	8/27/2007	C-Corp
Cushing Renaissance Fund	SZC	CEF	MLP-R	Cushing Asset Management (Swank Capital)	9/28/2012	RIC
Cushing Energy Income Fund	SRF	CEF	MLP-R	Cushing Asset Management (Swank Capital)	2/28/2012	C-Corp
Duff & Phelps Global Utility Income Fund	DPG	CEF	MLP-R	Duff & Phelps Investment Management Co.	7/27/2011	RIC

MLP-A-MLP and MLP Related Funds and Indices

Fund Name	Ticker Symbol(s) (1)	Fund Type (2)	MLP / MLP-R (3)	Sponsor/Managing Company	Inception Date	RIC or C-Corp (5)
Duff & Phelps Select Energy MLP Fund	DSE	CEF	MLP	Duff & Phelps Investment Management Co.	6/25/2014	C-Corp
Fiduciary/Claymore MLP Opportunity Fund	FMO	CEF	MLP	Guggenheim Funds and Advisory Research	12/22/2004	C-Corp
First Trust Energy Income and Growth Fund	FEN	CEF	MLP	First Trust / Energy Income Partners	6/24/2004	C-Corp
First Trust Energy Infrastructure Fund	FIF	CEF	MLP-R	First Trust / Energy Income Partners	9/27/2011	RIC
First Trust MLP and Energy Income Fund	FEI	CEF	MLP	First Trust / Energy Income Partners	11/27/2012	C-Corp
First Trust New Opportunities MLP and Energy Fund	FPL	CEF	MLP	First Trust / Energy Income Partners	3/27/2014	C-Corp
Goldman Sachs MLP and Energy Renaissance Fund	GER	CEF	MLP	Goldman Sachs Asset Management	9/26/14	C-Corp
Goldman Sachs MLP Income Opportunities Fund	GMZ	CEF	MLP	Goldman Sachs Asset Management	11/26/2013	C-Corp
Kayne Anderson Energy Development Company	KED	CEF	MLP-R	Kayne Anderson	9/20/2006	C-Corp
Kayne Anderson Energy Total Return Fund	KYE	CEF	MLP-R	Kayne Anderson	6/27/2005	RIC
Kayne Anderson Midstream / Energy Fund	KMF	CEF	MLP-R	Kayne Anderson	11/23/2010	RIC
Kayne Anderson MLP Investment Company	KYN	CEF	MLP	Kayne Anderson	9/27/2004	C-Corp
Neuberger Berman MLP Income Fund Inc.	NML	CEF	MLP	Neuberger Berman	3/26/2013	C-Corp
Nuveen All Cap Energy MLP Opportunities Fund	JMLP	CEF	MLP	Nuveen and Advisory Research	3/26/2014	C-Corp
Nuveen Energy MLP Total Return Fund	JMF	CEF	MLP	Nuveen and Advisory Research	2/24/2011	C-Corp
Salient Midstream and MLP Fund	SMM	CEF	MLP-R	Salient Capital Advisors, LLC	5/24/2012	RIC
Tortoise Energy Independence Fund, Inc.	NDP	CEF	MLP-R	Tortoise Capital Advisors, LLC	7/26/2012	RIC
Tortoise Energy Infrastructure Corp.	TYG	CEF	MLP	Tortoise Capital Advisors, LLC	2/24/2004	C-Corp
Tortoise MLP Fund, Inc.	NTG	CEF	MLP	Tortoise Capital Advisors, LLC	7/27/2010	C-Corp
Tortoise Pipeline & Energy Fund, Inc.	TTP	CEF	MLP-R	Tortoise Capital Advisors, LLC	10/31/2011	C-Corp
Tortoise Power and Energy Infrastructure	TPZ	CEF	MLP-R	Tortoise Capital Advisors, LLC	7/29/2009	RIC
Exchange Traded Funds (ETFs)						
Alerian MLP ETF	AMLP	ETF	MLP	ALPS Advisors	8/25/2010	C-Corp
Alerian Energy Infrastructure ETF	ENFR	ETF	MLP	ALPS Advisors	11/1/2013	C-Corp
American Energy Independence ETF	USAI	ETF	MLP-R	SL Advisors, LLC	12/12/2017	RIC
Direxion Zacks MLP High Income Shares	ZMLP	ETF	MLP	Direxion Investments	1/23/2014	C-Corp
First Trust North American Energy Infrastructure Fund	EMLP	ETF	MLP	First Trust Advisors L.P.	6/20/2012	RIC
Global X MLP & Energy Infrastructure ETF	MLPX	ETF	MLP	Global X Management Company LLC	8/6/2013	RIC

MLPA-MLP and MLP Related Funds and Indices

Fund Name	Ticker Symbol(s) (1)	Fund Type (2)	MLP / MLP-R (3)	Sponsor/Managing Company	Inception Date	RIC or C-Corp (5)
Global X MLP ETF	MLPA	ETF	MLP	Global X Management Company LLC	4/18/2012	C-Corp
InfraCap MLP ETF	AMZA	ETF	MLP	Infrastructure Capital Advisors	10/1/2014	C-Corp
Tortoise North American Pipeline Fund	TPYP	ETF	MLP-R	Tortoise Capital Advisors, LLC	6/15/2015	RIC
VnEck Vectors High Income Infrastructure ETF	YMLI	ETF	MLP	VanEck Associates Corp.	2/11/2013	C-Corp
VanEck Vectors High Income MLP ETF	YMLP	ETF	MLP	VanEck Associates Corp.	3/12/2012	C-Corp
Exchange Traded Notes (ETNs)						
Barclays ETN+ Select MLP ETN	ATMP	ETN	MLP	Barclays	3/12/2013	*
C-Tracks Miller Howard MLP ETN	MLPC	ETN	MLP	Citi	9/30/2013	*
Credit Suisse X-Links® Monthly Pay 2xLeveraged Alerian MLP Index ETN	AMJL	EYN	MLP	Credit Suisse	5/17/2016	*
iPath S&P MLP ETN	IMLP	ETN	MLP	Barclays	1/3/2013	*
J.P. Morgan -Alerian MLP Index ETN	AMJ	ETN	MLP	J. P. Morgan	4/2/2009	*
Morgan Stanley Cushing MLP High Income ETN	MLPY	ETN	MLP	Morgan Stanley	3/17/2011	*
RBC Yorkville MLP Distribution Growth Leader's ETN	YGRO	ETN	MLP	Royal Bank of Canada, Yorkville Capital Management LLC	7/29/2014	*
UBS ETRACS Alerian MLP Index ETN	AMU	ETN	MLP	UBS	7/17/2012	*
UBS ETRACS Alerian MLP Index ETN Series B	AMUB	ETN	MLP	UBS	10/8/2015	*
UBS E-TRACS Alerian MLP Infrastructure ETN	MLPI	ETN	MLP	UBS	4/1/2010	*
UBS E-TRACS Aler an MLP Infrastructure ETN Series B	MLPB	ETN	MLP	UBS	10/8/2015	*
UBS ETRACS Alerian Natural Gas MLP Index	MLPG	ETN	MLP	UBS	7/13/2010	*
UBS E-TRACS Monthly Pay 2x Leveraged Wells Fargo® MLP Ex-Energy ETN	LMLP	ETN	MLP	UBS	6/24/2014	*
ETRACS 2xMonthly Leveraged Alerian MLP Infrastructure Index ETN Series B	MLPQ	ETN	MLP	UBS	2/8/2016	*
UBS E-TRACS 1x Monthly Short MLP Infrastructure Index ETN	MLPS	ETN	MLP	UBS	9/29/2010	*
ETRACS 2xMonthly Leveraged S&P MLP Index ETN Series B	MLPZ	ETN	MLP	UBS	2/8/2016	*

Fund Name	Ticker Symbol(s) (1)	Fund Type (2)	MLP / MLP-R (3)	Sponsor/Managing Company	Inception Date	RIC or C-Corp (5)

(1) The various ticker symbols for each fund are for different classes of shares.

(2) OEF=open-end fund; CEF=closed-end fund; ETF=exchange traded fund; ETN= exchange traded note.

(3) MLP funds primarily invest in MLPs. MLP-Related (MLP-R) Funds include MLPs in a mix of investments.

(4) Primarily MLP GPs.

(5) If a fund qualifies as a RIC (MLPs must be ≤ 25% of fund assets) it pays no corporate tax as long as earnings are distributed. Otherwise it is treated as a C-corporation and must pay corporate tax. This does not apply to ETNs, which are not subject to corporate tax.

MLP Indices	
Alerian MLP Index	AMZ (Price Return) AMXT (Total Return)
Alerian MLP Infrastructure Index	AMZI (Price Return) AMZIX (Total Return)
Alerian Large Cap Index	AMLI (Price Return) AMLIX (Total Return)
Alerian Mid Cap MLP Index	AMMI (Price Return), AMMIX (Total Return)
Alerian Small Cap MLP Index	AMSI (Price Return), AMSIX (Total Return)
Alerian Energy Infrastructure Index	AMEI (Price Return), AMEIX (Total Return)
American Energy Independence Index	AEITR(Total Return)
Barclay's Atlantic Trust Select MLP Index	BXIIATMP (Price Return)
Citigroup® MLP Index	CITIMLP ALCI (Price Return) CITIMLPT (Total Return)
Cushing® 30 MLP Index	MLPX (Price Return) MLPXTR (Total Return)
Cushing® MLP Market Cap Index	CMCI (Price Return), CMCIT (Total Return)

74

Cushing® MLP High Income Index	MLPYY(Price Return), MLPYTR (Total Return)
Miller/Howard MLP Fundamental Index	MLPMP (Price Return), MLPMH (Total Return)
S&P MLP Index	SPMLP (Price Return) SPMLPT (Total Return)
Tortoise MLP Index	TMLP (Price Return) TMLPT (Total Return)
Wells Fargo MLP Index	WML (Price Return), WCHWMLPT (Total Return)
Wells Fargo MLP Ex-Energy Index	MLPXEPX (Price Return) MLPXE (Total Return)

EFTs
EXCHANGE TRADED FUNDS

Other securities traded on the exchanges that offer great returns and allow a steady wealth-building strategy are exchange-traded funds or ETFs for short. ETF represents a basket of securities that tracks an underlying index. It doesn't matter. It can be stocks or bonds, etc. What's good about this vehicle of investing is a fund that can own hundreds or thousands of stocks across various industries or focus solely on one industry or sector, which is great for diversification. Rather than trying to beat the market, you can own the market through funds and get positive returns. The advantages of buying ETFs and using a buy-and-hold strategy will yield great results. Using ETF allows you to see the whole market or sector instead of trying to analyze individual stocks to invest in.

Two of the most popular indexes are the S&P 500 (Standard & Poor's 500) and the NASDAQ Composite. The S&P 500 averages a 10% annual return. Getting this return means not selling when the stock market falls. Your protection against this is that you bought a collection of stocks that cross several industries and sectors. While these are the popular funds, "ETFs" have multiple different types that have different focuses, such as:

- **Passive Managed ETFs:** Typically, they do not target an index of securities but rather have a portfolio manager making decisions about securities.

- **Bond ETFs** are used to provide regular income to investors.

- **Stock (Equity) ETFs:** comprise a basket of stocks to track a single industry or sector. For example, a stock ETF has lower fees and doesn't involve actual ownership of securities.

- **Industry/Sector ETFs:** are funds focusing on a specific sector.

- **Commodity ETFs:** Invest in commodities, including crude oil or gold.

- **Currency ETFs:** pooled investment vehicles that track the performance of currency pairs consisting of domestic and foreign currencies.

- **Inverse ETFs:** These allow you to short stocks while earning gains from stock declines. Shorting is selling a stock, expecting a decline in value, and repurchasing it at a lower amount. An inverse ETF uses derivatives (Financial contracts whose value depends on an underlying asset, group of assets, or benchmark to short a stock. They bet that the market will decline and an inverse ETF will increase by a proportionate amount.

- **Leveraged ETFs:** Uses multiples (e.g. 2x or 3x) on the return of the underlying investment. So, if the S&P 500 ETF returns 2% (if the index falls by 1%, the ETF loses 2%), the Leveraged ETF uses options and futures contracts to leverage all returns. To begin this investing journey in ETFs, find an investing platform [see list below].

Research ETFs by checking the sector, not the individual stocks listed in the Index Fund, and build or follow a consistent trending strategy, such as:

- Buy and Hold: Basically, you do what the name suggests: you buy and hold it indefinitely. Using this strategy should be a 3 to 5-year journey to get the proven results you want.

- Dollar–Cost Averaging: What you do here is add money into your investments at regular intervals. Set a monthly (min.) to invest, like $100. Each month, you put $100 into the ETF, regardless of what the market is doing. This strategy allows you to spread out your buy points during different market conditions. Depending on your risk tolerance and capital, you can also do this weekly or daily. The ultimate goal you will reach by doing this is ensuring that you get an average purchase price over time, making sure you're not buying too high.

Investing Platforms

- **Fidelity Investments**

  www.fidelity.com or mobile app

  Min. $0

  Fees: $0 for stocks/ETF trades, $0 plus $0.65 per contract for options trade.

  Best lowest option for stocks and ETFs; Best mobile app

- **TD Ameritrade**

  www.tdamentrade.com

  Min investment: $0

  Fees: Free stock & ETF trades; $0.65 per option contract

- **Tastytrade**

  www.tastytrade.com

  Min. investment: $0

  Fees: $0 for stock trades; $1.00 to open option trades. $0.00 to close.

- Charles Schwab

  www.schwab.com

  Min investment: $0

  Fees: free stock and ETF Trades; $0.65 per option contract

  Best for ETF investing

- Interactive Brokers

  www.interactivebrokers.com

Min investment: $0

Fees: Max $0.005 per share for Pro Platform, or 1% of trade value, $0 for IBKR Lite

Best for Advanced trades, it is not recommended to start here

While many platforms exist to trade stocks, ETFs, and options, the above are the top ones. Sitting in prison, many of the technologies that exist on the outside seem advanced. But keeping up with the latest advancements in this field is critical so we won't be lost. Getting your outside support to set up these accounts is the best way to take advantage of these new technologies, such as Apps. For example, apps exist that you can use with your own name and bank account. Some are:

- **Public**: the setup is easy. You can use your name and SSN to set it up. Just have your people use your info. The public has stocks, ETFs, and cryptocurrency.

- **Plank** is another mobile investing app that can be easily set up in your home, funded by a bank account or debit card.

- **Moomoo**: Free commission. Min $0, up to $0 free stocks.

These basic Apps don't require much personal information, so it's an easier setup for you than TD Ameritrade, Fidelity, etc. Those will require your outside support to have ID and SSN to set up and get started in their name. Now that you have the investing strategies and platforms to do some investing in stocks and ETFs, let's get back to the ETF market. To get you started with investing in ETFs, I will give you a popular list of ETFs and specific sector ETFs that track certain sectors.

Popular ETFs

- SPDR S&P 500 (SPX)

  It is the oldest and most widely known ETF that tracks the S&P 500 Index.

- Invesco QQQ (QQQ)

  Tracks the Nasdaq 100 Index, which contains technology stocks

- iShares Russell 2000 (IWM)

  Tracks the Russel 2000 small-cap index

- SPDR Dow Jones Industrial Average (DTA)

  Represents the 30 stokes of the D.J.J.A.

Sector ETFs

- **Oil**: Vaneck Oil Services ETF (OIH)
- **Energy**: SPDR Select Sector Fund – Energy Select Sector (XLE)
- **Financial Services**: SPDR Select Sector Fund Financial (XLF)
- **Real Estate Investment Trust**: iShares U.S. Real Estate ETF (IXR)

- **Biotechnology**: Vaneck Biotech ETF (BBH)
- **Gold**: SPDR Gold Trust (GLD)
- **Silver**: iShares silver trust (SLV)
- **Crude Oil**: United States Oil Fund (USO)
- **Natural Gas**: United States Natural Gas Natural Gas Fund LP (UGN)

Closing out this part, ETFs are vehicles that allow you to invest in the whole market at a bargain price. Sector by sector can be invested depending on our economic environment at a specific time. Read, learn, and use your dollar for a bigger purpose: to build wealth. Lastly, below is a short list of ETFs for your use. Study these ETFs to suit your investment strategy best.

Core Equity Solutions

U.S. Equity	Exchange-Traded Fund	Ticker
All-Cap		
S&P Total Market Index	iShares Core S&P Total US Stock Market ETF	ITOT
Dow Jones U.S. Index	iShares Dow Jones U.S. ETF	IYY
Dow Jones U.S. Broad Stock Market Index	Schwab U.S. Broad Market ETF	SCHB
S&P Composite 1500	SPDR Portfolio S&P 1500 Composite Stock Market ETF	SPTM
Mega-Cap		
S&P 100®	iShares S&P 100 ETF	OEF
S&P 500 Top 50	Invesco S&P Top 50 ETF	XLG
Large-Cap		
S&P 500®	iShares Core S&P 500 ETF	IVV
	SPDR® S&P 500 ETF	SPY
	SPDR Portfolio S&P 500® ETF	SPLG
	Vanguard S&P 500 ETF	VOO
Dow Jones Industrial Average	SPDR Dow Jones Industrial Average ETF	DIA
Dow Jones U.S. Large-Cap Total Stock Market Index	Schwab U.S. Large-Cap ETF	SCHX
Mid-Cap		
S&P MidCap 400® Index	iShares Core S&P Mid-Cap ETF	IJH
	SPDR S&P MidCap 400 ETF	MDY
	SPDR Portfolio S&P 400 Mid Cap ETF	SPMD
	Vanguard S&P Mid-Cap 400 ETF	IVOO
Dow Jones U.S. Mid-Cap Total Stock Market Index	Schwab U.S. Mid-Cap ETF	SCHM
Small-/Mid-Cap		
S&P Completion Index	Vanguard Extended Market Index ETF	VXF
Small-Cap		
S&P SmallCap 600®	iShares S&P SmallCap 600 ETF	IJR
	SPDR S&P Small Cap 600 ETF	SLY
	SPDR Portfolio S&P 600 Small Cap ETF	SPSM
	Vanguard S&P Small-Cap 600 ETF	VIOO
Dow Jones U.S. Small-Cap Total Stock Market Index	Schwab U.S. Small-Cap ETF	SCHA
Dow Jones Select MicroCap Index	First Trust Dow Jones Select MicroCap Index ETF	FDM

International Equity	Exchange-Traded Fund	Ticker
Developed		
S&P Developed Ex-U.S. BMI	SPDR Portfolio Developed World ex-US ETF	SPDW
S&P Developed Ex-U.S. Cap Range <2 Bil	SPDR S&P International Small Cap ETF	GWX
S&P Europe 350®	iShares Europe ETF	IEV
Emerging		
S&P Asia 50	iShares Asia 50 ETF	AIA
S&P Asia Pacific Emerging BMI	SPDR S&P Emerging Asia Pacific ETF	GMF
S&P China BMI	SPDR S&P China ETF	GXC
S&P Emerging BMI	SPDR Portfolio Emerging Markets ETF	SPEM
S&P Emerging Under USD2 Billion	SPDR S&P Emerging Markets Small Cap ETF	EWX
S&P Latin America 40	iShares Latin America 40 ETF	ILF
Global Equity		
S&P Global 100	iShares Global 100 ETF	IOO
The Global Dow	SPDR Global Dow ETF	DGT

Environmental, Social, and Governance (ESG)

Core ESG	Exchange-Traded Fund	Ticker
S&P 500 ESG Index	Xtrackers S&P 500 ESG ETF	SNPE
	SPDR S&P 500 ESG ETF	EFIV
S&P 500 Equal Weight ESG Leaders Select Index	Invesco ESG S&P 500 Equal Weight ETF	RSPE
S&P 500 Sustainability Screened Index	iShares ESG Screened S&P 500 ETF	XVV
S&P MidCap 400 Sustainability Screened Index	iShares ESG Screened S&P Mid-Cap ETF	XJH
S&P SmallCap 600 Sustainability Screened Index	iShares ESG Screened S&P Small-Cap ETF	XJR

Climate	Exchange-Traded Fund	Ticker
S&P 500 Fossil Fuel Free Index	SPDR S&P 500 Fossil Fuel Reserves Free ETF	SPYX

Thematic ESG	Exchange-Traded Fund	Ticker
S&P Global Clean Energy Index	iShares Global Clean Energy ETF	ICLN
S&P Global Water Index	Invesco S&P Global Water Index ETF	CGW
S&P 500 Catholic Values Index	Global X S&P 500 Catholic Values ETF	CATH

Fixed Income ESG	Exchange-Traded Fund	Ticker
S&P Green Bond Select Index	VanEck Vectors Green Bond ETF	GRNB

Alternative ESG	Exchange-Traded Fund	Ticker
IHS Markit Global Carbon Index	KraneShares Global Carbon Strategy ETF	KRBN
IHS Markit Carbon CCA Index	KraneShares California Carbon Allowance Strategy ETF	KCCA
IHS Markit Carbon EUA Index	KraneShares European Carbon Allowance Strategy ETF	KEUA

Income Solutions

Equity Dividends	Exchange-Traded Fund	Ticker
U.S.		
S&P High Yield Dividend Aristocrats®	SPDR S&P Dividend ETF	SDY
S&P 500 Dividend Aristocrats	ProShares S&P 500 Dividend Aristocrats ETF	NOBL
Dow Jones U.S. Select Dividend Index	iShares Dow Jones Select Dividend Index Fund	DVY
S&P Technology Dividend Aristocrats Index	ProShares S&P Technology Dividend Aristocrats ETF	TDV
Dow Jones U.S. Dividend 100 Index	Schwab U.S. Dividend Equity ETF	SCHD
S&P 500 Low Volatility High Dividend Index	Invesco S&P 500 High Dividend Low Volatility Portfolio	SPHD
S&P MidCap 400 Dividend Aristocrats	ProShares S&P Midcap 400 Dividend Aristocrats ETF	REGL
S&P Small Cap 600 Low Volatility High Dividend Index	Invesco S&P SmallCap High Dividend Low Volatility Portfolio	XSHD
S&P 500 High Dividend Index	SPDR Portfolio S&P 500 High Dividend ETF	SPYD
International		
S&P International Dividend Opportunities Index	SPDR S&P International Dividend ETF	DWX
Dow Jones International Dividend 100 Index	Schwab International Dividend Equity ETF	SCHY
Dow Jones EPAC Select Dividend Index	iShares Dow Jones International Select Dividend Index Fund	IDV
Dow Jones Asia Pacific Select Dividend 30	iShares Asia/Pacific Dividend ETF	DVYA
Emerging		
S&P Emerging Markets Dividend Opportunities Index	SPDR S&P Emerging Markets Dividend ETF	EDIV
Dow Jones Emerging Markets Select Dividend Index	iShares Emerging Markets Dividend ETF	DVYE
Global		
S&P Global Dividend Aristocrats	SPDR S&P Global Dividend ETF	WDIV
Dow Jones Global Composite Yield Total Return Index	Arrow Dow Jones Global Yield ETF	GYLD
Dow Jones Global Select Dividend Index	First Trust Dow Jones Global Select Dividend Index ETF	FGD

Preferreds	Exchange-Traded Fund	Ticker
North American		
S&P Enhanced Yield North American Preferred Stock	Global X SuperIncome™ Preferred ETF	SPFF
International		
S&P International Preferred Stock Index	iShares S&P International Preferred Stock Index Fund	IPFF

MLPs	Exchange-Traded Fund	Ticker
S&P MLP Index	iPath S&P MLP ETN	IMLP

Municipals	Exchange-Traded Fund	Ticker
Investment Grade		
S&P National AMT-Free Municipal Bond Index	Vanguard Tax-Exempt Bond ETF	VTEB
S&P California AMT-Free Municipal Bond Index	iShares S&P California AMT-Free Municipal Index Fund	CMF
S&P New York AMT-Free Municipal Bond Index	iShares S&P New York AMT-Free Municipal Index Fund	NYF
S&P Short Term National AMT-Free Municipal Bond Index	iShares S&P Short Term AMT-Free Municipal Index Fund	SUB
Maturity-Based		
S&P AMT-Free Muni Series 2021 Index	iShares iBonds Dec 2021 AMT-Free Muni Bond ETF	IBMJ
S&P AMT-Free Muni Series 2022 Index	iShares iBonds Dec 2022 AMT-Free Muni Bond ETF	IBMK
S&P AMT-Free Muni Series 2023 Index	iShares iBonds Dec 2023 AMT-Free Muni Bond ETF	IBML
S&P AMT-Free Muni Series 2024 Index	iShares iBonds Dec 2024 AMT-Free Muni Bond ETF	IBMM
S&P AMT-Free Muni Series 2025 Index	iShares iBonds Dec 2025 AMT-Free Muni Bond ETF	IBMN
S&P AMT-Free Muni Series 2026 Index	iShares iBonds Dec 2026 AMT-Free Muni Bond ETF	IBMO
S&P AMT-Free Muni Series 2027 Index	iShares iBonds Dec 2027 AMT-Free Muni Bond ETF	IBMP
S&P AMT-Free Muni Series 2028 Index	iShares iBonds Dec 2028 AMT-Free Muni Bond ETF	IBMQ
High Yield		
S&P High Yield Municipal Bond Index	SPDR Nuveen S&P High Yield Municipal Bond ETF	HYMB

Global Treasury	Exchange-Traded Fund	Ticker
International Treasury Bonds		
S&P/Citigroup Int'l Treasury Bond Index Ex U.S. Index	iShares S&P/Citi Intl Treasury Bond Fund	IGOV
S&P/Citigroup Int'l Treasury Bond Index Ex U.S. 1-3 yr Index	iShares S&P/Citi 1-3 Yr International Treasury Bond Fund	ISHG

U.S. Corporate	Exchange-Traded Fund	Ticker
iBoxx USD Liquid Investment Grade Index	iShares iBoxx $ Investment Grade Corporate Bond ETF	LQD
Markit iBoxx USD Liquid Investment Grade 0-5 Index	iShares 0-5 Year Investment Grade Corporate Bond ETF	SLQD
iBoxx USD Liquid Investment Grade BBB 0+ Index	iShares BBB Rated Corporate Bond ETF	LQDB
iBoxx USD Liquid High Yield Index	iShares iBoxx $ High Yield Corporate Bond ETF	HYG
Markit iBoxx USD Liquid Investment Grade 0-5 Index	iShares 0-5 Year High Yield Corporate Bond ETF	SHYG
Markit iBoxx 5-Year Target Duration TIPS Index	FlexShares iBoxx 5-Year Target Duration TIPS Index Fund	TDTF
Markit iBoxx 3-Year Target Duration TIPS Index	FlexShares iBoxx 3-Year Target Duration TIPS Index Fund	TDTT
S&P 500/MarketAxess Investment Grade Corporate Bond Index	ProShares S&P 500 Bond ETF	SPXB

Global Corporate	Exchange-Traded Fund	Ticker
International Corporate Bonds		
S&P International Corporate Bond Index	Invesco International Corporate Bond Portfolio	PICB
Markit iBoxx Global Developed Markets High Yield Index	iShares Global High Yield Corporate Bond ETF	GHYG

Factor-Based	Exchange-Traded Fund	Ticker
S&P U.S. High Yield Low Volatility Corporate Bond Index	IQ S&P High Yield Low Volatility Bond ETF	HYLV

Alternative Fixed Income – ESG	Exchange-Traded Fund	Ticker
S&P Green Bond Select Index	VanEck Vectors Green Bond ETF	GRNB

Sector Solutions

Market Cap Weighted Sectors	Exchange-Traded Fund	Ticker
Domestic Market Cap Weighted – Large Cap		
S&P Select Sector Communication Services	SPDR - Communication Services Select Sector Fund	XLC
S&P Select Sector Consumer Discretionary	SPDR - Consumer Discretionary Select Sector Fund	XLY
S&P Select Sector Energy	SPDR - Energy Select Sector Fund	XLE
S&P Select Sector Financials	SPDR - Financials Select Sector Fund	XLF
S&P Select Sector Health Care	SPDR - Health Care Select Sector Fund	XLV
S&P Select Sector Industrials	SPDR - Industrials Select Sector Fund	XLI
S&P Select Sector Materials	SPDR - Materials Select Sector Fund	XLB
S&P Select Sector Real Estate	SPDR - Real Estate Select Sector Fund	XLRE
S&P Select Sector Technology	SPDR - Technology Select Sector Fund	XLK
S&P Select Sector Utilities	SPDR - Utilities Select Sector Fund	XLU
Domestic Market Cap Weighted – Small Cap		
S&P SmallCap 600 Capped Consumer Discretionary	Invesco S&P SmallCap Consumer Discretionary Portfolio	PSCD
S&P SmallCap 600 Capped Consumer Staples	Invesco S&P SmallCap Consumer Staples Portfolio	PSCC
S&P SmallCap 600 Capped Energy	Invesco S&P SmallCap Energy Portfolio	PSCE
S&P SmallCap 600 Capped Financials	Invesco S&P SmallCap Financials Portfolio	PSCF
S&P SmallCap 600 Capped Health Care	Invesco S&P SmallCap Health Care Portfolio	PSCH
S&P SmallCap 600 Capped Industrials	Invesco S&P SmallCap Industrials Portfolio	PSCI
S&P SmallCap 600 Capped Information Technology	Invesco S&P SmallCap Information Technology Portfolio	PSCT
S&P SmallCap 600 Capped Materials	Invesco S&P SmallCap Materials Portfolio	PSCM
S&P SmallCap 600 Capped Utilities & Communication Services	Invesco S&P SmallCap Utilities & Communication Services Portfolio	PSCU
Global Sectors		
S&P Global 1200 Communication Services	iShares Global Communication Services ETF	IXP
S&P Global 1200 Consumer Discretionary	iShares Global Consumer Discretionary ETF	RXI
S&P Global 1200 Consumer Staples	iShares Global Consumer Staples ETF	KXI
S&P Global 1200 Energy	iShares Global Energy ETF	IXC
S&P Global 1200 Financials	iShares Global Financials ETF	IXG
S&P Global 1200 Health Care	iShares Global Healthcare ETF	IXJ
S&P Global 1200 Industrials	iShares Global Industrials ETF	EXI
S&P Global 1200 Materials	iShares Global Materials ETF	MXI
S&P Global 1200 Information Technology	iShares Global Technology ETF	IXN
S&P Global 1200 Utilities	iShares Global Utilities ETF	JXI

Alternatively Weighted Sectors	Exchange-Traded Fund	Ticker
Domestic Equal Weighted – Large Cap		
S&P 500 Equal Weight Communication Services	Invesco S&P 500 Eql Wt Communication Services ETF	EWCO
S&P 500 Equal Weight Consumer Discretionary	Invesco S&P 500 Eql Wt Consumer Discretionary ETF	RCD
S&P 500 Equal Weight Consumer Staples	Invesco S&P 500 Eql Wt Consumer Staples ETF	RHS
S&P 500 Equal Weight Energy	Invesco S&P 500 Eql Wt Energy ETF	RYE
S&P 500 Equal Weight Financials	Invesco S&P 500 Eql Wt Financials ETF	RYF
S&P 500 Equal Weight Health Care	Invesco S&P 500 Eql Wt Health Care ETF	RYH
S&P 500 Equal Weight Industrials	Invesco S&P 500 Eql Wt Industrials ETF	RGI
S&P 500 Equal Weight Materials	Invesco S&P 500 Eql Wt Materials ETF	RTM
S&P 500 Equal Weight Technology	Invesco S&P 500 Eql Wt Technology ETF	RYT
S&P 500 Equal Weight Utilities	Invesco S&P 500 Eql Wt Utilities ETF	RYU
S&P 500 Equal Weight Real Estate	Invesco S&P 500 Eql Wt Real Estate ETF	EWRE

Kensho Sectors

S&P Kensho New Economies Composite Index	SPDR Kensho New Economies Composite ETF	KOMP
S&P Kensho Smart Transportation Index	SPDR Kensho Smart Mobility ETF	HAIL
S&P Kensho Future Security Index	SPDR Kensho Future Security ETF	FITE
S&P Kensho Intelligent Infrastructure Index	SPDR Kensho Intelligent Structures ETF	SIMS
S&P Kensho Final Frontiers Index	SPDR Kensho Final Frontiers ETF	ROKT
S&P Kensho Clean Power Index	SPDR Kensho Clean Power ETF	CNRG
S&P Kensho Moonshot Index	Direxion Moonshot Innovators ETF	MOON
S&P Kensho Cleantech Index	ProShares S&P Kensho Cleantech ETF	CTEX
S&P Kensho Smart Factories Index	ProShares S&P Kensho Smart Factories ETF	MAKX

ICB Industries	Exchange-Traded Fund	Ticker
Domestic Broad Market Sectors		
Dow Jones U.S. Health Care Providers Index	iShares US Healthcare Provider ETF	IHF

Narrow Sectors & Industries	Exchange-Traded Fund	Ticker
Financials		
S&P Banks Select Industry Index	SPDR S&P Bank ETF	KBE
S&P Regional Banks Select Industry Index	SPDR S&P Regional Banks ETF	KRE
S&P Insurance Select Industry Index	SPDR S&P Insurance ETF	KIE
Dow Jones U.S. Financial Services Index	iShares US Financial Services ETF	IYG
Dow Jones U.S. Select Regional Banks Index	iShares US Regional Banks ETF	IAT
Dow Jones U.S. Select Insurance Index	iShares U.S. Insurance ETF	IAK
Dow Jones U.S. Select Investment Services Index	iShares U.S. Broker-Dealers ETF	IAI
Health Care		
S&P Biotechnology Select Industry Index	SPDR S&P Biotechnology ETF	XBI
Dow Jones U.S. Select Pharmaceuticals Index	iShares US Pharmaceuticals ETF	IHE
S&P Pharmaceuticals Select Industry Index	SPDR S&P Pharmaceuticals ETF	XPH
Dow Jones U.S. Select Medical Equipment Index	iShares Dow Jones US Medical Devices	IHI
S&P Health Care Services Select Industry Index (TR)	SPDR S&P Health Care Services	XHS
S&P Health Care Equipment Select Industry Index	SPDR S&P Health Care Equipment ETF	XHE
Oil & Gas		
S&P Oil & Gas Equipment & Services Select Industry Index	SPDR S&P Oil & Gas Equipment & Services ETF	XES
Dow Jones U.S. Select Oil Equipment & Services Index	iShares US Oil Equipment & Services ETF	IEZ
S&P Oil & Gas Exploration & Production Select Industry Index	SPDR S&P Oil & Gas Exploration & Production ETF	XOP
Dow Jones U.S. Select Oil Exploration & Production Index	iShares US Oil & Gas Exploration ETF	IEO
S&P 500 Fossil Fuel Free Index	SPDR S&P 500 Fossil Fuel Reserves Free ETF	SPYX
Technology		
S&P North American Technology Sector Index	iShares North American Tech ETF	IGM
S&P North American Technology Software Index	iShares North Amer Tech-Software ETF	IGV
S&P North American Technology Multimedia Networking Index	iShares North American Tech-Multimedia Networking ETF	IGN
Dow Jones Internet Composite Index	First Trust Dow Jones Internet Index Fund	FDN
S&P Software & Services Select Industry Index	SPDR S&P Software & Services ETF	XSW
S&P Internet Select Industry Index	SPDR S&P Internet ETF	XWEB
Consumer Goods & Services		
Dow Jones U.S. Select Home Construction Index	iShares US Home Construction ETF	ITB
S&P Homebuilders Select Industry Index	SPDR S&P Homebuilders ETF	XHB
S&P Retail Select Industry Index	SPDR S&P Retail ETF	XRT
Dow Jones Emerging Markets Consumer Titans 30 Index	Columbia Emerging Markets Consumer ETF	ECON

Transportation

Dow Jones Transportation Average™	iShares Dow Jones Transportation Average	IYT
S&P Transportation Select Industry Index	SPDR S&P Tansportation ETF	XTN

Capital Markets

S&P Capital Markets Select Industry Index	SPDR S&P Capital Markets ETF	KCE

Semiconductor

S&P Semiconductor Select Industry Index	SPDR S&P Semiconductor ETF	XSD

Telecom

S&P Telecom Select Industry Index	SPDR S&P Telecom ETF	XTL

Aerospace & Defense

Dow Jones U.S. Select Aerospace & Defense Index	iShares US Aerospace & Defense	ITA
S&P Aerospace & Defense Select Industry Index	SPDR S&P Aerospace & Defense ETF	XAR

Sector-Based ESG

S&P Global Clean Energy Index	iShares Global Clean Energy ETF	ICLN

Real Asset Solutions

Equity-Based	Exchange-Traded Fund	Ticker
Commodities		
S&P North American Natural Resources Index	iShares North American Natural Resources ETF	IGE
S&P Global Natural Resources Index	SPDR S&P Global Natural Resources ETF	GNR
S&P Metals and Mining Index	SPDR S&P Metals and Mining ETF	XME
Infrastructure		
Dow Jones Brookfield Global Infrastructure Composite Index	ProShares DJ Brookfield Global Infrastructure ETF	TOLZ
S&P Global Infrastructure Index	iShares Global Infrastructure ETF	IGF
	SPDR S&P Global Infrastructure ETF	GII
S&P Emerging Markets Infrastructure Index	iShares Emerging Markets Infrastructure ETF	EMIF
Water		
S&P Global Water Index	Invesco S&P Global Water ETF	CGW
Timber & Forestry		
S&P Global Timber & Forestry Index	iShares Global Timber & Forestry ETF	WOOD
Real Estate		
Dow Jones U.S. Real Estate Index	iShares US Real Estate ETF	IYR
Dow Jones Global Ex-U.S. Select Real Estate Securities Index	SPDR Dow Jones International Real Estate	RWX
S&P Global Ex-US Property	Vanguard Global ex-US Real Estate ETF	VNQI
S&P Select Sector Real Estate	SPDR - Real Estate Select Sector Fund	XLRE
Dow Jones Global Select Real Estate Index	SPDR Dow Jones Global Real Estate	RWO
S&P Developed Ex-US Property	iShares International Developed Property ETF	WPS
REITs		
Dow Jones U.S. Select REIT Index	SPDR Dow Jones REIT	RWR
Dow Jones Equity All REIT Capped Index	Schwab U.S. REIT ETF	SCHH
S&P United States REIT	First Trust S&P REIT Index Fund	FRI
MLPs		
S&P MLP Index	iPath S&P MLP ETN	IMLP

Futures-Based	Exchange-Traded Fund	Ticker
S&P GSCI		
S&P GSCI TR	iShares S&P GSCI Commodity Indexed Trust	GSG

Smart Beta (Factor-Based and Alternatively Weighted) Solutions

Size & Style	Exchange-Traded Fund	Ticker
U.S. Large-Cap Growth		
S&P 500 Growth	iShares S&P 500 Growth ETF	IVW
	SPDR Portfolio S&P 500 Growth ETF	SPYG
	Vanguard S&P 500 Growth ETF	VOOG
Dow Jones U.S. Large-Cap Growth Total Stock Market Index	Schwab U.S. Large-Cap Growth ETF	SCHG
U.S. Large-Cap Value		
S&P 500 Value	iShares S&P 500 Value ETF	IVE
	SPDR Portfolio S&P 500 Value ETF	SPYV
	Vanguard S&P 500 Value ETF	VOOV
Dow Jones U.S. Large-Cap Value Total Stock Market Index	Schwab U.S. Large-Cap Value ETF	SCHV
U.S. Large/Mid-Cap Growth		
S&P 900 Growth	iShares Core S&P US Growth	IUSG
U.S. Large/Mid-Cap Value		
S&P 900 Value	iShares Core S&P US Value	IUSV
U.S. Mid-Cap Growth		
S&P MidCap 400 Growth	iShares S&P MidCap 400 Growth ETF	IJK
	SPDR S&P Mid Cap 400 Growth ETF	MDYG
	Vanguard S&P Mid-Cap 400 Growth ETF	IVOG
U.S. Mid-Cap Value		
S&P MidCap 400 Value	iShares S&P MidCap 400 Value ETF	IJJ
	SPDR S&P Mid Cap 400 Value ETF	MDYV
	Vanguard S&P Mid-Cap 400 Value ETF	IVOV
U.S. Small-Cap Growth		
S&P SmallCap 600 Growth	iShares S&P SmallCap 600 Growth ETF	IJT
	SPDR S&P Small Cap 600 Growth ETF	SLYG
	Vanguard S&P Small-Cap 600 Growth ETF	VIOG
U.S. Small-Cap Value		
S&P SmallCap 600 Value	iShares S&P SmallCap 600 Value ETF	IJS
	SPDR S&P Small Cap 600 Value ETF	SLYV
	Vanguard S&P Small-Cap 600 Value ETF	VIOV

Pure Style	Exchange-Traded Fund	Ticker
S&P 500 Pure Growth	Invesco S&P 500 Pure Growth ETF	RPG
S&P 500 Pure Value	Invesco S&P 500 Pure Value ETF	RPV
S&P MidCap 400 Pure Growth	Invesco S&P MidCap 400 Pure Growth ETF	RFG
S&P MidCap 400 Pure Value	Invesco S&P MidCap 400 Pure Value ETF	RFV
S&P SmallCap 600 Pure Growth	Invesco S&P SmallCap 600 Pure Growth ETF	RZG
S&P SmallCap 600 Pure Value	Invesco S&P SmallCap 600 Pure Value ETF	RZV

Enhanced Value	Exchange-Traded Fund	Ticker
S&P 500 Enhanced Value	Invesco S&P 500 Enhanced Value ETF	SPVU

Equal-Weight	Exchange-Traded Fund	Ticker
S&P 500 Equal Weight Index	Invesco S&P 500 Equal Weight ETF	RSP
S&P MidCap 400 Equal Weight Index	Invesco S&P MidCap 400 Equal Weight ETF	EWMC
S&P SmallCap 600 Equal Weight Index	Invesco S&P SmallCap 600 Equal Weight ETF	EWSC

Low Volatility	Exchange-Traded Fund	Ticker
S&P 500 Low Volatility Index	Invesco S&P 500 Low Volatility Portfolio	SPLV
S&P MidCap 400 Low Volatility Index	Invesco S&P Midcap Low Volatility Portfolio	XMLV
S&P SmallCap 600 Low Volatility Index (TR)	Invesco S&P Smallcap Low Volatility Portfolio	XSLV
S&P BMI Emerging Markets Low Volatility Index	Invesco S&P Emerging Markets Low Volatility Portfolio	EELV
S&P BMI International Developed Low Volatility Index	Invesco S&P Int'l Developed Low Volatility Portfolio	IDLV
S&P 500 Low Volatility Rate Response Index	Invesco S&P 500 ex-Rate Sensitive Low Volatility Portfolio	XRLV

Momentum	Exchange-Traded Fund	Ticker
S&P 500 Momentum	Invesco S&P 500 Momentum Portfolio	SPMO
S&P MidCap 400 Momentum Index	Invesco S&P MidCap Momentum ETF	XMMO
S&P Small Cap 600 Momentum Index	Invesco S&P SmallCap Momentum ETF	XSMO
S&P 1500 Positive Momentum Tilt Index	SPDR S&P 1500 Momentum Tilt ETF	MMTM
S&P Momentum Emerging Plus LargeMidCap Index	Invesco S&P Emerging Markets Momentum Portfolio	EEMO
S&P Momentum Developed Ex. U.S. & South Korea LargeMidCap Index	Invesco S&P International Developed Momentum Porttfolio	IDMO

Quality	Exchange -Traded Fund	Ticker
S&P 500 Quality Index	Invesco S&P 500 Quality ETF	SPHQ
S&P MidCap 400 Quality Index	Invesco S&P MidCap Quality ETF	XMHQ
S&P SmallCap 600 Quality Index	Invesco S&P SmallCap Quality ETF	XSHQ
S&P Quality Developed Ex U.S. LargeMidCap Index	Invesco S&P International Developed Quality ETF	IDHQ

Revenue-Weighted	Exchange-Traded Fund	Ticker
S&P 500 Revenue-Weighted Index	Invesco S&P 500 Revenue ETF	RWL
S&P MidCap 400 Revenue-Weighted Index	Invesco S&P MidCap 400 Revenue ETF	RWK
S&P SmallCap 600 Revenue-Weighted Index	Invesco S&P SmallCap 600 Revenue ETF	RWJ
S&P 900 Dividend Revenue-Weighted Index	Invesco S&P Ultra Dividend Revenue ETF	RDIV

Spin-Off	Exchange Traded Fund	Ticker
S&P U.S. Spin-Off Index	Invesco S&P Spin-Off ETF	CSD

Multi-Factor	Exchange-Traded Fund	Ticker
S&P 500 Low Volatility High Dividend Index	Invesco S&P 500 High Dividend Low Volatility Portfolio	SPHD
S&P Small Cap 600 Low Volatility High Dividend Index	Invesco S&P 600 High Dividend Low Volatility Portfolio	XSHD
S&P EPAC Ex-Korea Low Volatility High Dividend Index	Invesco S&P International Developed Low Volatility Portfolio	IDHD
S&P 500 Growth at a Reasonable Price (GARP) Index	Invesco S&P 500 GARP ETF	SPGP
S&P 500 High Momentum Value Index	Invesco S&P 500 Value with Momentum ETF	SPVM
S&P MidCap 400 High Momentum Value Index	Invesco S&P MidCap Value with Momentum ETF	XMVM
S&P SmallCap 600 High Momentum Value Index	Invesco S&P SmallCap Value with Momentum ETF	XSVM
S&P U.S. High Yield Low Volatility Corporate Bond Index	IQ S&P High Yield Low Volatility Bond ETF	HYLV

Kensho	Exchange-Traded Fund	Ticker
S&P Kensho New Economies Composite Index	SPDR Kensho New Economies Composite ETF	KOMP
S&P Kensho Smart Transportation Index	SPDR Kensho Smart Mobility ETF	HAIL
S&P Kensho Future Security Index	SPDR Kensho Future Security ETF	FITE
S&P Kensho Intelligent Infrastructure Index	SPDR Kensho Intelligent Structures ETF	SIMS
S&P Kensho Final Frontiers Index	SPDR Kensho Final Frontiers ETF	ROKT
S&P Kensho Clean Power Index	SPDR Kensho Clean Power ETF	CRNG
S&P Kensho Moonshots Index	Direxion Moonshot Innovators ETF	MOON

Risk Management and Asset Allocation Solutions

Volatility	Exchange-Traded Fund	Ticker
VIX®		
S&P 500 VIX Short-Term Futures Index	iPath S&P 500 VIX Short-Term Futures ETN	VXX
	ProShares VIX Short-Term Futures ETF	VIXY
S&P 500 VIX Mid-Term Futures Index	ProShares VIX Mid-Term Futures ETF	VIXM
Dynamic Equity		
S&P 500 Dynamic VEQTOR Index	Invesco S&P 500 Downside Hedged Portfolio	PHDG
Low Volatility		
S&P 500 Low Volatility Index	Invesco S&P 500 Low Volatility	SPLV
S&P BMI International Developed Low Volatility Index	Invesco S&P International Developed Low Volatility Portfolio	IDLV
S&P BMI Emerging Markets Low Volatility Index	Invesco S&P Emerging Markets Low Volatility Portfolio	EELV
S&P 500 Low Volatility Rate Response index	Invesco S&P 500 ex-Rate Sensitive Low Volatility Portfolio	XRLV
Buy-Write		
CBOE S&P 500 Buywrite Index (BXM)	Invesco S&P 500 BuyWrite Portfolio	PBP

Asset Allocation	Exchange-Traded Fund	Ticker
S&P Target Risk Conservative Index	IShares Core Conservative Allocation	AOK
S&P Target Risk Moderate Index	iShares Core Moderate Allocation	AOM
S&P Target Risk Growth Index	iShares Core Growth Allocation	AOR
S&P Target Risk Aggressive Index	iShares Core Aggressive Allocation	AOA

Managed Risk	Exchange-Traded Fund	Ticker
Managed Risk Equity		
S&P 500 Managed Risk 2.0 Index	DeltaShares S&P 500 Managed Risk ETF	DMRL
S&P 400 Managed Risk 2.0 Index	DeltaShares S&P 400 Managed Risk ETF	DMRM
S&P 600 Managed Risk 2.0 Index	Delta Shares S&P 600 Managed Risk ETF	DMRS
S&P EPAC Ex. Korea LargeMidCap Managed Risk 2.0 Index	DeltaShares S&P International Managed Risk ETF	DMRI

Defined Outcome	Exchange-Traded Fund	Ticker
S&P 500 Price Return	Allianz U.S. Large Cap 10% Buffer - January	AZAJ
	Allianz U.S. Large Cap 20% Buffer - January	AZBJ
	Allianz U.S. Large Cap 10% Buffer - April	AZAA
	Allianz U.S. Large Cap 20% Buffer - April	AZBA
	Allianz U.S. Large Cap 10% Buffer - July	AZAL
	Allianz U.S. Large Cap 20% Buffer - July	AZBL
	Allianz U.S. Large Cap 10% Buffer - October	AZAO
	Allianz U.S. Large Cap 20% Buffer - October	AZBO
	FT Cboe Vest U.S. Equity Buffer ETF - January	FJAN
	FT Cboe Vest U.S. Equity Deep Buffer ETF - January	DJAN
	FT Cboe Vest U.S. Equity Buffer ETF - February	FFEB
	FT Cboe Vest U.S. Equity Deep Buffer ETF - February	DFEB
	FT Cboe Vest U.S. Equity Buffer ETF - May	FMAY
	FT Cboe Vest U.S. Equity Deep Buffer ETF - May	DMAY
	FT Cboe Vest U.S. Equity Buffer ETF - June	FJUN
	FT Cboe Vest U.S. Equity Deep Buffer ETF - June	DJUN
	FT Cboe Vest U.S. Equity Buffer ETF - July	FJUL
	FT Cboe Vest U.S. Equity Deep Buffer ETF - July	DJUL

Defined Outcome	Exchange-Traded Fund	Ticker
S&P 500 Price Return	FT Cboe Vest U.S. Equity Buffer ETF - August	FAUG
	FT Cboe Vest U.S. Equity Deep Buffer ETF - August	DAUG
	FT Cboe Vest U.S. Equity Buffer ETF - September	FSEP
	FT Cboe Vest U.S. Equity Deep Buffer ETF - September	DSEP
	FT Cboe Vest U.S. Equity Buffer ETF - October	FOCT
	FT Cboe Vest U.S. Equity Deep Buffer ETF - October	DOCT
	FT Cboe Vest U.S. Equity Buffer ETF - November	FNOV
	FT Cboe Vest U.S. Equity Deep Buffer ETF - November	DNOV
	FT Cboe Vest U.S. Equity Buffer ETF - December	FDEC
	FT Cboe Vest U.S. Equity Deep Buffer ETF - December	DDEC
	Innovator S&P 500 Buffer ETF January	BJAN
	Innovator S&P 500 Power Buffer ETF January	PJAN
	Innovator S&P 500 Ultra Buffer ETF January	UJAN
	Innovator S&P 500 Buffer ETF February	BFEB
	Innovator S&P 500 Power Buffer ETF February	PFEB
	Innovator S&P 500 Ultra ETF February	UFEB
	Innovator S&P 500 Buffer ETF March	BMAR
	Innovator S&P 500 Power Buffer ETF March	PMAR
	Innovator S&P 500 Ultra ETF March	UMAR
	Innovator S&P 500 Buffer ETF April	BAPR
	Innovator S&P 500 Power Buffer ETF April	PAPR
	Innovator S&P 500 Ultra Buffer ETF April	UAPR
	Innovator S&P 500 Buffer ETF May	BMAY
	Innovator S&P 500 Power Buffer ETF May	PMAY
	Innovator S&P 500 Ultra Buffer ETF May	UMAY
	Innovator S&P 500 Buffer ETF June	BJUN
	Innovator S&P 500 Power Buffer ETF June	PJUN
	Innovator S&P 500 Ultra Buffer ETF June	UJUN
	Innovator S&P 500 Buffer ETF July	BJUL
	Innovator S&P 500 Power Buffer ETF July	PJUL
	Innovator S&P 500 Ultra Buffer ETF July	UJUL
	Innovator S&P 500 Buffer ETF August	BAUG
	Innovator S&P 500 Power Buffer ETF August	PAUG
	Innovator S&P 500 Ultra Buffer ETF August	UAUG
	Innovator S&P 500 Buffer ETF September	BSEP
	Innovator S&P 500 Power Buffer ETF September	PSEP
	Innovator S&P 500 Ultra Buffer ETF September	USEP
	Innovator S&P 500 Buffer ETF October	BOCT
	Innovator S&P 500 Power Buffer ETF October	POCT
	Innovator S&P 500 Ultra Buffer ETF October	UOCT
	Innovator S&P 500 Buffer ETF November	BNOV
	Innovator S&P 500 Power Buffer ETF November	PNOV
	Innovator S&P 500 Ultra Buffer ETF November	UNOV
	Innovator S&P 500 Buffer ETF December	BDEC
	Innovator S&P 500 Power Buffer ETF December	PDEC
	Innovator S&P 500 Ultra ETF December	UDEC

iShares
by BlackRock

GET INVESTED.

iShares U.S. ETF Product List as of 8/1/2022

Flat 9x12 - 1 - 9

iShares Core ETFs

Low-cost stock and bond ETFs to build the foundation of a portfolio.

U.S. stocks

Fund name	Trading symbol	Expense ratio (%)
iShares Core S&P 500 ETF	IVV	0.03
iShares Core S&P Total U.S. Stock Market ETF	ITOT	0.03
iShares Core S&P Mid-Cap ETF	IJH	0.05
iShares Core S&P Small-Cap ETF	IJR	0.06
iShares Core S&P U.S. Growth ETF	IUSG	0.04
iShares Core S&P U.S. Value ETF	IUSV	0.04
iShares Core High Dividend ETF	HDV	0.08
iShares Core Dividend Growth ETF	DGRO	0.08
iShares Core U.S. REIT ETF	USRT	0.08

International stocks

Fund name	Trading symbol	Expense ratio (%)
iShares Core MSCI Total International Stock ETF	IXUS	0.07
iShares Core MSCI EAFE ETF	IEFA	0.07
iShares Core MSCI International Developed Markets ETF	IDEV	0.04
iShares Core MSCI Emerging Markets ETF	IEMG	0.09
iShares Core MSCI Europe ETF	IEUR	0.09
iShares Core MSCI Pacific ETF	IPAC	0.09

Bonds

Fund name	Trading symbol	Expense ratio (%)
iShares Core U.S. Aggregate Bond ETF	AGG	0.03
iShares Core Total USD Bond Market ETF	IUSB	0.06¹
iShares Core 1-5 Year USD Bond ETF	ISTB	0.06
iShares Core 5-10 Year USD Bond ETF	IMTB	0.06¹
iShares Core 10+ Year USD Bond ETF	ILTB	0.06
iShares Core International Aggregate Bond ETF	IAGG	0.07

iShares Core Allocation ETFs

	Trading symbol	Expense ratio (%)
iShares Core Conservative Allocation ETF	AOK	0.15¹
iShares Core Moderate Allocation ETF	AOM	0.15¹
iShares Core Growth Allocation ETF	AOR	0.15¹
iShares Core Aggressive Allocation ETF	AOA	0.15¹

THE COMPLETE iSHARES ETF LINEUP ▶

iShares.com

iShares Core ETFs are bolded

1

Regions

U.S. – Broad market

	Trading symbol	Inception date	Exp. ratio (%)
iShares Core S&P Total U.S. Stock Market ETF	ITOT	1/20/04	0.03
iShares Core S&P U.S. Value ETF	IUSV	7/24/00	0.04
iShares Core S&P U.S. Growth ETF	IUSG	7/24/00	0.04
iShares Russell 3000 ETF	IWV	5/22/00	0.20
iShares Dow Jones U.S. ETF	IYY	6/12/00	0.20

U.S. – Large cap

	Trading symbol	Inception date	Exp. ratio (%)
iShares Core S&P 500 ETF	IVV	5/15/00	0.03
iShares Core High Dividend ETF	HDV	3/29/11	0.08
iShares Core Dividend Growth ETF	DGRO	6/10/14	0.08
iShares MSCI USA Min Vol Factor ETF	USMV	10/18/11	0.15
iShares MSCI USA Quality Factor ETF	QUAL	7/16/13	0.15
iShares MSCI USA Momentum Factor ETF	MTUM	4/16/13	0.15
iShares MSCI USA Size Factor ETF	SIZE	4/16/13	0.15
iShares MSCI USA Value Factor ETF	VLUE	4/16/13	0.15
iShares Morningstar U.S. Equity ETF	ILCB	6/28/04	0.03
iShares Morningstar Growth ETF	ILCG	6/28/04	0.04
iShares Morningstar Value ETF	ILCV	6/28/04	0.04
iShares Russell 1000 ETF	IWB	5/15/00	0.15
iShares Russell 1000 Growth ETF	IWF	5/22/00	0.18
iShares Russell 1000 Value ETF	IWD	5/22/00	0.18
iShares Russell Top 200 ETF	IWL	9/22/09	0.15
iShares Russell Top 200 Growth ETF	IWY	9/22/09	0.20

U.S. – Large cap (continued)

	Trading symbol	Inception date	Exp. ratio (%)
iShares Russell Top 200 Value ETF	IWX	9/22/09	0.20
iShares S&P 100 ETF	OEF	10/23/00	0.20
iShares S&P 500 Growth ETF	IVW	5/22/00	0.18
iShares S&P 500 Value ETF	IVE	5/22/00	0.18
iShares Select Dividend ETF	DVY	11/3/03	0.38
iShares U.S. Dividend and Buyback ETF	DIVB	11/7/17	0.25
iShares MSCI USA Equal Weighted ETF	EUSA	5/5/10	0.09
iShares U.S Equity Factor ETF	LRGF	4/28/15	0.08
iShares MSCI KLD 400 Social ETF	DSI	11/14/06	0.25
iShares MSCI USA ESG Select ETF	SUSA	1/24/05	0.25
iShares ESG Aware MSCI USA ETF	ESGU	12/1/16	0.15
iShares Factors U.S. Growth Style ETF	STLG	1/14/20	0.25
iShares Factors U.S. Value Style ETF	STLV	1/14/20	0.25

U.S. – Mid cap

	Trading symbol	Inception date	Exp. ratio (%)
iShares Core S&P Mid-Cap ETF	IJH	5/22/00	0.05
iShares S&P Mid-Cap 400 Growth ETF	IJK	7/24/00	0.17
iShares S&P Mid-Cap 400 Value ETF	IJJ	7/24/00	0.18
iShares Morningstar Mid-Cap ETF	IMCB	6/28/04	0.04
iShares Morningstar Mid-Cap Growth ETF	IMCG	6/28/04	0.06
iShares Morningstar Mid-Cap Value ETF	IMCV	6/28/04	0.06
iShares Russell Mid-Cap ETF	IWR	7/17/01	0.18
iShares Russell Mid-Cap Growth ETF	IWP	7/17/01	0.23
iShares Russell Mid-Cap Value ETF	IWS	7/17/01	0.23
iShares Russell 2500 ETF	SMMD	7/6/17	0.15'

U.S. – Small cap

	Trading symbol	Inception date	Exp. ratio (%)
iShares Core S&P Small-Cap ETF	IJR	5/22/00	0.06
iShares Russell 2000 ETF	IWM	5/22/00	0.19
iShares Russell 2000 Growth ETF	IWO	7/24/00	0.23
iShares Russell 2000 Value ETF	IWN	7/24/00	0.23
iShares S&P Small-Cap 600 Growth ETF	IJT	7/24/00	0.18
iShares S&P Small-Cap 600 Value ETF	IJS	7/24/00	0.18
iShares Morningstar Small-Cap ETF	ISCB	6/28/04	0.04
iShares Morningstar Small-Cap Growth ETF	ISCG	6/28/04	0.06
iShares Morningstar Small-Cap Value ETF	ISCV	6/28/04	0.06
iShares Micro-Cap ETF	IWC	8/12/05	0.60
iShares MSCI USA Small-Cap Min Vol Factor ETF	SMMV	9/7/16	0.20
iShares MSCI USA Small-Cap Multifactor ETF	SMLF	4/28/15	0.30
iShares ESG Aware MSCI USA Small-Cap ETF	ESML	4/10/18	0.17

Global

	Trading symbol	Inception date	Exp. ratio (%)
iShares Core MSCI Total International Stock ETF	IXUS	10/18/12	0.07
iShares MSCI ACWI ETF	ACWI	3/26/08	0.32
iShares MSCI Global Min Vol Factor ETF	ACWV	10/18/11	0.20'
iShares MSCI ACWI ex U.S. ETF	ACWX	3/26/08	0.32
iShares Currency Hedged MSCI ACWI ex U.S. ETF	HAWX	6/29/15	0.35'
iShares Exponential Technologies ETF	XT	3/19/15	0.46
iShares Self-Driving EV and Tech ETF	IDRV	4/16/19	0.47
iShares Global 100 ETF	IOO	12/5/00	0.40
iShares MSCI Global Sustainable Development Goals ETF	SDG	4/20/16	0.49

Europe

	Trading symbol	Inception date	Exp. ratio (%)
iShares Core MSCI Europe ETF	IEUR	6/10/14	0.09
iShares Europe ETF	IEV	7/25/00	0.58
iShares MSCI Eurozone ETF	EZU	7/25/00	0.50
iShares Currency Hedged MSCI Eurozone ETF	HEZU	7/9/14	0.53'
iShares MSCI Europe Small-Cap ETF	IEUS	11/12/07	0.40
iShares MSCI Europe Financials ETF	EUFN	1/20/10	0.48

Asia Pacific

	Trading symbol	Inception date	Exp. ratio (%)
iShares Core MSCI Pacific ETF	IPAC	6/10/14	0.09
iShares Asia 50 ETF	AIA	11/13/07	0.50
iShares Asia/Pacific Dividend ETF	DVYA	2/23/12	0.49
iShares MSCI All Country Asia ex Japan ETF	AAXJ	8/13/08	0.69
iShares MSCI Emerging Markets Asia ETF	EEMA	2/8/12	0.50
iShares MSCI Pacific ex Japan ETF	EPP	10/25/01	0.47

Latin America

	Trading symbol	Inception date	Exp. ratio (%)
iShares Latin America 40 ETF	ILF	10/25/01	0.47

Markets

Developed markets

	Trading symbol	Inception date	Exp. ratio (%)
iShares Core MSCI Total International Stock ETF	IXUS	10/18/12	0.07
iShares Core MSCI EAFE ETF	IEFA	10/18/12	0.07
iShares Core MSCI International Developed Markets ETF	IDEV	3/21/17	0.04

Developed markets (continued)

	Trading symbol	Inception date	Exp. ratio (%)
iShares Core MSCI Europe ETF	IEUR	6/10/14	0.09
iShares Core MSCI Pacific ETF	IPAC	6/10/14	0.09
iShares Asia 50 ETF	AIA	11/13/07	0.50
iShares Asia/Pacific Dividend ETF	DVYA	2/23/12	0.49
iShares Currency Hedged MSCI ACWI ex U.S. ETF	HAWX	6/29/15	0.35¹
iShares MSCI EAFE ETF	EFA	8/14/01	0.32
iShares Currency Hedged MSCI EAFE ETF	HEFA	1/31/14	0.35¹
iShares Currency Hedged MSCI EAFE Small-Cap ETF	HSCZ	6/29/15	0.42¹
iShares MSCI Eurozone ETF	EZU	7/25/00	0.50
iShares Currency Hedged MSCI Eurozone ETF	HEZU	7/9/14	0.53¹
iShares Europe ETF	IEV	7/25/00	0.58
iShares Global 100 ETF	IOO	12/5/00	0.40
iShares International Select Dividend ETF	IDV	6/11/07	0.49
iShares MSCI ACWI ETF	ACWI	3/26/08	0.32
iShares MSCI ACWI ex U.S. ETF	ACWX	3/26/08	0.32
iShares MSCI ACWI Low Carbon Target ETF	CRBN	12/8/14	0.20
iShares MSCI Global Min Vol Factor ETF	ACWV	10/18/11	0.20¹
iShares ESG Aware MSCI EAFE ETF	ESGD	6/28/16	0.20
iShares MSCI EAFE Growth ETF	EFG	8/1/05	0.35
iShares MSCI EAFE Min Vol Factor ETF	EFAV	10/18/11	0.20¹
iShares MSCI EAFE Small-Cap ETF	SCZ	12/10/07	0.39
iShares MSCI EAFE Value ETF	EFV	8/1/05	0.35
iShares MSCI Europe Small-Cap ETF	IEUS	11/12/07	0.40

Developed markets (continued)

	Trading symbol	Inception date	Exp. ratio (%)
iShares MSCI Intl Momentum Factor ETF	IMTM	1/13/15	0.30
iShares MSCI Intl Quality Factor ETF	IQLT	1/13/15	0.30
iShares MSCI Intl Size Factor ETF	ISZE	6/16/15	0.30
iShares MSCI Intl Value Factor ETF	IVLU	6/16/15	0.30
iShares MSCI Kokusai ETF	TOK	12/10/07	0.25
iShares MSCI Pacific ex Japan ETF	EPP	10/25/01	0.47
iShares MSCI World ETF	URTH	1/10/12	0.24
iShares MSCI Global Multifactor ETF	ACWF	4/28/15	0.35
iShares International Equity Factor ETF	INTF	4/28/15	0.15
iShares MSCI Intl Small-Cap Multifactor ETF	ISCF	4/28/15	0.40

Emerging markets

	Trading symbol	Inception date	Exp. ratio (%)
iShares Core MSCI Emerging Markets ETF	IEMG	10/18/12	0.09
iShares MSCI Emerging Markets ETF	EEM	4/7/03	0.68
iShares Currency Hedged MSCI Emerging Markets ETF	HEEM	9/23/14	0.68¹
iShares MSCI Emerging Markets ex China ETF	EMXC	7/18/17	0.25¹
iShares Emerging Markets Dividend ETF	DVYE	2/23/12	0.49
iShares MSCI Emerging Markets Multifactor ETF	EMGF	12/8/15	0.45¹
iShares Latin America 40 ETF	ILF	10/25/01	0.47
iShares MSCI All Country Asia ex Japan ETF	AAXJ	8/13/08	0.69
iShares MSCI BIC ETF	BKF	11/12/07	0.70
iShares MSCI Emerging Markets Asia ETF	EEMA	2/8/12	0.50
iShares ESG Aware MSCI EM ETF	ESGE	6/28/16	0.25
iShares MSCI Emerging Markets Min Vol Factor ETF	EEMV	10/18/11	0.25¹
iShares MSCI Emerging Markets Small-Cap ETF	EEMS	8/16/11	0.68

Frontier markets

	Trading symbol	Inception date	Exp. ratio (%)
iShares MSCI Frontier 100 ETF	FM	9/12/12	0.79
iShares MSCI Kuwait ETF	KWT	9/1/20	0.74

Geographies

Developed markets

	Trading symbol	Inception date	Exp. ratio (%)
iShares Currency Hedged MSCI United Kingdom ETF	HEWU	6/29/15	0.50¹
iShares MSCI Australia ETF	EWA	3/12/96	0.50
iShares Currency Hedged MSCI Canada ETF	HEWC	6/29/15	0.53¹
iShares MSCI Austria ETF	EWO	3/12/96	0.50
iShares MSCI Belgium ETF	EWK	3/12/96	0.50
iShares MSCI Canada ETF	EWC	3/12/96	0.50
iShares MSCI Denmark ETF	EDEN	1/25/12	0.53
iShares MSCI Finland ETF	EFNL	1/25/12	0.55
iShares MSCI France ETF	EWQ	3/12/96	0.50
iShares MSCI Germany ETF	EWG	3/12/96	0.50
iShares MSCI Germany Small-Cap ETF	EWGS	1/25/12	0.59
iShares MSCI Hong Kong ETF	EWH	3/12/96	0.50
iShares MSCI Ireland ETF	EIRL	5/5/10	0.50
iShares MSCI Israel ETF	EIS	3/26/08	0.57
iShares MSCI Italy ETF	EWI	3/12/96	0.50
iShares MSCI Japan ETF	EWJ	3/12/96	0.50
iShares Currency Hedged MSCI Japan ETF	HEWJ	1/31/14	0.50¹
iShares Currency Hedged JPX-Nikkei 400 ETF	HJPX	9/29/15	0.48¹
iShares JPX-Nikkei 400 ETF	JPXN	10/23/01	0.48
iShares MSCI Japan Equal Weighted ETF	EWJE	3/5/19	0.15

Developed markets (continued)

	Trading symbol	Inception date	Exp. ratio (%)
iShares MSCI Japan Value ETF	EWJV	3/5/19	0.15
iShares MSCI Japan Small-Cap ETF	SCJ	12/20/07	0.50
iShares MSCI Netherlands ETF	EWN	3/12/96	0.50
iShares MSCI New Zealand ETF	ENZL	9/1/10	0.50
iShares Currency Hedged MSCI Germany ETF	HEWG	1/31/14	0.53¹
iShares MSCI Norway ETF	ENOR	1/23/12	0.53
iShares MSCI Singapore ETF	EWS	3/12/96	0.50
iShares MSCI Spain ETF	EWP	3/12/96	0.50
iShares MSCI Sweden ETF	EWD	3/12/96	0.54
iShares MSCI Switzerland ETF	EWL	3/12/96	0.50
iShares MSCI United Kingdom ETF	EWU	3/12/96	0.50
iShares MSCI United Kingdom Small-Cap ETF	EWUS	1/25/12	0.59

Emerging markets

	Trading symbol	Inception date	Exp. ratio (%)
iShares China Large-Cap ETF	FXI	10/5/04	0.74
iShares MSCI China ETF	MCHI	3/29/11	0.57
iShares MSCI China Small-Cap ETF	ECNS	9/28/10	0.57
iShares MSCI China Multisector Tech ETF	TCHI	1/25/22	0.59
iShares MSCI China A ETF	CNYA	6/13/16	0.60
iShares India 50 ETF	INDY	11/18/09	0.89
iShares MSCI All Peru ETF	EPU	6/19/09	0.57
iShares MSCI Argentina and Global Exposure ETF	AGT	4/25/17	0.59
iShares MSCI Brazil ETF	EWZ	7/10/00	0.57
iShares MSCI Brazil Small-Cap ETF	EWZS	9/28/10	0.57
iShares MSCI Chile ETF	ECH	11/12/07	0.57
iShares MSCI Colombia ETF	ICOL	6/18/13	0.61

Emerging markets (continued)

	Trading symbol	Inception date	Exp. ratio (%)
iShares MSCI India ETF	INDA	2/2/12	0.65
iShares MSCI India Small-Cap ETF	SMIN	2/8/12	0.74
iShares MSCI Indonesia ETF	EIDO	5/5/10	0.57
iShares MSCI Malaysia ETF	EWM	3/12/96	0.50
iShares MSCI Mexico ETF	EWW	3/12/96	0.40
iShares MSCI Philippines ETF	EPHE	9/28/10	0.57
iShares MSCI Poland ETF	EPOL	5/25/10	0.57
iShares MSCI Qatar ETF	QAT	4/29/14	0.57
iShares MSCI Russia ETF	ERUS	11/9/10	0.57
iShares MSCI Saudi Arabia ETF	KSA	9/16/15	0.74
iShares MSCI South Africa ETF	EZA	2/3/03	0.57
iShares MSCI South Korea ETF	EWY	5/9/00	0.57
iShares MSCI Taiwan ETF	EWT	6/20/00	0.57
iShares MSCI Thailand ETF	THD	3/26/08	0.57
iShares MSCI Turkey ETF	TUR	3/26/08	0.57
iShares MSCI UAE ETF	UAE	4/29/14	0.57

Bonds

Broad market bonds

	Trading symbol	Inception date	Exp. ratio (%)
iShares Core U.S. Aggregate Bond ETF	AGG	9/22/03	0.03
iShares Core Total USD Bond Market ETF	IUSB	6/10/14	0.06[1]
iShares Core 1-5 Year USD Bond ETF	ISTB	10/18/12	0.06
iShares Core 5-10 Year USD Bond ETF	IMTB	11/1/16	0.06[1]
iShares Core 10+ Year USD Bond ETF	ILTB	12/8/09	0.06

Broad market bonds (continued)

	Trading symbol	Inception date	Exp. ratio (%)
iShares ESG Aware U.S. Aggregate Bond ETF	EAGG	10/18/18	0.10[1]
iShares Government/Credit Bond ETF	GBF	1/5/07	0.20
iShares Intermediate Government/ Credit Bond ETF	GVI	1/5/07	0.20
BlackRock Short Maturity Bond ETF[1]	NEAR	9/25/13	0.25
iShares U.S. Fixed-Income Balanced Risk Factor ETF	FIBR	2/24/15	0.25[1]
BlackRock Ultra Short-Term ETF[1]	ICSH	12/11/13	0.08
iShares Yield Optimized Bond ETF	BYLD	4/22/14	0.20[1]
iShares USD Bond Factor ETF	USBF	10/12/21	0.18

U.S. government bonds

	Trading symbol	Inception date	Exp. ratio (%)
iShares 0-3 Month Treasury Bond ETF	SGOV	5/26/20	0.05[1]
iShares Short Treasury Bond ETF	SHV	1/5/07	0.15
iShares 1-3 Year Treasury Bond ETF	SHY	7/22/02	0.15
iShares 3-7 Year Treasury Bond ETF	IEI	1/5/07	0.15
iShares 7-10 Year Treasury Bond ETF	IEF	7/22/02	0.15
iShares 10-20 Year Treasury Bond ETF	TLH	1/5/07	0.15
iShares 20+ Year Treasury Bond ETF	TLT	7/22/02	0.15
iShares 20+ Year Treasury Bond BuyWrite Strategy ETF	TLTW	7/26/02	0.35
iShares 25+ Year Treasury STRIPS Bond ETF	GOVZ	9/22/20	0.15
iShares U.S. Treasury Bond ETF	GOVT	2/14/12	0.05
iShares Treasury Floating Rate Bond ETF	TFLO	2/3/14	0.15
iShares Agency Bond ETF	AGZ	11/5/08	0.20
iBonds® Dec 2022 Term Treasury ETF[29]	IBTB	2/25/20	0.07
iBonds® Dec 2023 Term Treasury ETF[30]	IBTD	2/25/20	0.07
iBonds® Dec 2024 Term Treasury ETF[31]	IBTE	2/25/20	0.07
iBonds® Dec 2025 Term Treasury ETF[32]	IBTF	2/25/20	0.07

U.S. government bonds (continued)

	Trading symbol	Inception date	Exp. ratio (%)
iBonds® Dec 2026 Term Treasury ETF[33]	IBTG	2/25/20	0.07
iBonds® Dec 2027 Term Treasury ETF[34]	IBTH	2/25/20	0.07
iBonds® Dec 2028 Term Treasury ETF[35]	IBTI	2/25/20	0.07
iBonds® Dec 2029 Term Treasury ETF[35]	IBTJ	2/25/20	0.07
iBonds® Dec 2030 Term Treasury ETF[37]	IBTK	7/14/20	0.07
iBonds® Dec 2031 Term Treasury ETF[38]	IBTL	7/13/21	0.07
iBonds® Dec 2032 Term Treasury ETF[39]	IBTM	7/6/22	0.07

Municipal bonds

	Trading symbol	Inception date	Exp. ratio (%)
iShares National Muni Bond ETF	MUB	9/7/07	0.07
iShares California Muni Bond ETF	CMF	10/4/07	0.25
iShares New York Muni Bond ETF	NYF	10/4/07	0.25
BlackRock Short Maturity Municipal Bond ETF†	MEAR	3/3/15	0.25
iShares Short-Term National Muni Bond ETF	SUB	11/5/08	0.07
BlackRock Intermediate Muni Income Bond ETF†	INMU	3/16/21	0.30†
BlackRock High Yield Muni Income Bond ETF†	HYMU	3/16/21	0.35†
iBonds Dec 2022 Term Muni Bond ETF[13]	IBMK	9/1/15	0.18
iBonds Dec 2023 Term Muni Bond ETF[1/1]	IBML	4/11/17	0.18
iBonds Dec 2024 Term Muni Bond ETF[15]	IBMM	3/20/18	0.18
iBonds Dec 2025 Term Muni Bond ETF[16]	IBMN	11/13/18	0.18
iBonds Dec 2026 Term Muni Bond ETF[17]	IBMO	4/2/19	0.18
iBonds Dec 2027 Term Muni Bond ETF[18]	IBMP	4/9/19	0.18
iBonds Dec 2028 Term Muni Bond ETF[19]	IBMQ	4/16/19	0.18

Inflation-linked bonds

	Trading symbol	Inception date	Exp. ratio (%)
iShares 0-5 Year TIPS Bond ETF	STIP	12/1/10	0.03
iShares TIPS Bond ETF	TIP	12/4/03	0.19

Mortgage-backed bonds

	Trading symbol	Inception date	Exp. ratio (%)
iShares CMBS ETF	CMBS	2/14/12	0.25
iShares GNMA Bond ETF	GNMA	2/14/12	0.10†
iShares MBS ETF	MBB	3/13/07	0.04†

Investment grade bonds

	Trading symbol	Inception date	Exp. ratio (%)
iShares Broad USD Investment Grade Corporate Bond ETF	USIG	1/5/07	0.04
iShares iBoxx $ Investment Grade Corporate Bond ETF	LQD	7/22/02	0.14
iShares ESG Advanced Investment Grade Corporate Bond ETF	ELQD	11/08/21	0.18
iShares 0-5 Year Investment Grade Corporate Bond ETF	SLQD	10/15/13	0.06
iShares BBB Rated Corporate Bond ETF	LQDB	5/18/21	0.15
iShares Interest Rate Hedged U.S. Aggregate Bond ETF	AGRH	6/22/22	0.13†
iShares Inflation Hedged U.S. Aggregate Bond ETF	AGIH	6/22/22	0.13†
iShares Inflation Hedged High Yield Bond ETF	HYGI	6/22/22	0.52†
iShares Interest Rate Hedged Corporate Bond ETF	LQDH	5/27/14	0.24†
iShares Inflation Hedged Corporate Bond ETF	LQDI	5/8/18	0.19†
iShares Investment Grade Corporate Bond BuyWrite Strategy ETF	LQDW	7/26/22	0.35
iShares ESG Aware USD Corporate Bond ETF	SUSC	7/11/17	0.18
iShares ESG Aware 1-5 Year USD Corporate Bond ETF	SUSB	7/11/17	0.12
iShares Investment Grade Bond Factor ETF	IGEB	7/11/17	0.18
iShares Floating Rate Bond ETF	FLOT	6/14/11	0.15
iShares 1-5 Year Investment Grade Corporate Bond ETF	IGSB	1/5/07	0.06
iShares 5-10 Year Investment Grade Corporate Bond ETF	IGIB	1/5/07	0.06
iShares 10+ Year Investment Grade Corporate Bond ETF	IGLB	12/8/09	0.06
iShares Interest Rate Hedged Long-Term Corporate Bond ETF	IGBH	7/22/15	0.15†
iShares AAA - A Rated Corporate Bond ETF	QLTA	2/14/12	0.15
iShares USD Green Bond ETF	BGRN	11/13/18	0.20
iBonds® Mar 2023 Term Corporate ETF[2]	IBDD	7/9/13	0.10
iBonds® Dec 2022 Term Corporate ETF[1]	IBDN	3/10/15	0.10

Investment grade bonds (continued)

	Trading symbol	Inception date	Exp. ratio (%)
iBonds® Dec 2023 Term Corporate ETF[3]	IBDO	3/11/15	0.10
iBonds® Dec 2024 Term Corporate ETF[4]	IBDP	3/11/15	0.10
iBonds® Dec 2025 Term Corporate ETF[5]	IBDQ	3/11/15	0.10
iBonds® Dec 2026 Term Corporate ETF[6]	IBDR	9/13/16	0.10
iBonds® Dec 2027 Term Corporate ETF[7]	IBDS	9/12/17	0.10
iBonds® Dec 2028 Term Corporate ETF[8]	IBDT	9/18/18	0.10
iBonds® Dec 2029 Term Corporate ETF[9]	IBDU	9/17/19	0.10
iBonds® Dec 2030 Term Corporate ETF[10]	IBDV	6/23/20	0.10
iBonds® Dec 2031 Term Corporate ETF[11]	IBDW	6/22/21	0.10
iBonds® Dec 2032 Term Corporate ETF[12]	IBDX	6/28/22	0.10
iBonds® Mar 2023 Term Corporate ex-Financials ETF[13]	IBCE	4/17/13	0.10

High yield bonds

	Trading symbol	Inception date	Exp. ratio (%)
iShares iBoxx $ High Yield Corporate Bond ETF	HYG	4/4/07	0.48
iShares High Yield Corporate Bond BuyWrite Strategy ETF	HYGW	7/26/22	0.70
iShares Broad USD High Yield Corporate Bond ETF	USHY	10/25/17	0.15†
iShares 0-5 Year High Yield Corporate Bond ETF	SHYG	10/15/13	0.30
iShares BB Rated Corporate Bond ETF	HYBB	10/6/20	0.25
iShares U.S. Fallen Angels ETF	FALN	6/14/16	0.25
iShares High Yield Bond Factor ETF	HYDB	7/11/17	0.35
iShares J.P. Morgan EM High Yield Bond ETF	EMHY	4/3/12	0.50
iShares International High Yield Corporate Bond ETF	HYXU	4/3/12	0.40
iShares U.S. & Intl High Yield Corp Bond ETF	GHYG	4/3/12	0.40
iShares Interest Rate Hedged High Yield Bond ETF	HYGH	5/27/14	0.53†
BlackRock High Yield Muni Income Bond ETF†	HYMU	3/16/21	0.35†
iBonds® 2022 Term High Yield and Income ETF[21]	IBHB	5/7/19	0.35
iBonds® 2023 Term High Yield and Income ETF[22]	IBHC	5/7/19	0.35
iBonds® 2024 Term High Yield and Income ETF[23]	IBHD	5/7/19	0.35

High yield bonds (continued)

	Trading symbol	Inception date	Exp. ratio (%)
iBonds® 2025 Term High Yield and Income ETF[24]	IBHE	5/7/19	0.35
iBonds® 2026 Term High Yield and Income ETF[25]	IBHF	11/10/20	0.35
iBonds® 2027 Term High Yield and Income ETF[26]	IBHG	7/7/21	0.35
iBonds® 2028 Term High Yield and Income ETF[27]	IBHH	3/8/22	0.35
iBonds® 2029 Term High Yield and Income ETF[28]	IBHI	3/8/22	0.35

International bonds

	Trading symbol	Inception date	Exp. ratio (%)
iShares Core International Aggregate Bond ETF	IAGG	11/10/15	0.07
iShares 1-3 Year International Treasury Bond ETF	ISHG	1/21/09	0.35
iShares J.P. Morgan EM Corporate Bond ETF	CEMB	4/17/12	0.50
iShares J.P. Morgan EM High Yield Bond ETF	EMHY	4/3/12	0.50
iShares J.P. Morgan EM Local Currency Bond ETF	LEMB	10/18/11	0.30
iShares International High Yield Corporate Bond ETF	HYXU	4/3/12	0.40
iShares U.S. & Intl High Yield Corp Bond ETF	GHYG	4/3/12	0.40
iShares International Treasury Bond ETF	IGOV	1/21/09	0.35
iShares J.P. Morgan USD Emerging Markets Bond ETF	EMB	12/17/07	0.39

Emerging markets bonds

	Trading symbol	Inception date	Exp. ratio (%)
iShares J.P. Morgan EM Corporate Bond ETF	CEMB	4/17/12	0.50
iShares J.P. Morgan EM High Yield Bond ETF	EMHY	4/3/12	0.50
iShares J.P. Morgan EM Local Currency Bond ETF	LEMB	10/18/11	0.30
iShares Interest Rate Hedged Emerging Markets Bond ETF	EMBH	7/22/15	0.48†
iShares J.P. Morgan USD Emerging Markets Bond ETF	EMB	12/17/07	0.39

Convertible bonds

	Trading symbol	Inception date	Exp. ratio (%)
iShares Convertible Bond ETF	ICVT	6/2/15	0.20

Short duration bonds

	Trading symbol	Inception date	Exp. ratio (%)
iShares Core 1-5 Year USD Bond ETF	ISTB	10/18/12	0.06

Short duration bonds (continued)

	Trading symbol	Inception date	Exp. ratio (%)
iShares 0–5 Year Investment Grade Corporate Bond ETF	SLQD	10/15/13	0.06
iShares 0–5 Year High Yield Corporate Bond ETF	SHYG	10/15/13	0.30
iShares 0–5 Year TIPS Bond ETF	STIP	12/1/10	0.03
iShares 0–3 Month Treasury Bond ETF	SGOV	5/26/20	0.05[t]
iShares Short Treasury Bond ETF	SHV	1/5/07	0.15
iShares 1–3 Year Treasury Bond ETF	SHY	7/22/02	0.15
iShares 1–3 Year International Treasury Bond ETF	ISHG	1/21/09	0.35
iShares Treasury Floating Rate Bond ETF	TFLO	2/3/14	0.15
iShares Floating Rate Bond ETF	FLOT	6/14/11	0.15
iShares 1-5 Year Investment Grade Corporate Bond ETF	IGSB	1/5/07	0.06
BlackRock Ultra Short-Term ETF[t]	ICSH	12/11/13	0.08
BlackRock Short Maturity Bond ETF[t]	NEAR	9/25/13	0.25
BlackRock Short Maturity Municipal Bond ETF[t]	MEAR	3/3/15	0.25
iShares Short-Term National Muni Bond ETF	SUB	11/5/08	0.07

Intermediate duration bonds

	Trading symbol	Inception date	Exp. ratio (%)
iShares Core 5–10 Year USD Bond ETF	IMTB	11/1/16	0.06[t]
iShares 3–7 Year Treasury Bond ETF	IEI	1/5/07	0.15
iShares 7–10 Year Treasury Bond ETF	IEF	7/22/02	0.15
iShares Intermediate Government/ Credit Bond ETF	GVI	1/5/07	0.20
iShares 5-10 Year Investment Grade Corporate Bond ETF	IGIB	1/5/07	0.06

Long duration bonds

	Trading symbol	Inception date	Exp. ratio (%)
iShares Core 10+ Year USD Bond ETF	ILTB	12/8/09	0.06
iShares 10–20 Year Treasury Bond ETF	TLH	1/5/07	0.15
iShares 10+ Year Investment Grade Corporate Bond ETF	IGLB	12/8/09	0.06
iShares 20+ Year Treasury Bond ETF	TLT	7/22/02	0.15
iShares 20+ Year Treasury Bond BuyWrite Strategy ETF	TLTW	7/26/22	0.35
iShares 25+ Year Treasury STRIPS Bond ETF	GOVZ	9/22/20	0.15

Interest rate hedged bonds

	Trading symbol	Inception date	Exp. ratio (%)
iShares Interest Rate Hedged Long-Term Corporate Bond ETF	IGBH	7/22/15	0.15[t]
iShares Interest Rate Hedged U.S. Aggregate Bond ETF	AGRH	6/22/22	0.13[t]
iShares Interest Rate Hedged Corporate Bond ETF	LQDH	5/27/14	0.24[t]
iShares Interest Rate Hedged Emerging Markets Bond ETF	EMBH	7/22/15	0.48[t]
iShares Interest Rate Hedged High Yield Bond ETF	HYGH	5/27/14	0.53[t]

Term maturity – iBonds®

Corporate series

	Trading symbol	Inception date	Exp. ratio (%)
iBonds® Mar 2023 Term Corporate ETF[2]	IBDD	7/9/13	0.10
iBonds® Dec 2022 Term Corporate ETF[1]	IBDN	3/10/15	0.10
iBonds® Dec 2023 Term Corporate ETF[3]	IBDO	3/11/15	0.10
iBonds® Dec 2024 Term Corporate ETF[4]	IBDP	3/11/15	0.10
iBonds® Dec 2025 Term Corporate ETF[5]	IBDQ	3/11/15	0.10
iBonds® Dec 2026 Term Corporate ETF[6]	IBDR	9/13/16	0.10
iBonds® Dec 2027 Term Corporate ETF[7]	IBDS	9/12/17	0.10
iBonds® Dec 2028 Term Corporate ETF[8]	IBDT	9/18/18	0.10
iBonds® Dec 2029 Term Corporate ETF[9]	IBDU	9/17/19	0.10
iBonds® Dec 2030 Term Corporate ETF[10]	IBDV	6/23/20	0.10
iBonds® Dec 2031 Term Corporate ETF[11]	IBDW	6/22/21	0.10
iBonds® Dec 2032 Term Corporate ETF[12]	IBDX	6/28/22	0.10

Corporate ex-financials series

	Trading symbol	Inception date	Exp. ratio (%)
iBonds® Mar 2023 Term Corporate ex-Financials ETF[12]	IBCE	4/17/13	0.10

Muni series

	Trading symbol	Inception date	Exp. ratio (%)
iBonds® Dec 2022 Term Muni Bond ETF[13]	IBMK	9/1/15	0.18
iBonds® Dec 2023 Term Muni Bond ETF[14]	IBML	4/11/17	0.18
iBonds® Dec 2024 Term Muni Bond ETF[15]	IBMM	3/20/18	0.18

Muni series (continued)

	Trading symbol	Inception date	Exp. ratio (%)
iBonds® Dec 2025 Term Muni Bond ETF[16]	IBMN	11/13/18	0.18
iBonds® Dec 2026 Term Muni Bond ETF[17]	IBMO	4/2/19	0.18
iBonds® Dec 2027 Term Muni Bond ETF[18]	IBMP	4/9/19	0.18
iBonds® Dec 2028 Term Muni Bond ETF[19]	IBMQ	4/16/19	0.18

High yield and income series

	Trading symbol	Inception date	Exp. ratio (%)
iBonds® 2022 Term High Yield and Income ETF[21]	IBHB	5/7/19	0.35
iBonds® 2023 Term High Yield and Income ETF[22]	IBHC	5/7/19	0.35
iBonds® 2024 Term High Yield and Income ETF[23]	IBHD	5/7/19	0.35
iBonds® 2025 Term High Yield and Income ETF[24]	IBHE	5/7/19	0.35
iBonds® 2026 Term High Yield and Income ETF[25]	IBHF	11/10/20	0.35
iBonds® 2027 Term High Yield and Income ETF[26]	IBHG	7/7/21	0.35
iBonds® 2028 Term High Yield and Income ETF[27]	IBHH	3/8/22	0.35
iBonds® 2029 Term High Yield and Income ETF[28]	IBHI	3/8/22	0.35

U.S. Treasury series

	Trading symbol	Inception date	Exp. ratio (%)
iBonds® Dec 2022 Term Treasury ETF[29]	IBTB	2/25/20	0.07
iBonds® Dec 2023 Term Treasury ETF[30]	IBTD	2/25/20	0.07
iBonds® Dec 2024 Term Treasury ETF[31]	IBTE	2/25/20	0.07
iBonds® Dec 2025 Term Treasury ETF[32]	IBTF	2/25/20	0.07
iBonds® Dec 2026 Term Treasury ETF[33]	IBTG	2/25/20	0.07
iBonds® Dec 2027 Term Treasury ETF[34]	IBTH	2/25/20	0.07
iBonds® Dec 2028 Term Treasury ETF[35]	IBTI	2/25/20	0.07
iBonds® Dec 2029 Term Treasury ETF[36]	IBTJ	2/25/20	0.07
iBonds® Dec 2030 Term Treasury ETF[37]	IBTK	7/14/20	0.07
iBonds® Dec 2031 Term Treasury ETF[38]	IBTL	7/13/21	0.07
iBonds® Dec 2032 Term Treasury ETF[39]	IBTM	7/6/22	0.07

Factors

Minimum volatility

	Trading symbol	Inception date	Exp. ratio (%)
iShares MSCI USA Min Vol Factor ETF	USMV	10/18/11	0.15
iShares ESG MSCI USA Min Vol Factor ETF	ESMV	11/02/21	0.18
iShares MSCI EAFE Min Vol Factor ETF	EFAV	10/18/11	0.20'
iShares MSCI Emerging Markets Min Vol Factor ETF	EEMV	10/18/11	0.25'
iShares MSCI Global Min Vol Factor ETF	ACWV	10/18/11	0.20'
iShares MSCI USA Small-Cap Min Vol Factor ETF	SMMV	9/7/16	0.20

Single factor

iShares MSCI USA Momentum Factor ETF	MTUM	4/16/13	0.15
iShares MSCI USA Quality Factor ETF	QUAL	7/16/13	0.15
iShares MSCI USA Size Factor ETF	SIZE	4/16/13	0.15
iShares MSCI USA Value Factor ETF	VLUE	4/16/13	0.15
iShares Focused Value Factor ETF	FOVL	3/19/19	0.25
iShares US Small Cap Value Factor ETF	SVAL	10/29/20	0.20'
iShares International Developed Small Cap Value Factor ETF	ISVL	3/22/21	0.30'
iShares MSCI Intl Momentum Factor ETF	IMTM	1/13/15	0.30
iShares MSCI Intl Quality Factor ETF	IQLT	1/13/15	0.30
iShares MSCI Intl Size Factor ETF	ISZE	6/16/15	0.30
iShares MSCI Intl Value Factor ETF	IVLU	6/16/15	0.30

Multifactor

iShares U.S Equity Factor ETF	LRGF	4/28/15	0.08
iShares MSCI USA Mid-Cap Multifactor ETF	MIDF	6/4/19	0.25
iShares MSCI USA Small-Cap Multifactor ETF	SMLF	4/28/15	0.30
iShares International Equity Factor ETF	INTF	4/28/15	0.15

Minimum volatility

	Trading symbol	Inception date	Exp. ratio (%)
iShares MSCI Emerging Markets Multifactor ETF	EMGF	12/8/15	0.45[1]
iShares MSCI Global Multifactor ETF	ACWF	4/28/15	0.35
iShares MSCI Intl Small-Cap Multifactor ETF	ISCF	4/28/15	0.40
BlackRock U.S. Equity Factor Rotation ETF[1]	DYNF	3/19/19	0.30
iShares Factors U.S. Growth Style ETF	STLG	1/14/20	0.25
iShares Factors U.S. Value Style ETF	STLV	1/14/20	0.25

Equal weighted

iShares MSCI USA Equal Weighted ETF	EUSA	5/5/10	0.09
iShares MSCI Japan Equal Weighted ETF	EWJE	3/5/19	0.15

Dividend weighted

iShares Core High Dividend ETF	HDV	3/29/11	0.08
iShares Core Dividend Growth ETF	DGRO	6/10/14	0.08
iShares Select Dividend ETF	DVY	11/3/03	0.38
iShares U.S. Dividend and Buyback ETF	DIVB	11/7/17	0.25
iShares International Dividend Growth ETF	IGRO	5/17/16	0.15
iShares International Select Dividend ETF	IDV	6/11/07	0.49
iShares Asia/Pacific Dividend ETF	DVYA	2/23/12	0.49
iShares Emerging Markets Dividend ETF	DVYE	2/23/12	0.49

Fixed income factors

iShares U.S. Fallen Angels ETF	FALN	6/14/16	0.25
iShares U.S. Fixed Income Balanced Risk Factor ETF	FIBR	2/24/15	0.25[1]
iShares Yield Optimized Bond ETF	BYLD	4/22/14	0.20[1]
iShares Investment Grade Bond Factor ETF	IGEB	7/11/17	0.18
iShares High Yield Bond Factor ETF	HYDB	7/11/17	0.35
iShares USD Bond Factor ETF	USBF	10/12/21	0.18

Sustainable

Screened

	Trading symbol	Inception date	Exp. ratio (%)
iShares ESG Screened S&P 500 ETF	XVV	9/22/20	0.08
iShares ESG Screened S&P Mid-cap ETF	XJH	9/22/20	0.12
iShares ESG Screened S&P Small-cap ETF	XJR	9/22/20	0.12

Broad ESG

iShares ESG Aware MSCI USA ETF	ESGU	12/1/16	0.15
iShares ESG Aware MSCI USA Small-Cap ETF	ESML	4/10/18	0.17
iShares ESG Aware MSCI EAFE ETF	ESGD	6/28/16	0.20
iShares ESG Aware MSCI EM ETF	ESGE	6/28/16	0.25
iShares ESG Aware 1-5 Year USD Corporate Bond ETF	SUSB	7/11/17	0.12
iShares ESG Aware USD Corporate Bond ETF	SUSC	7/11/17	0.18
iShares ESG Aware U.S. Aggregate Bond ETF	EAGG	10/18/18	0.10[1]
iShares ESG Advanced MSCI USA ETF	USXF	6/18/20	0.10
iShares ESG Advanced MSCI EAFE ETF	DMXF	6/18/20	0.12
iShares ESG Advanced MSCI EM ETF	EMXF	10/06/20	0.16
iShares ESG Advanced Total USD Bond Market ETF	EUSB	6/23/20	0.12[1]
iShares ESG Advanced Investment Grade Corporate Bond ETF	ELQD	11/8/21	0.18
iShares ESG Advanced High Yield Corporate Bond ETF	HYXF	6/14/16	0.35
iShares ESG MSCI USA Min Vol Factor ETF	ESMV	11/2/21	0.18
iShares MSCI USA ESG Select ETF	SUSA	1/24/05	0.25
iShares MSCI KLD 400 Social ETF	DSI	11/14/06	0.25
iShares ESG MSCI USA Leaders ETF	SUSL	5/7/19	0.10
iShares ESG MSCI EM Leaders ETF	LDEM	2/5/20	0.16

ESG Allocation

	Trading symbol	Inception date	Exp. ratio (%)
iShares ESG Aware Conservative Allocation ETF	EAOK	6/12/20	0.18[‡]
iShares ESG Aware Moderate Allocation ETF	EAOM	6/12/20	0.18[‡]
iShares ESG Aware Growth Allocation ETF	EAOR	6/12/20	0.18[‡]
iShares ESG Aware Aggressive Allocation ETF	EAOA	6/12/20	0.18[‡]

Thematic

	Trading symbol	Inception date	Exp. ratio (%)
BlackRock U.S. Carbon Transition Readiness ETF[†]	LCTU	4/6/21	0.14[‡]
BlackRock World ex U.S. Carbon Transition Readiness ETF[†]	LCTD	4/6/21	0.20[‡]
iShares Paris-Aligned Climate MSCI USA ETF	PABU	2/8/22	0.10
iShares MSCI ACWI Low Carbon Target ETF	CRBN	12/8/14	0.20
iShares MSCI Global Sustainable Development Goals ETF	SDG	4/20/16	0.49
iShares Global Clean Energy ETF	ICLN	6/24/08	0.42
BlackRock Future Climate and Sustainable Economy ETF	BECO	8/3/21	0.70

Impact

	Trading symbol	Inception date	Exp. ratio (%)
iShares USD Green Bond ETF	BGRN	11/13/18	0.20

Megatrends

	Trading symbol	Inception date	Exp. ratio (%)
iShares Exponential Technologies ETF	XT	3/19/15	0.46
iShares U.S. Tech Breakthrough Multisector ETF	TECB	1/8/20	0.40
iShares Robotics and Artificial Intelligence Multisector ETF	IRBO	6/26/18	0.47
iShares Cybersecurity and Tech ETF	IHAK	6/11/19	0.47
iShares Cloud 5G and Tech ETF	IDAT	6/8/21	0.47
iShares Blockchain and Tech ETF	IBLC	4/25/22	0.47
iShares Virtual Work and Life Multisector ETF	IWFH	9/29/20	0.47
iShares Genomics Immunology and Healthcare ETF	IDNA	6/11/19	0.47
BlackRock Future Innovators ETF[†]	BFTR	9/29/20	0.80
BlackRock Future Tech ETF[†]	BTEK	9/29/20	0.88
BlackRock Future Health ETF[†]	BMED	9/29/20	0.85
BlackRock Future U.S. Themes ETF[†]	BTHM	12/14/21	0.60

Megatrends (continued)

	Trading symbol	Inception date	Exp. ratio (%)
iShares Global Infrastructure ETF	IGF	12/10/07	0.40
iShares U.S. Infrastructure ETF	IFRA	4/3/18	0.30
iShares Emerging Markets Infrastructure ETF	EMIF	6/16/09	0.60
iShares Emergent Food and AgTech Multisector ETF	IVEG	4/25/22	0.47
iShares Global Clean Energy ETF	ICLN	6/24/08	0.42
iShares Self-Driving EV and Tech ETF	IDRV	4/16/19	0.47
BlackRock Future Climate and Sustainable Economy ETF	BECO	8/3/21	0.70
iShares MSCI China Multisector Tech ETF	TCHI	1/25/22	0.59
iShares MSCI China A ETF	CNYA	3/29/11	0.60
iShares MSCI India ETF	INDA	2/2/12	0.69

Currency hedged

	Trading symbol	Inception date	Exp. ratio (%)
iShares Currency Hedged MSCI ACWI ex U.S. ETF	HAWX	6/29/15	0.35[‡]
iShares Currency Hedged MSCI EAFE ETF	HEFA	1/31/14	0.35[‡]
iShares Currency Hedged MSCI EAFE Small-Cap ETF	HSCZ	6/29/15	0.42[‡]
iShares Currency Hedged MSCI Emerging Markets ETF	HEEM	9/23/14	0.68[‡]
iShares Currency Hedged MSCI Eurozone ETF	HEZU	7/9/14	0.53[‡]
iShares Currency Hedged JPX-Nikkei 400 ETF	HJPX	9/29/15	0.48[‡]
iShares Currency Hedged MSCI Canada ETF	HEWC	6/29/15	0.53[‡]
iShares Currency Hedged MSCI Germany ETF	HEWG	1/31/14	0.53[‡]
iShares Currency Hedged MSCI Japan ETF	HEWJ	1/31/14	0.50[‡]
iShares Currency Hedged MSCI United Kingdom ETF	HEWU	6/29/15	0.50[‡]

Equity income

	Trading symbol	Inception date	Exp. ratio (%)
iShares Core High Dividend ETF	HDV	3/29/11	0.08
iShares Core Dividend Growth ETF	DGRO	6/10/14	0.08
iShares Select Dividend ETF	DVY	11/3/03	0.38
iShares U.S. Dividend and Buyback ETF	DIVB	11/7/17	0.25
iShares International Select Dividend ETF	IDV	6/11/07	0.49

Equity income (continued)

	Trading symbol	Inception date	Exp. ratio (%)
iShares Asia/Pacific Dividend ETF	DVYA	2/23/12	0.49
iShares Emerging Markets Dividend ETF	DVYE	2/23/12	0.49
iShares International Dividend Growth ETF	IGRO	5/17/16	0.15
iShares Morningstar Multi-Asset Income ETF	IYLD	4/3/12	0.60[†]
iShares Preferred and Income Securities ETF	PFF	3/26/07	0.45

Sectors

Consumer

	Trading symbol	Inception date	Exp. ratio (%)
iShares Evolved U.S. Consumer Staples ETF[†]	IECS	3/21/18	0.18
iShares Evolved U.S. Discretionary Spending ETF[†]	IEDI	3/21/18	0.18
iShares Global Consumer Discretionary ETF	RXI	9/12/06	0.40
iShares Global Consumer Staples ETF	KXI	9/12/06	0.40
iShares U.S. Consumer Staples ETF	IYK	6/12/00	0.41
iShares U.S. Consumer Discretionary ETF	IYC	6/12/00	0.41
iShares U.S. Home Construction ETF	ITB	5/1/06	0.39

Energy

	Trading symbol	Inception date	Exp. ratio (%)
iShares Global Clean Energy ETF	ICLN	6/24/08	0.42
iShares Global Energy ETF	IXC	11/12/01	0.40
iShares MSCI Global Energy Producers ETF	FILL	1/31/12	0.39
iShares U.S. Energy ETF	IYE	6/12/00	0.41
iShares U.S. Oil & Gas Exploration & Production ETF	IEO	5/1/06	0.39
iShares U.S. Oil Equipment & Services ETF	IEZ	5/1/06	0.39

Financials

	Trading symbol	Inception date	Exp. ratio (%)
iShares Evolved U.S. Financials ETF[†]	IEFN	3/21/18	0.18
iShares Global Financials ETF	IXG	11/12/01	0.40
iShares MSCI Europe Financials ETF	EUFN	1/20/10	0.48
iShares U.S. Broker-Dealers & Securities Exchanges ETF	IAI	5/1/06	0.39
iShares U.S. Financial Services ETF	IYG	6/12/00	0.41

Financials (continued)

	Trading symbol	Inception date	Exp. ratio (%)
iShares U.S. Financials ETF	IYF	5/22/00	0.41
iShares U.S. Insurance ETF	IAK	5/1/06	0.39
iShares U.S. Regional Banks ETF	IAT	5/1/06	0.39

Healthcare

	Trading symbol	Inception date	Exp. ratio (%)
iShares Evolved U.S. Innovative Healthcare ETF[†]	IEIH	3/21/18	0.18
iShares Evolved U.S. Healthcare Staples ETF[†]	IEHS	3/21/18	0.18
iShares Genomics Immunology and Healthcare ETF	IDNA	6/11/19	0.47
iShares Global Healthcare ETF	IXJ	11/13/01	0.40
iShares Biotechnology ETF	IBB	2/5/01	0.44
iShares U.S. Healthcare ETF	IYH	6/12/00	0.41
iShares U.S. Healthcare Providers ETF	IHF	5/1/06	0.39
iShares U.S. Medical Devices ETF	IHI	5/1/06	0.39
iShares U.S. Pharmaceuticals ETF	IHE	5/1/06	0.39

Industrials

	Trading symbol	Inception date	Exp. ratio (%)
iShares Global Industrials ETF	EXI	9/12/06	0.40
iShares U.S. Transportation ETF	IYT	10/6/03	0.41
iShares U.S. Aerospace & Defense ETF	ITA	5/1/06	0.39
iShares U.S. Industrials ETF	IYJ	6/12/00	0.41

Infrastructure

	Trading symbol	Inception date	Exp. ratio (%)
iShares Emerging Markets Infrastructure ETF	EMIF	6/16/09	0.60
iShares U.S. Infrastructure ETF	IFRA	4/3/18	0.30
iShares Global Infrastructure ETF	IGF	12/10/07	0.40

Materials

	Trading symbol	Inception date	Exp. ratio (%)
iShares Global Materials ETF	MXI	9/12/06	0.40
iShares U.S. Basic Materials ETF	IYM	6/12/00	0.41

Natural resources and commodity producer equities

	Trading symbol	Inception date	Exp. ratio (%)
iShares North American Natural Resources ETF	IGE	10/22/01	0.40
iShares Global Timber & Forestry ETF	WOOD	6/24/08	0.40
iShares MSCI Global Agriculture Producers ETF	VEGI	1/31/12	0.39[1]
iShares Emergent Food and AgTech Multisector ETF	IVEG	4/25/22	0.47
iShares MSCI Global Energy Producers ETF	FILL	1/31/12	0.39
iShares MSCI Global Metals & Mining Producers ETF	PICK	1/31/12	0.39
iShares MSCI Global Gold Miners ETF	RING	1/31/12	0.39
iShares MSCI Global Silver and Metals Miners ETF	SLVP	1/31/12	0.39

Real estate

	Trading symbol	Inception date	Exp. ratio (%)
iShares Core U.S. REIT ETF	USRT	5/1/07	0.08
iShares U.S. Real Estate ETF	IYR	6/12/00	0.39
iShares Cohen & Steers REIT ETF	ICF	1/29/01	0.33
iShares Global REIT ETF	REET	7/8/14	0.14
iShares International Developed Property ETF	WPS	7/30/07	0.48
iShares International Developed Real Estate ETF	IFGL	11/12/07	0.48
iShares Mortgage Real Estate ETF	REM	5/1/07	0.48
iShares Residential Real Estate ETF	REZ	5/1/07	0.48

Technology

	Trading symbol	Inception date	Exp. ratio (%)
iShares Evolved U.S. Technology ETF[1]	IETC	3/21/18	0.18
iShares Exponential Technologies ETF	XT	3/19/15	0.46
iShares Global Tech ETF	IXN	11/12/01	0.40
iShares Expanded Tech Sector ETF	IGM	3/13/01	0.40
iShares North American Tech-Multimedia Networking ETF	IGN	7/10/01	0.40
iShares Expanded Tech-Software Sector ETF	IGV	7/10/01	0.40
iShares Semiconductor ETF	SOXX	7/10/01	0.40
iShares U.S. Technology ETF	IYW	5/15/00	0.41
iShares MSCI China Multisector Tech ETF	TCHI	1/25/22	0.59

Technology (continued)

	Trading symbol	Inception date	Exp. ratio (%)
iShares Cybersecurity and Tech ETF	IHAK	6/11/19	0.47
iShares Cloud 5G and Tech ETF	IDAT	6/8/21	0.47
iShares Robotics and Artificial Intelligence Multisector ETF	IRBO	6/26/18	0.47
iShares Blockchain and Tech ETF	IBLC	4/25/22	0.47

Communications services

	Trading symbol	Inception date	Exp. ratio (%)
iShares Global Comm Services ETF	IXP	11/12/01	0.40
iShares Evolved U.S. Media and Entertainment ETF[1]	IEME	3/21/18	0.18
iShares U.S. Telecommunications ETF	IYZ	5/22/00	0.39

Utilities

	Trading symbol	Inception date	Exp. ratio (%)
iShares Global Utilities ETF	JXI	9/12/06	0.40
iShares U.S. Utilities ETF	IDU	6/12/00	0.41

Commodities–'40 Act Funds

Futures and equities-based

	Trading symbol	Inception date	Exp. ratio (%)
iShares Commodity Curve Carry Strategy ETF	CCRV	9/1/20	0.40
iShares Commodities Select Strategy ETF	COMT	10/15/14	0.48
iShares Bloomberg Roll Select Commodity Strategy ETF	CMDY	4/3/18	0.28
iShares Gold Strategy ETF	IAUF	6/6/18	0.25[1]

Commodities–'33 Act Trusts

	Trading symbol	Inception date
iShares Gold Trust	IAU	1/21/05
iShares Gold Trust Micro	IAUM	6/15/21
iShares Silver Trust	SLV	4/21/06

Futures-based products

	Trading symbol	Inception date
iShares S&P GSCI Commodity-Indexed Trust	GSG	7/10/06

The iShares Trusts are not investment companies registered under the Investment Company Act of 1940, and therefore are not subject to the same regulatory requirements as mutual funds or ETFs registered under the Investment Company Act of 1940. Investments in these products are speculative and involve a high degree of risk.

Visit www.iShares.com for a prospectus, which includes investment objectives, risks, fees, expenses and other information that you should read and consider carefully before investing.

FOREX AND OPTIONS TRADING

The ability to understand these monetary and asset systems is important to creating wealth. Forex (FX) is no different; Forex is a part of foreign currency and exchange (foreign exchange is the process of changing one currency into another for a variety of reasons, such as, but not limited to, commerce, trading, or tourism). My goal is to focus solely on trading here in this section. The almost $7 trillion dollar trading volume for forex is the largest asset market in the world, so why not get involved in this form of asset purchase?

In its simplest form, Forex trading is when a trader buys one currency and sells to another, with the exchange rate constantly fluctuating based on supply and demand. Multiple currencies trade against each other as exchange rates always pair (ex., EUR/USD is a currency for trading Ero against the U.S. Dollar). The first currency always means against, so EUR-7 against USD.

All trades on these markets happen electronically, over the counter, on vast computer networks rather than on centralized exchanges. This allows Forex trading markets to be open 24 hours a day, five ½ days a week. Worldwide access, in multiple time zones, even after U.S. trading in stocks ends, the Forex market in Tokyo and Hong Kong rings its bells to open and begin trading.

There were events in the 1970's that allowed Forex trading to explode. During the Bretton Woods collapse (under Bretton Wood's System, gold was the basis for the U.S. dollar, and other currencies were pegged to the U.S. dollar valve. President Nixon ended this in the 1970s'), allowing multiple currencies to move into the Forex markets against each other. Nixon's removal of the U.S. from the gold standard pushed Forex trading to become the largest asset class in the world in the coming years. While commercial and Investment banks control the majority of the trading in the Forex markets, investing tools and trading platforms have started to pop up that allow individuals like you to have the same access to these markets.

Some asset classes in this area include:

1. You can earn the interest rate differential between two currencies.

2. You can also profit from changes in the exchange rate by buying certain currencies with higher interest rates while at the same time shortening the currency with the lowest interest rate. We will talk about different strategies later, but this is called: "Carry Trade" [a strategy whereby a high-yielding currency funds the trade with a low-yielding currency]

Some other brief notes that should be taken are currency trades, which are not subject to mandatory disclosures because they trade in OTC markets. Forex is traded in (3) three markets or main venues.

1. **SPOT MARKETS**: This market is the largest of the three (3) markets listed here. Because

it is the "underlying" asset on which forwards and futures markets are based, where currencies are bought and sold based on their trading price, that price is determined by supply and demand [A theory that explains the interaction between the seller of a resource and the buys for that resource].

2. **Forward and Future Markets**: A forward contract is a private agreement between two parties to buy currency at a future date and a predetermined price in the OTC.

A **future contract** is a standardized agreement between two parties to take delivery of a currency at a future date and a predetermined price. Futures trade on exchanges and not OTC (e.g., Chicago Mercantile Exchange)

Forex trading offers many advantages; another one is "Forex Hedging," a business that does most of its business overseas is at higher risk for its currency to fluctuate in value. Businesses like these must use Foreign Exchange Markets [**An investment that intends to reduce the risk of adverse price movement in an asset**] to hedge currency risk by fixing a rate at which the transaction will be completed. This allows businesses to sort through the fluctuation in the currency's value. Forex Hedging is performed by buying and selling currencies in the Swap Market [**involves the exchange of interest and sometimes principal – in one currency for the same in another – currency. Interest payments are exchanged at fixed dates through the contract's life**] in advance, which locks the particular exchange rate in. Speculation can bring massive gains in the Forex space. Opportunities in "Forex Speculation" exist to profit from changes that may increase or reduce the currency's value compared to another. Forecasting that one currency will weaken is essentially the same as assuming that the other currency in the pair will strengthen because currencies are traded as pairs. For example, take a trader who expects interest rates to rise in the United States compared to the Euro. Union, the exchange rate between the two currencies (EUR/USD) is 0.71 (i.e., it takes $0.71 USD to buy $1.00 EUR). The trader believes a higher U.S. interest rate will increase demand for USD, and the EUR/USD exchange rate will fall because it will require fewer, stronger USDs to buy a EUR. So, using Forex speculation, you can profit from the changes that may increase or reduce the currency's value compared to another.

How Currencies are Traded

Each currency is assigned a three-letter code in the Forex market, similar to a stock's "Ticker" symbol. There are more than 170 currencies worldwide, but the U.S. dollar (USD) involves the vast majority of forex trading. I'm not going to name all the currencies here, but the most popular in the Forex marketplace are the Japanese Yen (JPY), the British pound (GBP), the Australian dollar (AND), the Canadian dollar (CAD), the Swiss Franc (CHF) and the New Zealand dollar (NZD).

Forex trading is mostly expressed as a combination of exchanging the two currencies. 75% of the Forex market uses "the Majors" below the most:

EUR/USD
USD/JPY
GBP/USD
AUD/USD

USD/CAD
USD/CHF
NED/USD

Each of the above currency pairs represents the current exchange rate for the two currencies. But now we need to interpret the above information more deeply to break down the exchange rate and what it is. So, use the USD/JPY or the U.S. dollar to Japanese yen exchange rate as an example. The currency on the left (the U.S. Dollar) is the **base currency, and** on the right (the Japanese Yen) is the quote currency. Looking at this pair, the exchange rate represents how much of **the quote** currency is needed to buy (1 unit) of the base currency. Because of this, the base currency is always expressed as (1 unit), while the quote currency varies based on the circumstances of the market and how much you need to purchase (1 unit) of the actual base currency.

So, suppose the USD/JPY exchange rate is 1.2, which means $1 will buy 1.20 Japanese yen (or flip this way, it will cost 1.20 Japanese yen to purchase $1). Another part of this is when the exchange rate rises, all that means is the base currency (here the U.S. Dollar) has risen in value relative to the quote currency (here Japanese Yen) because $1 U.S. Dollar will purchase more Japanese Yen, and if the opposite happens. The exchange rate falls, which means that the base currency has fallen in value.

Remember, this market is like any other. The supply and demand of sellers and buyers set prices. Other things like interest rates, Central bank policy (Federal Reserve Bank), and, as always, economic growth will also play a factor in the Forex Market. With this Forex Market, research is needed to look at global financial news and papers (newspapers, research work, etc.) because each country listed here has several factors that will impact their country's currency. (Think Global) 24 hours a day, five days a week gives you many more opportunities than the stock market, which has an open and closed time. Speaking back about value, also consider that Forex trading requires leverage. At the same time, currency prices fluctuate in small amounts, and you, as a trader, must execute large trades using (leverage) to make a profit.

This market may seem foreign to you now, but recently, the U.S. Dollar has strengthened relative to the Euro, which means traveling abroad is cheaper (Your U.S. Dollar can buy more Euros), and you can buy imported goods like cars and clothes cheaper, mainly because of the Russian war with Ukraine and the fact that Russia provided Europe with its energy supply, which caused economic problems for the Euro. Russia cut off oil and gas pipelines, and Europe struggled to recover. Hence, the U.S. dollar strengthened against the euro because travel and imported goods are cheaper in that part of the world. Anybody in the investing world could look at this war and predict Russia would do this because they are backed in a corner, so it will cause an energy crisis in Europe to hurt them, which was an investment opportunity for you and me. Because, like it or not, the "Spot Market" will impact the amount you and your family pay for exports and travel abroad, so become a consumer of all global news that looks to have an economic impact and invest in making a profit off of that information.

Brokers and Trading Platforms

Most of all, the Forex brokers and trading platforms don't charge commissions. Instead, they make money through spreads or pips (between buying and selling). When doing research, keep in mind that when choosing one of these platforms, focus on the "Leverage Ratio" (which is any one of several financial measurements that look at how much capital comes in the form of debt (loans) or assesses the ability of a company to meet its financial obligations. These brokers will allow you to leverage your account, which will allow you to buy larger trades.

Top Forex Brokers

Broker	Min. Deposit $	Website
Hot Forex	$5	Register.hFm.com
XM.com	$5	Xm.com
Exness	$5	My.exness.com
FXTM	$5	Forextime.com
IQ Option	$1	IQoption.com
NordFX		NordFx.com
QANDA (App), the best starter app	$0	Qanda.com
AvaTrade	$100	AvaTrade.com
IG	$500 / get $250 bonus	Ig.com
JustForex	$1	JustForex.com
Pepperstone	$10	Secure.Pepperstone.com
MetaTrader4 (app)		MT4 (App)
eToro (app) Advanced Traders Only		eToro (App)

Pro se Tip: (!)

Poor is a state of mind, Being broke is a temporary condition.
   -Unknown

Strategies for Forex Trading

The ones who succeed in Forex are the ones who have a strategy to make trades with. There are several common ones and even more complex ones. Eventually, you will develop your own strategies to trade in Forex; that's when gains will come faster, and losses will be small because of a strategy you created to invest your hard-earned money.

Some strategies include:

Scalp Trade: consists of positions held for seconds or minutes at most.

Day Trade: These are short-term trades in which positions are held and liquidated on the same day.

Swing Trade: The trader holds the position for a period longer than a day, i.e., holds positions for days or weeks.

Trend Trading: is one of the most reliable and simple Forex trading strategies. This type of strategy involves trading in the direction of the current price trend. To do so effectively, you first identify the overarching trend, direction, duration, and strength.

EMA Trading: The Exponential Moving Average (EMA) is one of the most commonly used Forex trading tools. EMA reacts faster to recent price changes. You would enter "buy orders" when the short-term EMA crosses above the long-term EMA or enter a "sell order" when the short-term EMA crosses below the long-term EMA. A 20 EMA or 10 EMA signifies the proceeding time period selected by you. Remember the number you set the EMA to means an average of the proceeding (20 EMA) days, a (50 EMA) days, and so on. You get a snapshot of the average for up to 200 days. Some of the most commonly used are the 5, 10, 12, 20, 26, 50, 100, and 200 (EMA) day averages. When you use the short-term timeframe charts set at 5 or 15, you are more likely to use EMAs such as 5 and 10-day averages. 50, 100, and 100 EMAs are for longer-term trend trading.

For example, there are three moving averages on most platforms that can be set using colors: the MA (13 green), (21 yellow), (55 red), and the set of the EMA length (8). But when the red line crosses to the bottom, hold it till it crosses to the top. If it only crosses one line, don't sell; only sell if the (Red 55) line is all the way to the top. See the different charts at the end of the chapter to see how this looks.

Bollinger Bonds Trading: a form of technical analysis that traders use to plot trend lines that are two standard deviations away from the Simple Moving Average (SMA) price of a security. The goal is to help you know when to enter or exit a position by identifying when an asset has been overbought or oversold.

One of the best features of using Bollinger Bonds is that it helps signal changes in volatility in the currency pairs. As you will see at the back of this chapter, there are an upper and a lower band, each set at a distance of two standard deviations from the security's 21-day Simple Moving Average (SMA). These bonds will show you the price volatility in relation to the average, allowing you to see movement in the price anywhere between the two bonds. You should always place "sell orders" at the upper band limit and "buy orders" at the lower band limit. Most of these strategies are based on tools on these trading platforms that can be modified using all these strategies; not one is better than the other; you just have to see what works for you or combine multiple strategies until you see what's best for you.

RSI Trading: the Relative Strength Index (RSI) is commonly used to indicate temporarily overbought or oversold conditions in a market. This is a widely used technical indicator (***pattern-based signals produced by the price, volume, and/or open interest of a security or contract***

used by most traders who follow technical analysis) and oscillator (*tools that construct high and low bands between extreme values, and then builds a trend indicator that fluctuates within these bounds*) that indicates a market is overbought when the RSI value is over 70 and indicates oversold conditions when RIS readings are under 30. RSI is used as momentum; it shows you momentum or whether it's no momentum.

A feature of using these strategies on charts can show you what tools you need to help you best read these charts better. I prefer changing the chart settings to: "Candlestick Pattern", a technical tool that packs data for multiple time frames into a single price bar. It builds patterns that predict price direction once completed. Another commonly used pattern in Forex trading is the "Head and Shoulder Pattern," which appears as a baseline with three peaks, where the outside two are close in height, and the middle is highest. Head and shoulders can be a topping formation after an uptrend or a bottoming formation after a downtrend. A topping is a price high, followed by a retracement, a higher price high, a retracement, and a lower low. The bottoming pattern is a low ("shoulder"), a retracement followed by a lower low, "the head")

Remember, there are multiple strategies, but unlike strategies, charts like Candlestick help to read the market better. First used by the Japanese rice traders in the 18th century, they are easier to read. The upper portion of a candle is used for the opening price and the highest price used by a currency, and the lower portion of a candle is used to indicate the closing price and lowest price point. When looking at the candlestick, a down candle means a period of declining prices and is colored ("red") or ("black"), while an up candle is a period of increase in prices and is colored ("green") or ("white"). A picture of candlesticks is provided later in this section for you to view. Another chart used to represent specific time periods for trading is the "bar chart." These charts allow Forex traders like you to identify whether it's a buyer's or seller's market. This means they provide more information, with each bar representing one day of trading and containing the opening price, highest price, lowest price, and closing price (OHLC) for a trade. The dash on the left is the day's opening price, and a similar dash on the right represents the closing price. So, it's up to you how you utilize these charts, but make sure you at least use both to see what fits you.

Commonly Used Forex Terms

- Forex Account: used to make trades. There are currently (3) types of accounts.

    - Micro Forex Account: allows you to trade up to $1,000 in one lot.

    - Mini Forex Account: allows you to trade up to $10,000 in one lot.

    - Standard Forex Account: allows you to trade up to $100,000 in one lot.

    Also, remember that the trading limit for each lot includes margin money used for leverage. You would only need to use $10 from your own funds to trade currencies worth $1,000 because of the leverage by the broker that is extended to you.

- **Ask**: an ask (or offer) is the lowest price at which you are willing to buy a currency. (ex.) if you place an ask of $1.3891 for JPY, then the figure mentioned is the lowest that you are willing to pay for a Japanese Yen in USD. The asking price is greater than the bid price.

- **Bid**: a bid is the price at which you are willing to sell a currency. A market maker in a given currency is responsible for continuously putting out bids in response to buying queries.

- **Bear Market**: a bear market is one in which prices decline among currencies.

- Bull Market: a bull market is one in which prices increase for all currencies.

- **Contract For Difference**: (CFD) is a derivative that enables traders to speculate on price movements for currencies without actually owning the underlying asset.

- **Leverage**: the use of borrowed capital to multiply returns. An example is when a trader puts up $1,000 of their own capital and borrows $9,000 from the broker to bet against the U.S. Dollar in trade against the EUR.

- **Lot size**: currencies traded in standard sizes known as lots. There are four common lot sizes: standard, mini, micro, and nano. Which equals 100,000 units, 10,000 units, 1,000 units, and 100 units respectively.

- **Margin**: is the money set aside in an account for currency trade. Margin money helps assure a broker that the trader will remain solvent and be able to meet financial obligations.

- **PIP**: a "pip" is a "Percentage in Point" or "Price Interest Point." It is the minimum price move made in the currency market, equal to four decimal points. One pip is equal to 0.0001.

- **Spread**: the difference between the bid (sell) price and ask (buy) price for a currency.

- **Sniping and Hunting**: Sniping and hunting is purchasing and selling currencies near predetermined points to maximize profits.

- **Currency Pair**: All Forex trades involve a currency pair (i.e. USD/JPY)

Tools For Forex Trading

- **Trading View.com** – Charts platform that shows trendlines, Fib trace tool, and long and short trading tool. Free for the regular version, the pro plan costs monthly to use.

- **MetaTrader4 App**

- **Babypip.com**

- **Myfxbook.com**

- **Admiralmarkets.com/analytics/market-heat-map**

Forex Trading Strategies and Chart Images

TYPES OF CHARTS

Heiken Ashi Chart

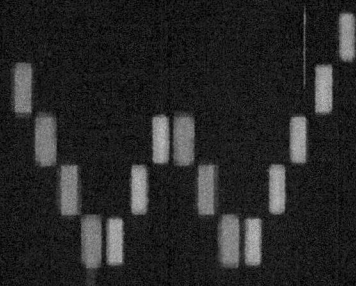

Renko Chart

Line Chart

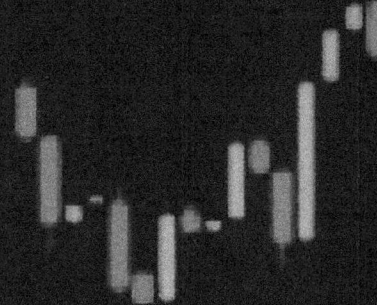

Candlestick Chart

BEST CANDLE PATTERNS

SHOTTING STAR

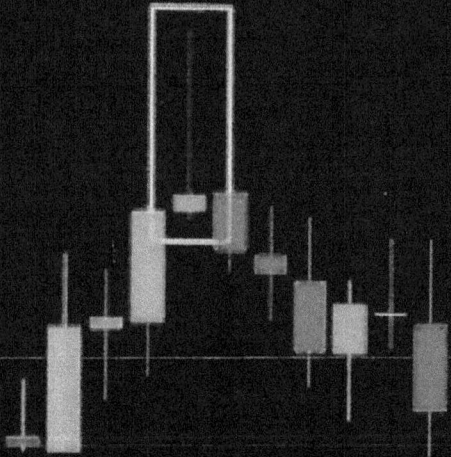

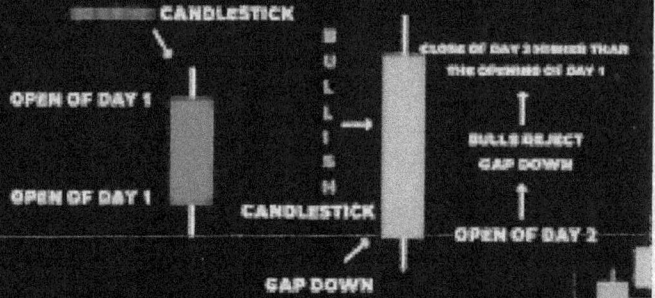

CANDLESTICK

OPEN OF DAY 1

OPEN OF DAY 1

BULLISH CANDLESTICK

CLOSE OF DAY 2 HIGHER THAN THE OPENING OF DAY 1

BULLS REJECT GAP DOWN

OPEN OF DAY 2

GAP DOWN

INSIDE BARS

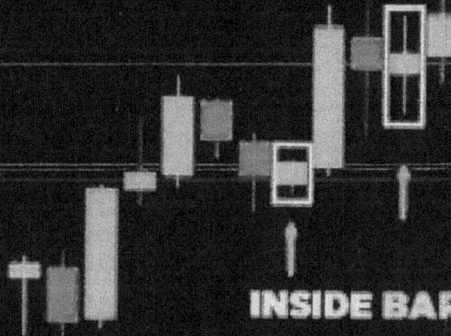

HAMMER PATTERN

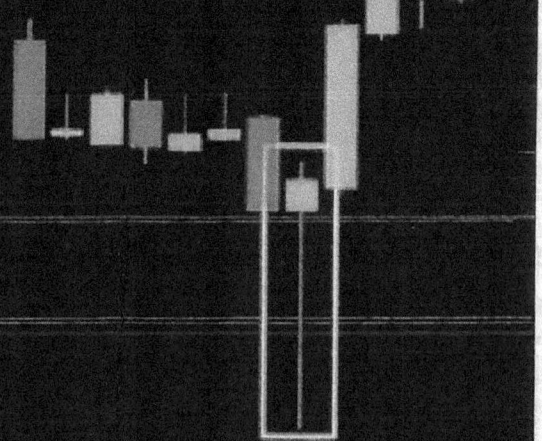

CANDLESTICKS SIGNALS

     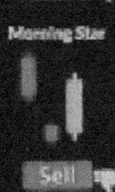

CANDLESTICK PATTERNS GUIDE

BULLISH PIN BAR

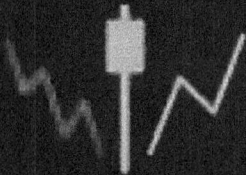

BUY

BULLISH HARAMI

BUY

TWEEZER BOTTOM

BUY

BEARISH PIN BAR

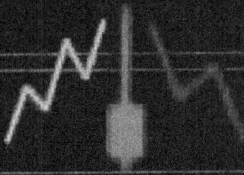

SELL

BEARISH HARAMI

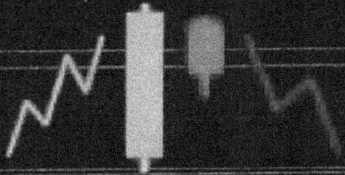

SELL

TWEEZER TOP

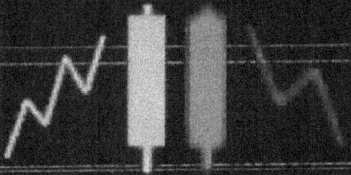

SELL

CANDLESTICK PATTERNS GUIDE

BULLISH PIN BAR

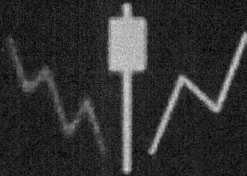

BUY

BULLISH HARAMI

BUY

TWEEZER BOTTOM

BUY

BEARISH PIN BAR

SELL

BEARISH HARAMI

SELL

TWEEZER TOP

SELL

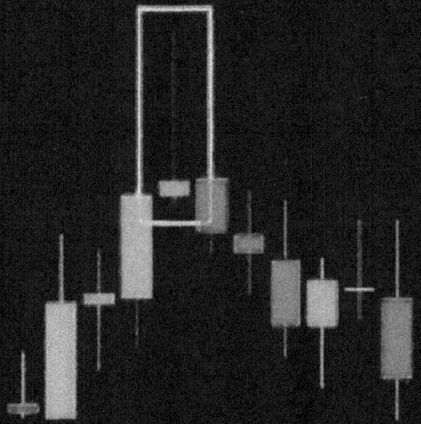
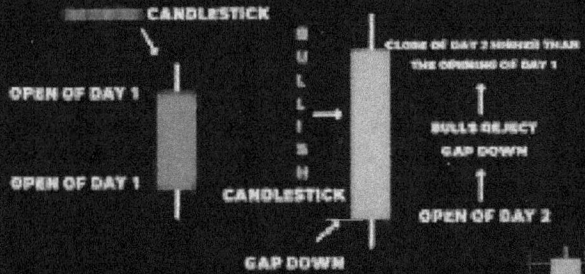

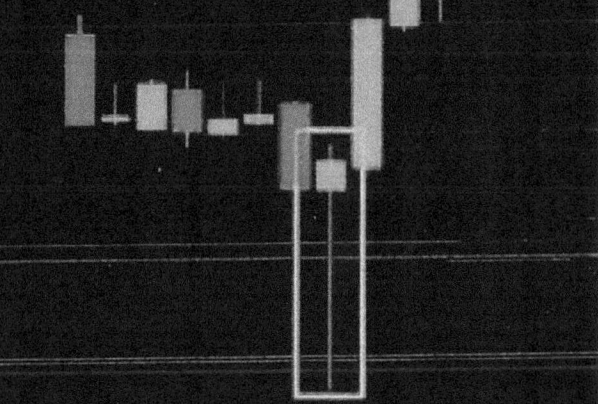

CANDLESTICKS SIGNALS

Dragonfly Doji	Gravestone Doji	Bullish Harami	Hammer	Hanging Man	Bullish Kicker
 Buy	 Sell	 Buy	 Buy	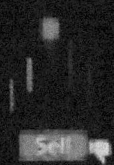 Sell	 Buy

Bearish Harami	Three Inside Up	Three Inside Down	Bearish Kicker	Three White Soldiers	Three Black Crows
 Sell	 Buy	 Sell	 Sell	 Buy	 Sell

Three Outside Up	Three Outside Down	Morning Star	Piercing Line	Bullish Abandoned Baby	Dark Cloud Cover
 Buy	 Sell	 Sell	 Buy	 Buy	 Sell

			Bearish Harami	Three Inside Up	Three Inside Down
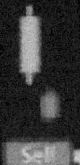 Sell	 Buy	 Sell	 Sell	 Buy	 Sell

Piercing Line	Bullish Abandoned Baby	Dark Cloud Cover	Three Outside Up	Three Outside Down	Morning Star
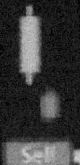 Buy	Buy	Sell	 Buy	 Sell	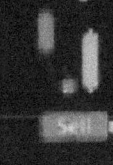 Sell

STOCK TRADING FLOWCHART

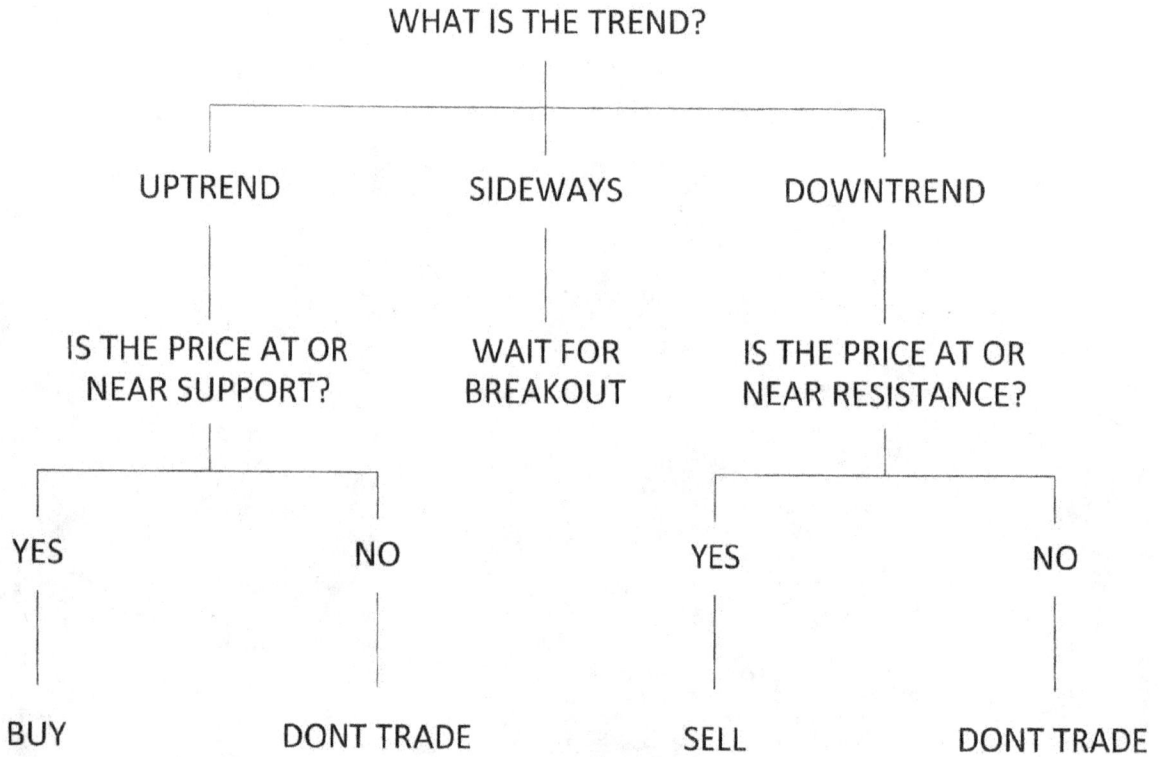

WHAT IS THE TREND?

UPTREND   SIDEWAYS   DOWNTREND

IS THE PRICE AT OR   WAIT FOR   IS THE PRICE AT OR
NEAR SUPPORT?   BREAKOUT   NEAR RESISTANCE?

YES   NO   YES   NO

BUY   DONT TRADE   SELL   DONT TRADE

RULES TO SUCCESSFUL TRADING

1.   ALWAYS USE A TRADING PLAN.

2.   ALWAYS USE A STOP LOSS.

3.   TREAT YOUR TRADING LIKE A BUSINESS.

4.   PROTECT YOUR CAPITAL.

5.   RISK ONLY WHAT YOU CAN AFFORD TO LOSE.

6.   STUDY THE MARKETS, TRENDS AND SECTORS YOU WILL PARTICIPATE IN.

7.   DEVELOP A TRADING METHOD BASED ON WHAT YOU HAVE LEARNED.

8.   ALWAYS TRY NEW METHODS OUT IN A PAPER ACCOUNT.

9.   YOU DONT NEED TO TRADE EVERY DAY.

10. KNOW WHEN TO STOP TRADING IF CONSECUTIVE LOSES OCCUR.

POPULAR TRADING INDICATORS

MACD   =   COMMONLY USED FOR BUY / SELL SIGNALS

RSI   =   LETS YOU KNOW IF THE STOCK IS OVERBOUGHT / OVERSOLD

VWAP   =   COMMONLY USED FOR DAY TRADING

9 EMA   =   COMMONLY USED FOR DAY TRADING

21 EMA   =   COMMONLY USED FOR DAY TRADING

50 EMA   =   COMMONLY USED FOR TREND ANALYSIS

200 EMA =   COMMONLY USED FOR TREND ANALYSIS

NOTES
SOME WILL USE THE SIMPLE MOVING AVERAGE (SMA) INSTEAD OF THE
EXPONENTIAL MOVING AVERAGE (EMA). THE EMA SEEMS TO BE A BIT
QUICKER AND MORE REACTIVE, SO MANY USE IT FOR THAT REASON.

TOPICS TO KNOW TO BE A SUCCESSFUL TRADER

1. CANDLESTICK PATTERNS

2. CHARTING PATTERNS

3. TRENDLINES

4. SUPPORT AND RESISTANCE

5. ATR

6. KEY LEVELS

7. MOMENTUM

8. CONFLUENCE

9. MOVING AVERAGES (SMA & EMA)

10. FIBONACCI

11. MACD

12. RSI

13. RISK / REWARD

14. STOCK FUNDAMENTALS

15. CANDLES RETESTING

16. PSYCHOLOGY

TIMEFRAME GUIDELINES

TRADING STYLE	TIME PERIOD	CHARTING TIME FRAME
Scalper	Seconds to Minutes	1minute - 15 minute
Day Trading	Minutes to Hours	60 Minute
Swing Trading	2 days - A few weeks	4-hour / Daily
Position Trading	A month or longer	Daily / Weekly

INVESTMENT RISK PYRAMID

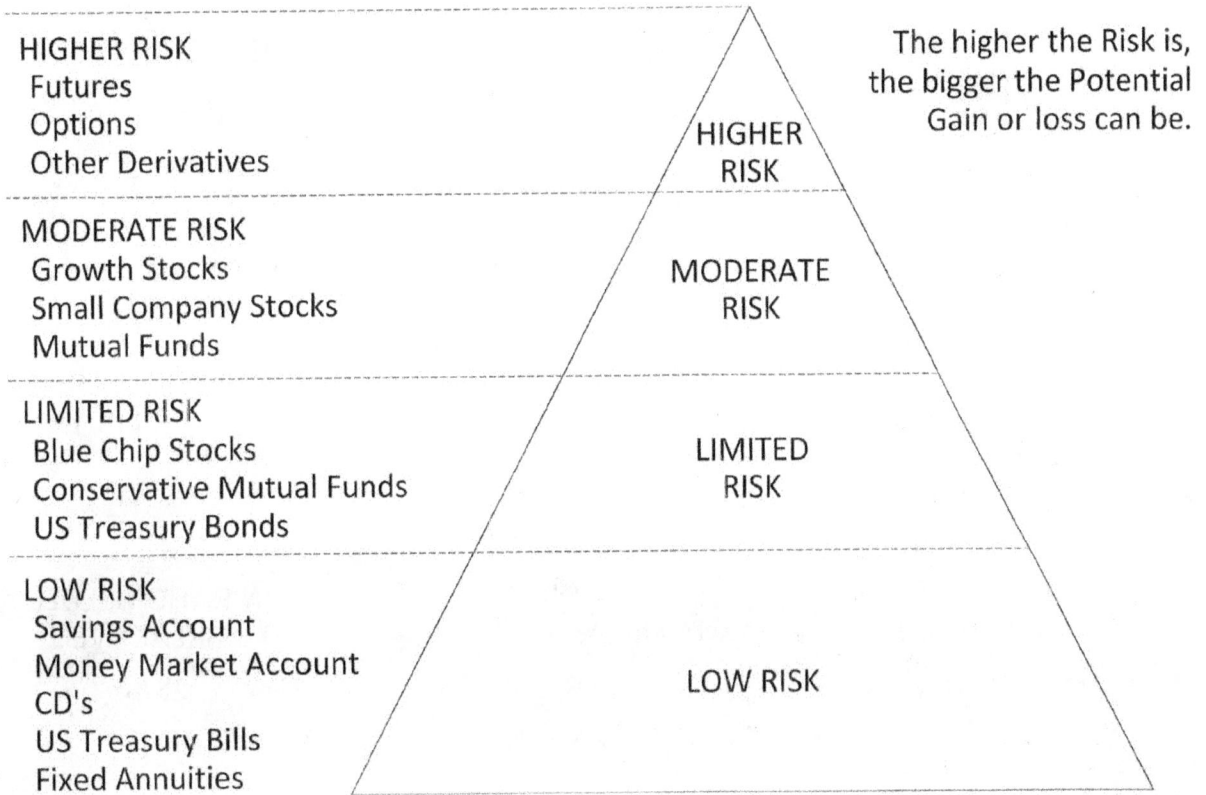

HIGHER RISK
Futures
Options
Other Derivatives

MODERATE RISK
Growth Stocks
Small Company Stocks
Mutual Funds

LIMITED RISK
Blue Chip Stocks
Conservative Mutual Funds
US Treasury Bonds

LOW RISK
Savings Account
Money Market Account
CD's
US Treasury Bills
Fixed Annuities

HIGHER
RISK

MODERATE
RISK

LIMITED
RISK

LOW RISK

The higher the Risk is,
the bigger the Potential
Gain or loss can be.

WIN RATE VS. RISK / REWARD

RISK TO REWARD 1:1	RISK TO REWARD 1:2	RISK TO REWARD 1:3

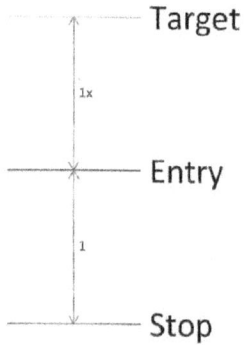

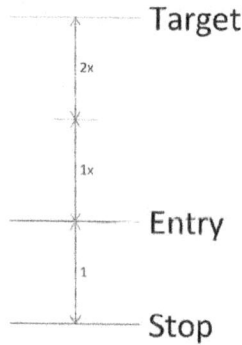

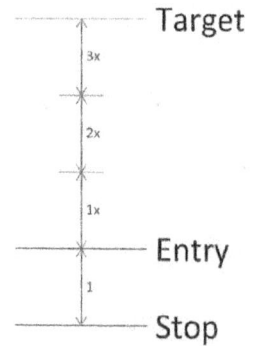

WIN RATIO NEEDED TO BREAK EVEN 50%	WIN RATIO NEEDED TO BREAK EVEN 33%	WIN RATIO NEEDED TO BREAK EVEN 25%

THE BIGGER THE RISK TO REWARD IS, THE LESS YOU NEED TO WIN TO BREAK EVEN. IF YOU WIN OVER 25% ON A 1:3 RISK REWARD, YOU ARE MAKING MONEY.

PROFITABILITY BASED ON RISK VS REWARD

	20%	30%	40%	50%	60%
5:1	PROFITABLE	PROFITABLE	PROFITABLE	PROFITABLE	PROFITABLE
4:1	BREAKEVEN	PROFITABLE	PROFITABLE	PROFITABLE	PROFITABLE
3:1	NOT PROFITABLE	PROFITABLE	PROFITABLE	PROFITABLE	PROFITABLE
2:1	NOT PROFITABLE	NOT PROFITABLE	PROFITABLE	PROFITABLE	PROFITABLE
1:1	NOT PROFITABLE	NOT PROFITABLE	NOT PROFITABLE	BREAKEVEN	PROFITABLE

EVERY TRADER NEEDS TO KNOW THIS CHART. THE HIGHER THE RISK/REWARD RATIO IS, THE LESS YOU NEED TO WIN TO BE PROFITABLE. WITH A 3:1 RISK/REWARD, YOU ONLY NEED TO BE RIGHT 3 OUT OF 10 TIMES TO MAKE MONEY.

WATCH YOUR LOSES

% LOSS	% GAIN NEEDED TO BREAKEVEN
5%	5.3%
10%	11.1%
15%	17.6%
20%	25%
25%	33.3%
30%	42.9%
35%	53.8%
40%	66.7%
45%	81.8%
50%	100%
55%	122.2%

THIS IS VERY IMPORTANT TO KEEP IN MIND. MANY THINK THAT IF YOU LOSE 50%, THAT YOU NEED TO WIN 50% TO BREAK EVEN, BUT THAT IS NOT THE CASE. THIS CHART WILL SHOW YOU WHAT YOU NEED TO BREAK EVEN FROM A LOSS. THIS IS WHY HAVING A STOP LOSS AND POSITION SIZING IS SO IMPORTANT.

DESIGN YOUR TRADING PLAN

TIMEFRAME

Day Trader 15 - 60 minutes
Trend Trader 15 - 60 minutes
Swing Trader 4 hours - 1 day

RISK MANAGEMENT

Risk 1% - 3% of your account max

MARKET CONDITION

Uptrend
Sideways (Trending)
Downtrend

MARKET TO TRADE

Equity
Options
Futures
Forex

ENTRY

Cross over
Breakout
Pullback
Trend Change

Stop Loss

Dollar Value
Percentage
Based on pattern
Trailing
Trend Change

TARGET

Dollar Value
Percentage
Based on pattern
3:1 or 5:1
Trailing Stop
Trend Change

UNDERSTANDING A CANDLESTICK

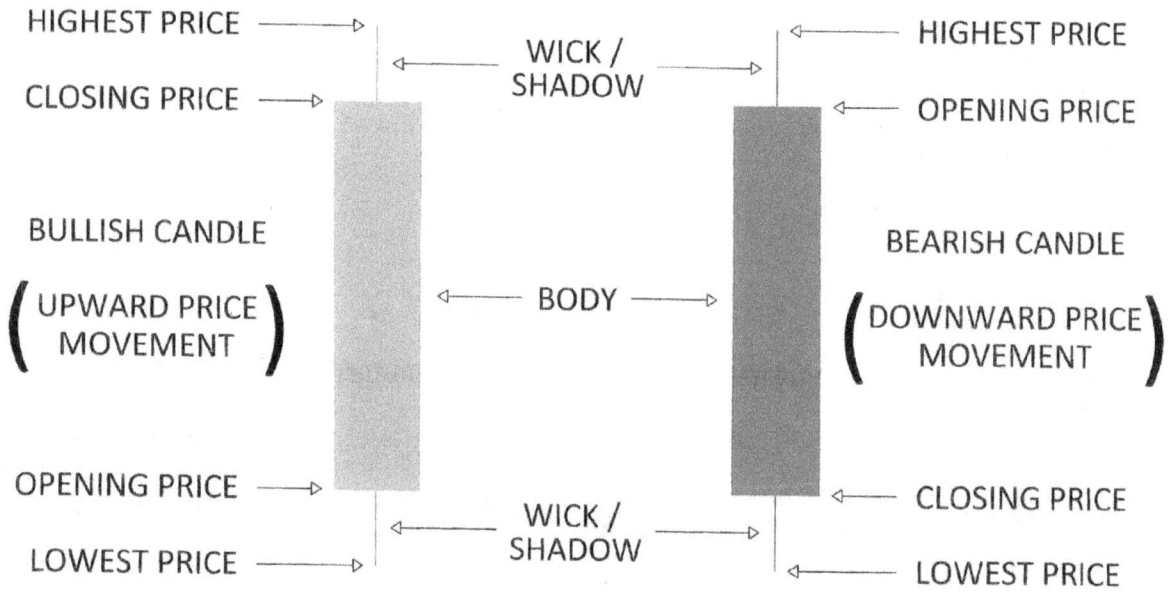

HIGHEST PRICE ────▷

CLOSING PRICE ────▷

WICK / SHADOW

HIGHEST PRICE

OPENING PRICE

BULLISH CANDLE

(UPWARD PRICE MOVEMENT)

◁──── BODY ────▷

BEARISH CANDLE

(DOWNWARD PRICE MOVEMENT)

OPENING PRICE ────▷

LOWEST PRICE ────▷

WICK / SHADOW

CLOSING PRICE

LOWEST PRICE

LEVELS OF BULLISH AND BEARISH CANDLES

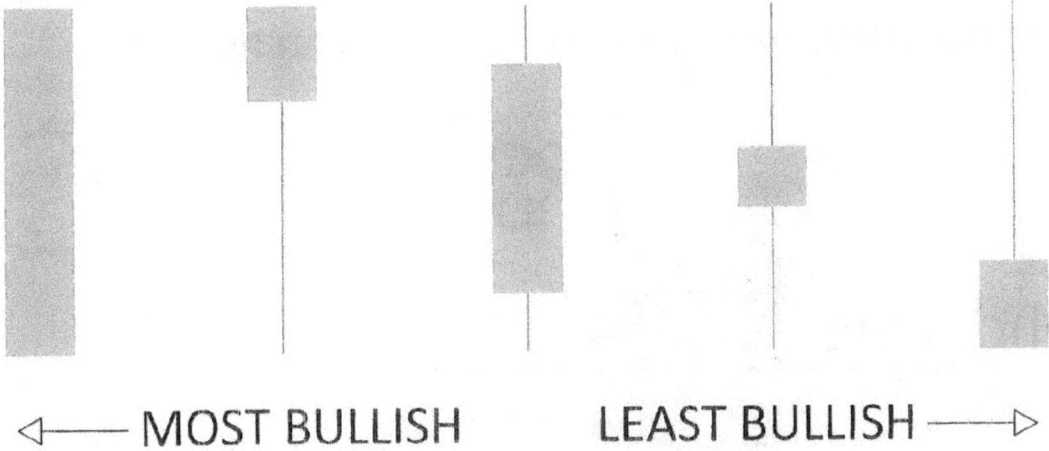

◁——— MOST BULLISH   LEAST BULLISH ———▷

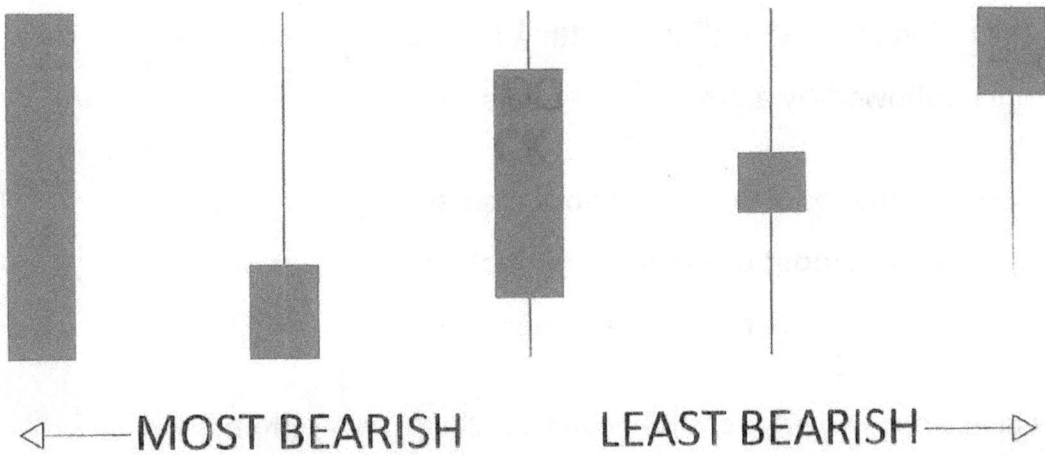

◁——— MOST BEARISH   LEAST BEARISH ———▷

THRUSTING LINE CANDLESTICK

WHAT IS A THRUSTING LINE CANDLESTICK PATTERN?

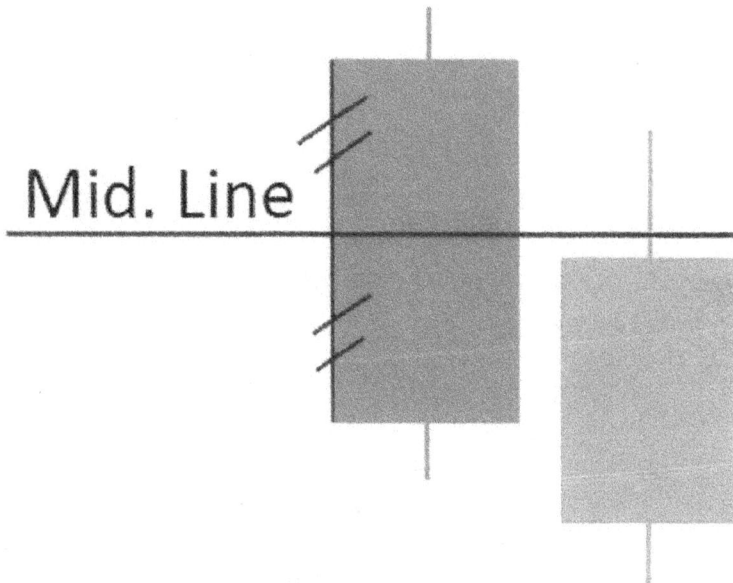

Mid. Line

A valid thrusting line pattern starts with a bearish candle on the chart, followed by a "thrusting" bullish candlestick.

This pattern leads to further downward pressure on the stock. So, as a trader in most cases you will look to get short once the pattern develops.

It is crucial the opening price of the second candle gap down from the closing price of the previous candle. The other important requirement is the closing level of the second candle not cross the mid-point of the first candle's body.

THRUSTING LINE CANDLESTICK

TYPES OF THRUSTING LINE CANDLESTICK PATTERNS

1. STRONG CONTINUATION THRUSTING LINE

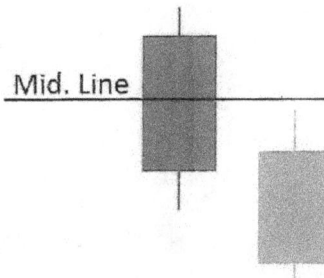

Mid. Line

2. MEDIUM CONTINUATION THRUSTING LINE

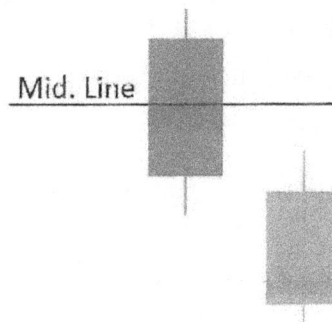

Mid. Line

3. REVERSAL THRUSTING LINE

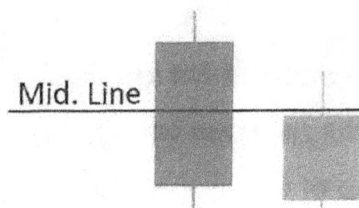

Mid. Line

THRUSTING LINE CANDLESTICK

STRONG CONTINUATION THRUSTING LINE

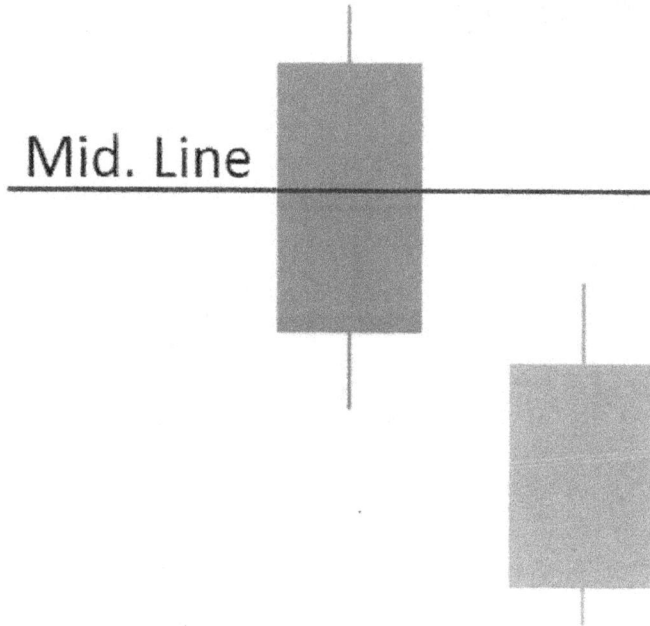

Mid. Line

The thrusting line with a strong continuation of the bearish trend

CHARACTERISTICS

• The opening of the second candle is relatively lower than the close of the first candle.

• The closing of the second candle is barely touching the close of the first candle.

THRUSTING LINE CANDLESTICK

MEDIUM CONTINUATION THRUSTING LINE

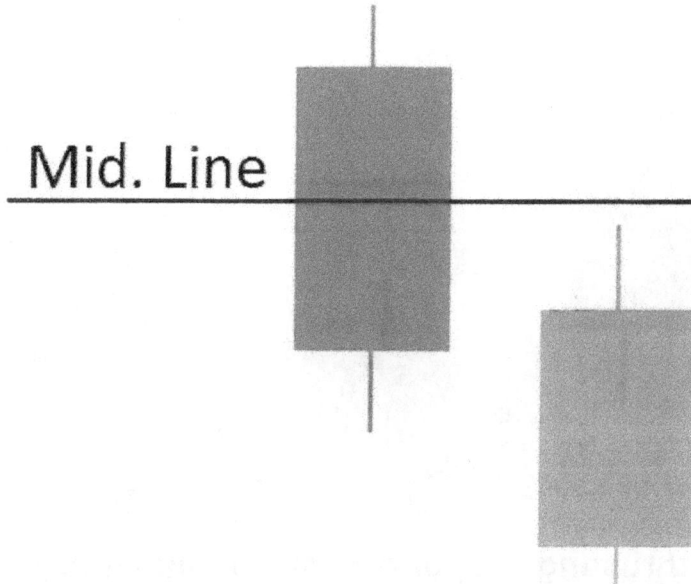

Mid. Line

The medium continuation thrust line pattern has the potential to send prices up or down.

CHARACTERISTICS

• The opening of the second candle is relatively distanced (downwards) from the close of the first candle.

• The closing of the second candle is relatively distanced from the mid-point of the first candle; however, both candles need to overlap.

THRUSTING LINE CANDLESTICK

REVERSAL THRUSTING LINE

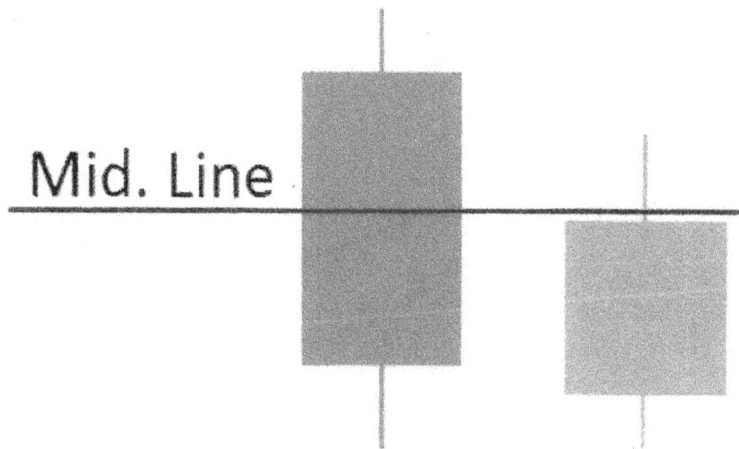

Mid. Line

It is also called a bullish thrusting line, or a weak continuation thrusting line. This type of thrusting line candle formation is more likely to reverse the price action, rather than continue in the direction of the bearish trend.

CHARACTERISTICS

• The opening of the second candle is almost on the same level with the close of the first candle.

• The closing of the second candle is almost on the same level with the middle point of the first candle.

THRUSTING LINE CANDLESTICK

TRADING THE BEARISH THRUST LINE PATTERN

TRADE ENTRY:-

Prior to entry, you first need to confirm the pattern. This happens when a third candle is created and closes below the body of the second candle. This means that the third candle should be bearish. When this candle closes below the body of the second candle, we have received confirmation of the bearish thrusting pattern on the chart.

STOPLOSS:-

The proper Stoploss location for your bearish Thrusting Line continuation pattern is above the upper candlewick of the second candle.

PROFIT TARGET:-

There isn't a fixed target when trading the thrusting line continuation pattern. After all, a continuation pattern can run without stopping.

We stay in the trade until the price action breaks the blue bearish trend in a bullish direction. This is shown in the red circle on the chart. We close our Twitter trade and collect profits.

THRUSTING LINE CANDLESTICK

TRADING THE BULLISH THRUSTING LINES CANDLESTICK PATTERN

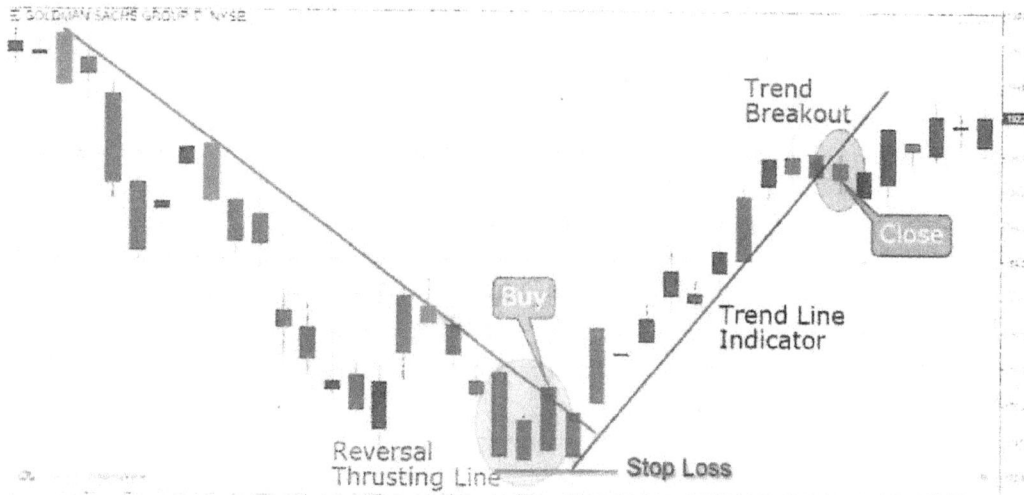

TRADE ENTRY:-

you would first need to attain the confirmation of the pattern. Again, this happens with a third candle. This time, the third candle needs to be bullish and it needs to break the middle line of the first candle. If the third candle closes above this level, then you would need to go long.

STOPLOSS:-

The right place for your stop loss would be below the lower candlewick of the second candle.

PROFIT TARGET:-

The profit target rules for the bullish thrusting line strategy are same as for the bearish thrusting line. To find the right exit point of your bullish thrusting trade, again, I recommend you use price action rules and time and sales.

THRUSTING LINE CANDLESTICK

The Set-up

Step 1:

Daily Chart

BULLISH THRUSTING LINE

minor price support

(1)

moving average
(10 MA, 20 MA, or 50 MA)

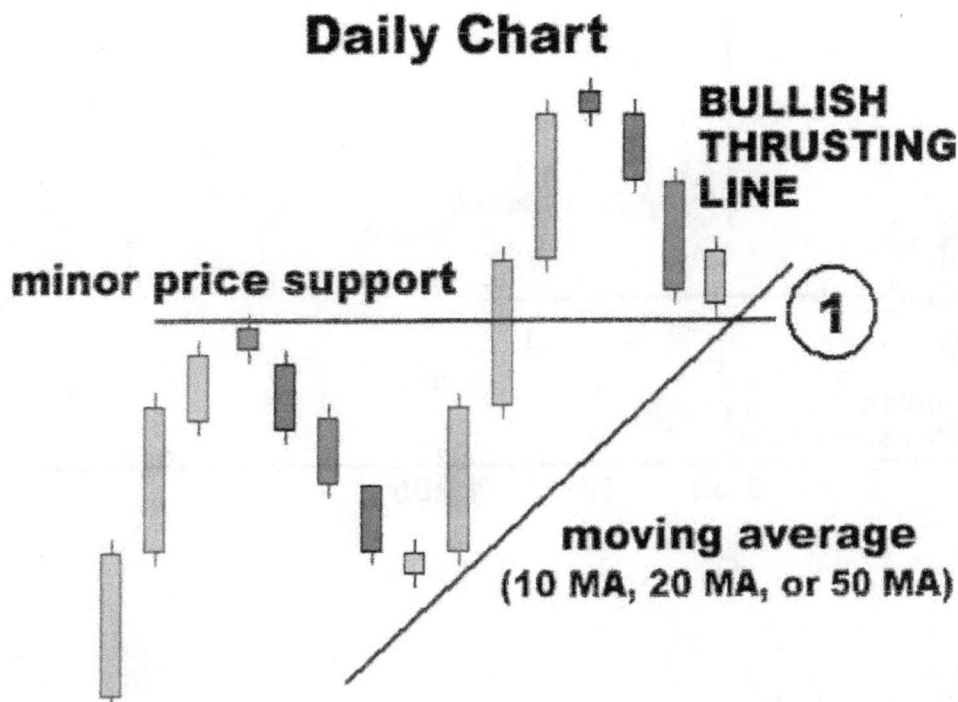

Look for a BULLISH THRUSTING LINE resting on MINOR PRICE SUPPORT, and/or a rising Major Moving Average (10 MA, 20 MA, or 50 MA) on the daily chart.

THRUSTING LINE CANDLESTICK

ENTRY

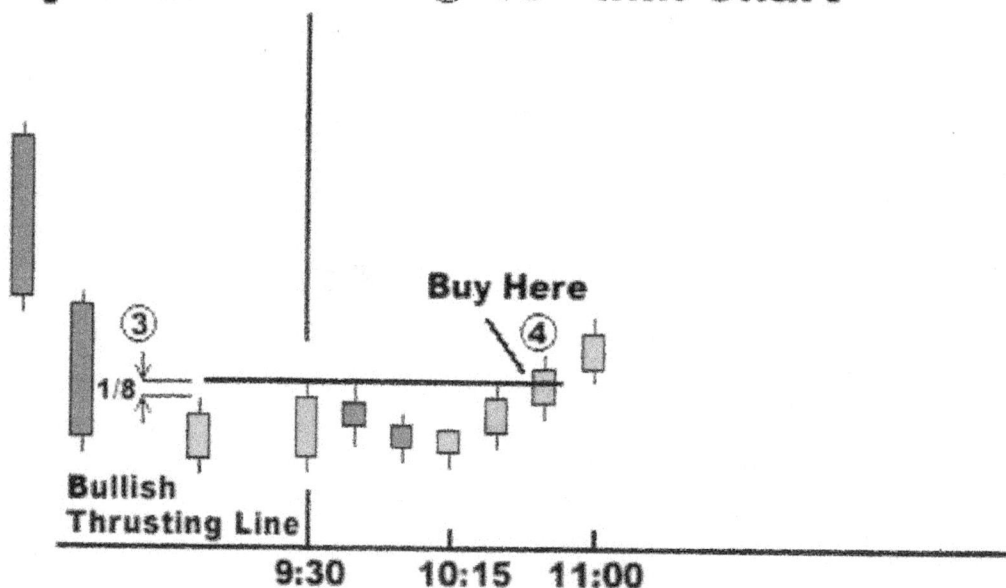

Step 4:

On the following day, allow the stock to trade for 5 minutes before entering.
Enter the stock only if it breaks above the entry criteria (1/8th above previous
day's high) and only after it has traded for 5 minutes. If the stock does not
break above the entry point, do not enter.

THRUSTING LINE CANDLESTICK

ENTRY

Step 2: Pull up a 15 min. chart of the stock.

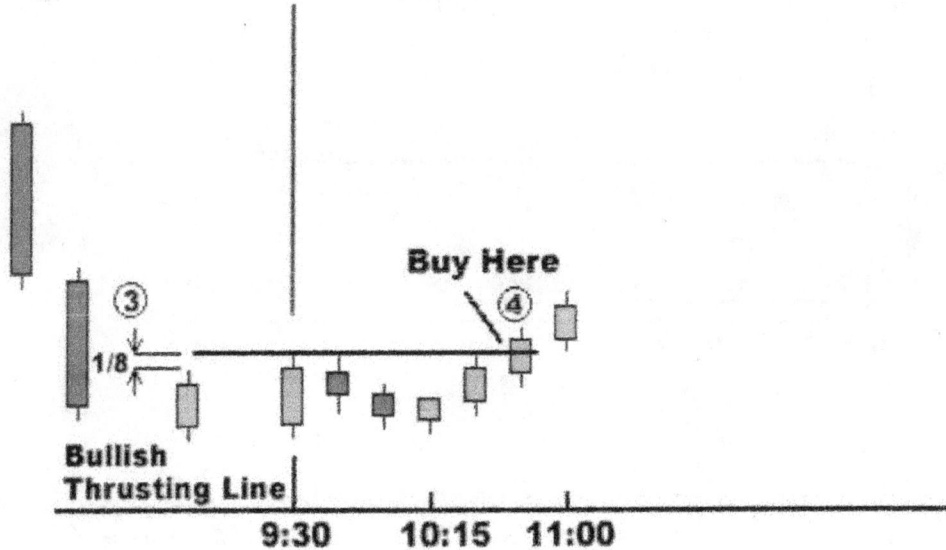

Step 3:

Note the high price of the previous day's daily THRUSTING LINE candlestick. Your entry point is 1/8th above this price.

THRUSTING LINE CANDLESTICK

THE PROTECTIVE STOP

15 - min Chart

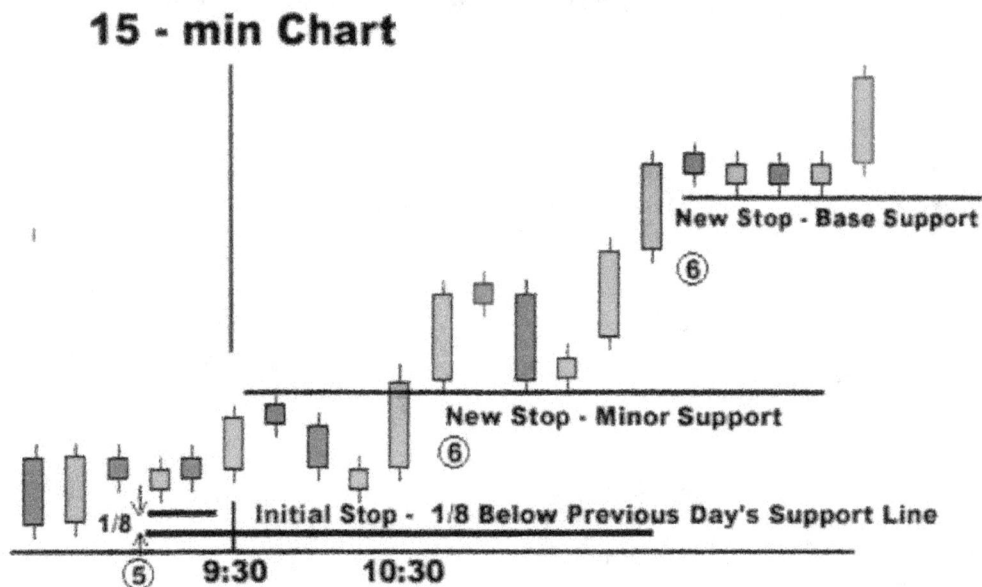

New Stop - Base Support
⑥

New Stop - Minor Support
⑥

1/8   Initial Stop - 1/8 Below Previous Day's Support Line

⑤   9:30   10:30

Step 5:

Observe the previous day's candlesticks on a 15 min chart. Find an internal line of support that is formed on the 15 min. chart. This will usually be an intra-day area where the stock moves down to and then rallies multiple times during the day. Place the initial protective stop 1/8 below the area of intraday support. Exit the stock for a small loss immediately if the stock breaks below this price.

Step 6:

Monitor the stock as it continues to rally upward. Look for areas of support (either minor price support or base price support) on the 15 minute chart, and re-adjust your protective stop price upward as the stock continues to rally. This will protect your profits, and/or minimize your losses if the stock should turn against you.

THRUSTING LINE CANDLESTICK

TAKING PROFITS

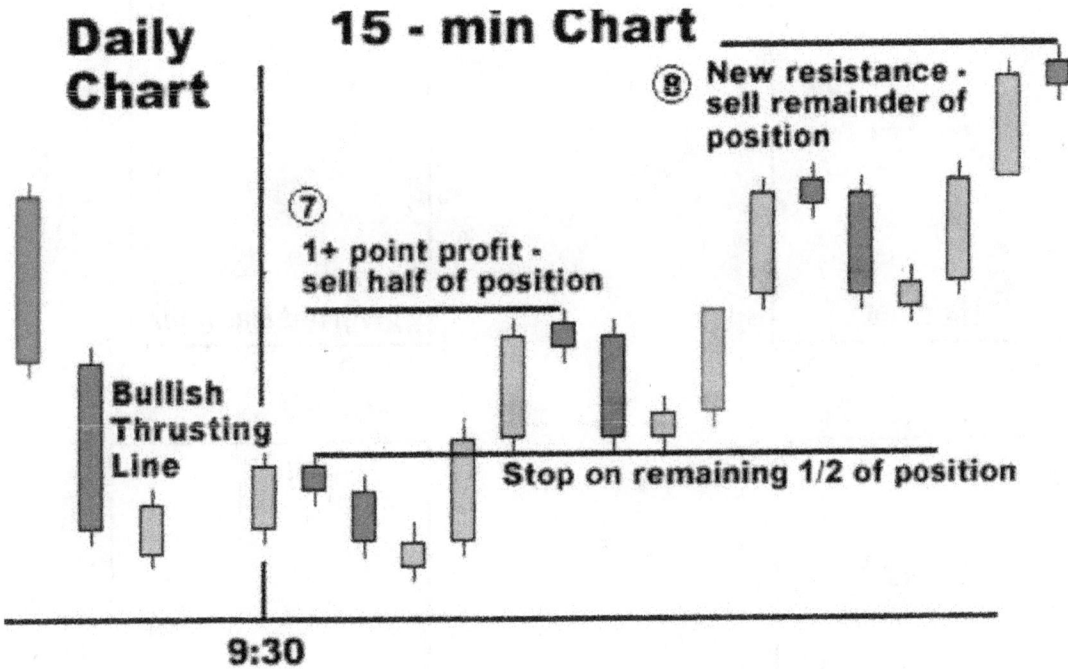

Daily Chart

15 - min Chart

⑧ New resistance - sell remainder of position

⑦ 1+ point profit - sell half of position

Bullish Thrusting Line

Stop on remaining 1/2 of position

9:30

Use price action rules and time and sales to exit your position.

THE HAMMER FAMILY

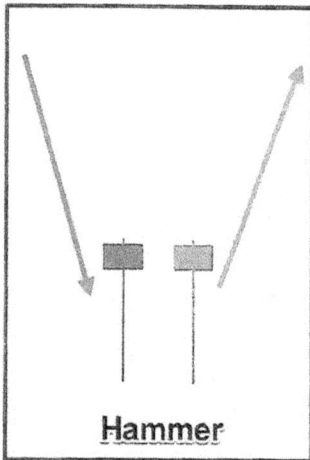

Hammer

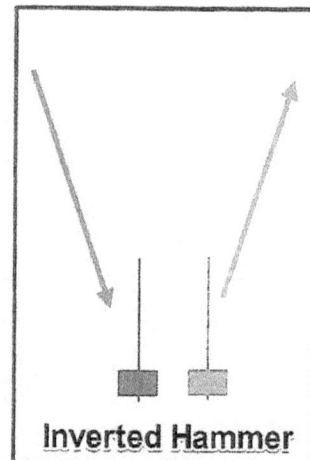

Inverted Hammer

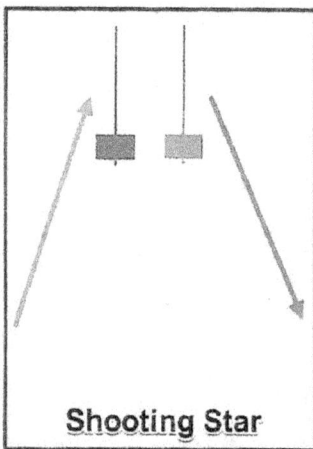

Shooting Star

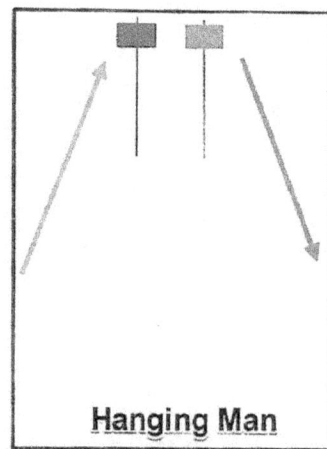

Hanging Man

THE TWEEZER FAMILY

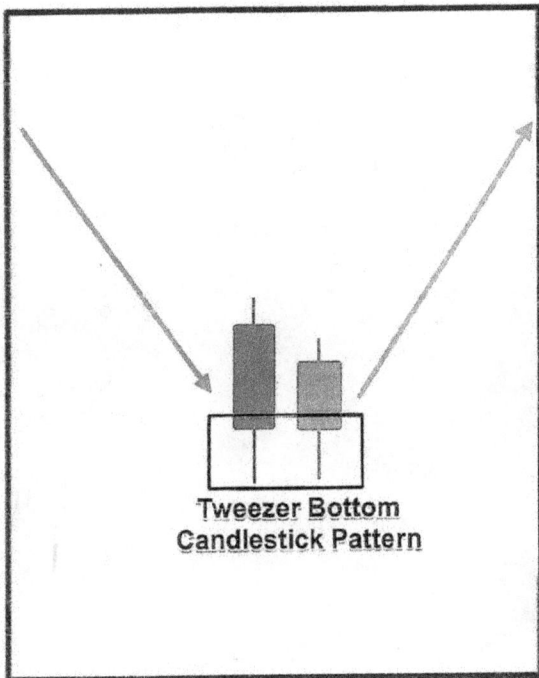

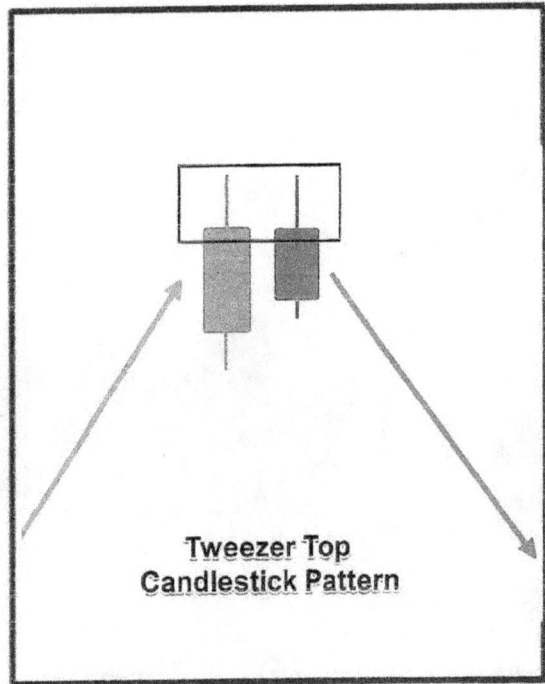

Tweezer Bottom
Candlestick Pattern

Tweezer Top
Candlestick Pattern

THREE INSIDE UPS / DOWNS

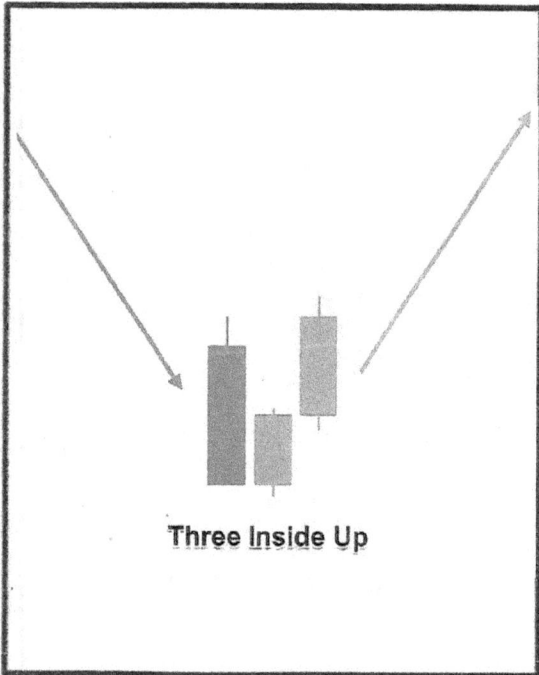

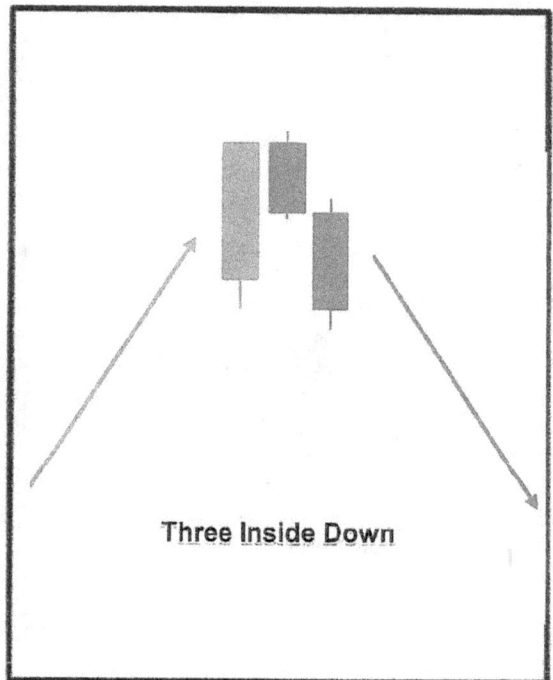

Three Inside Up

Three Inside Down

EVENING STAR / MORNING STAR

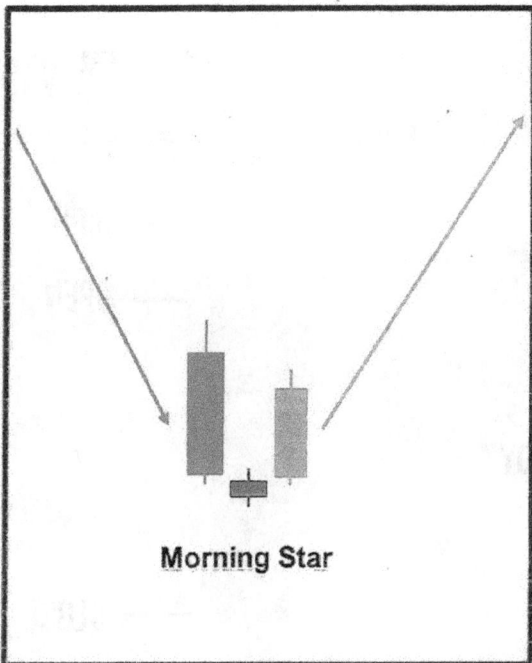

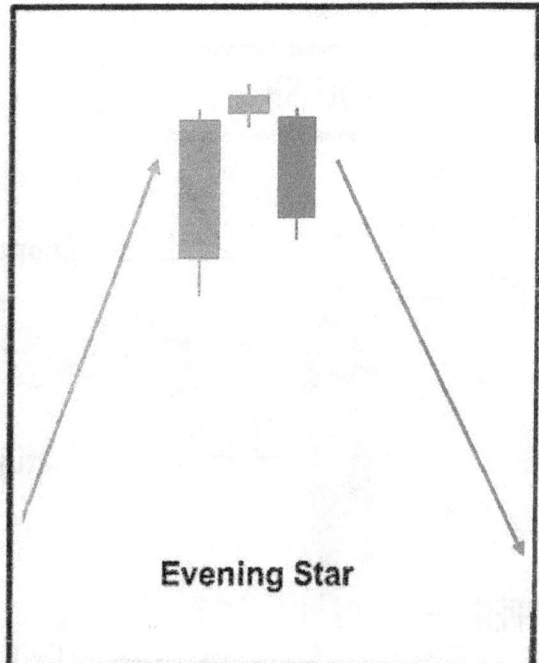

Morning Star

Evening Star

HOW TO READ
CANDLESTICKS

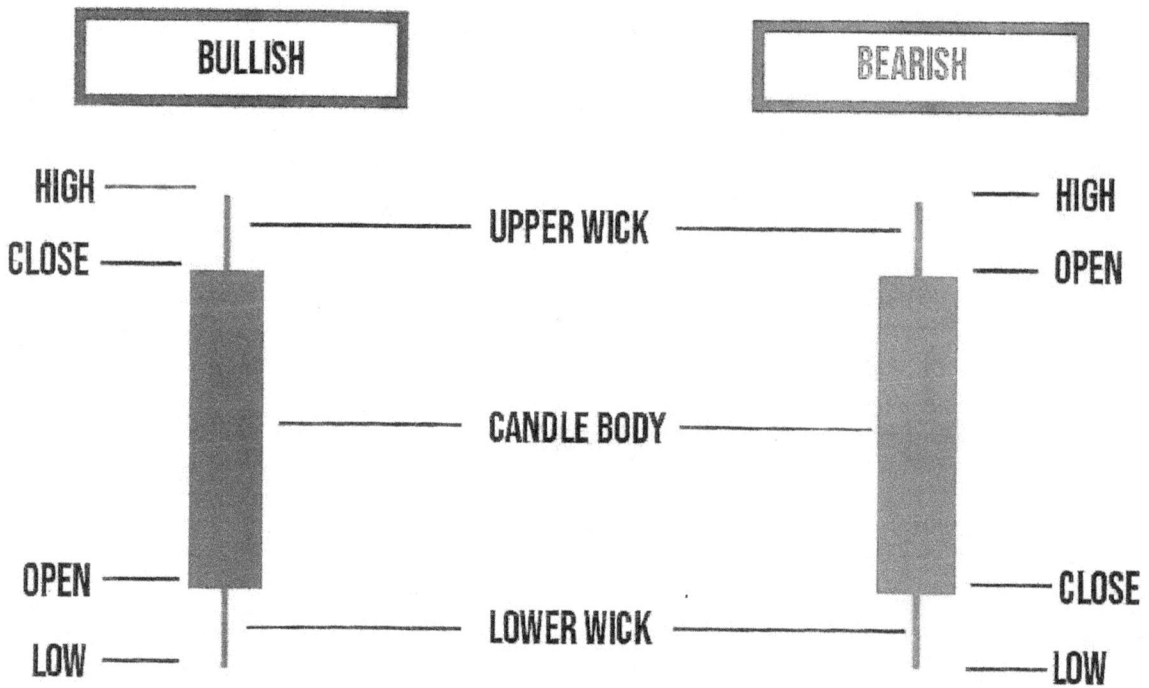

BULLISH		BEARISH

HIGH —

CLOSE —

OPEN —

LOW —

—————— UPPER WICK ——————

—————— CANDLE BODY ——————

—————— LOWER WICK ——————

— HIGH

— OPEN

— CLOSE

— LOW

CANDLESTICK STRENGTH

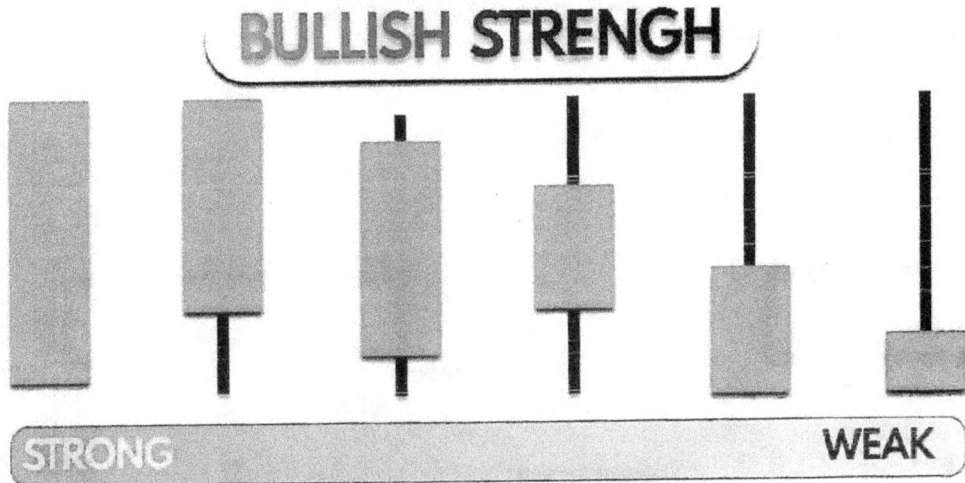

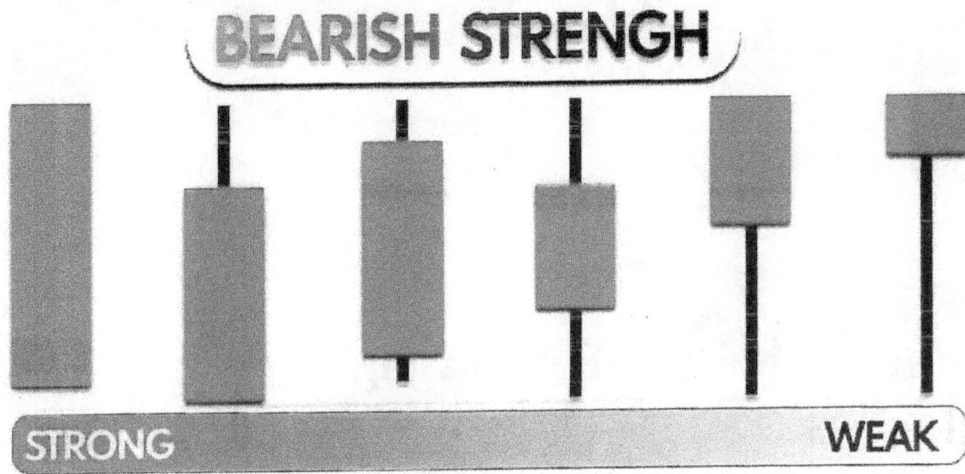

BULLISH STRENGH

| STRONG | | | | | WEAK |

BEARISH STRENGH

| STRONG | | | | | WEAK |

Buying pressure is increasing

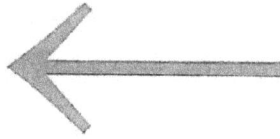

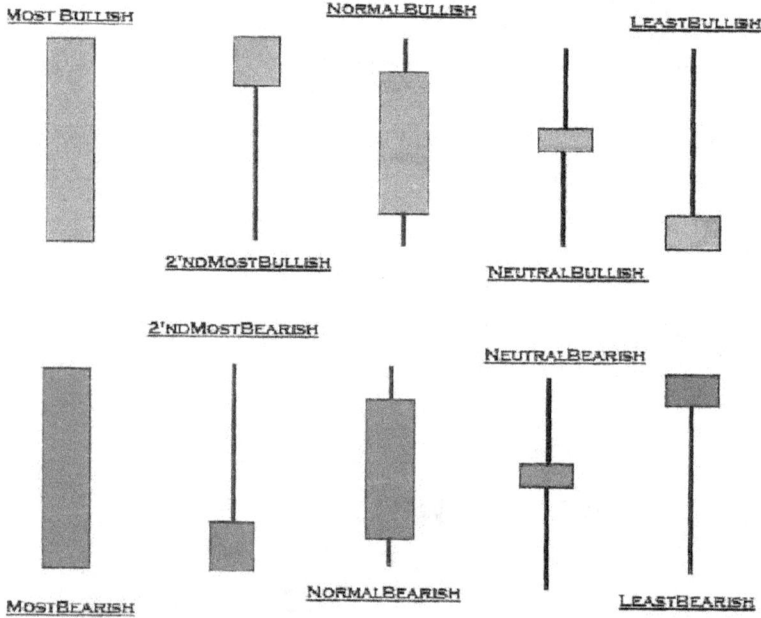

MOST BULLISH

NORMALBULLISH

LEASTBULLISH

DOJI CANDLES

2'NDMOSTBULLISH

NEUTRALBULLISH

2'NDMOSTBEARISH

NEUTRALBEARISH

MOSTBEARISH

NORMALBEARISH

LEASTBEARISH

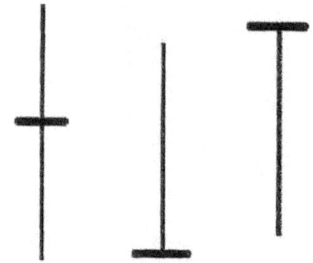

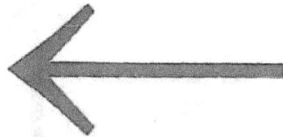

Selling pressure is increasing

TYPES OF CANDLESTICK PATTERNS

BASICS

HIGH → | UPPER SHADOW | ← HIGH
CLOSE → | | ← OPEN
| BODY |
OPEN → | | ← CLOSE
LOW → | LOWER SHADOW | ← LOW

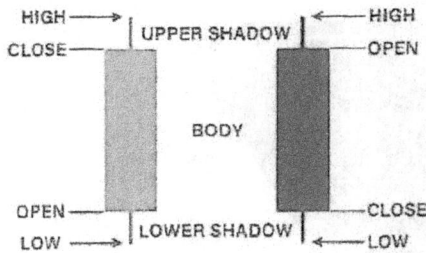

NEUTRAL CANDLESTICKS

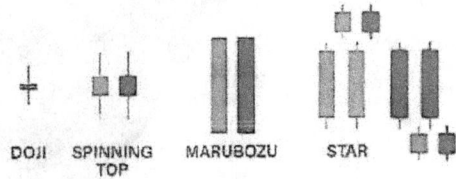

DOJI   SPINNING   MARUBOZU   STAR
        TOP

SINGLE CANDLE PATTERNS

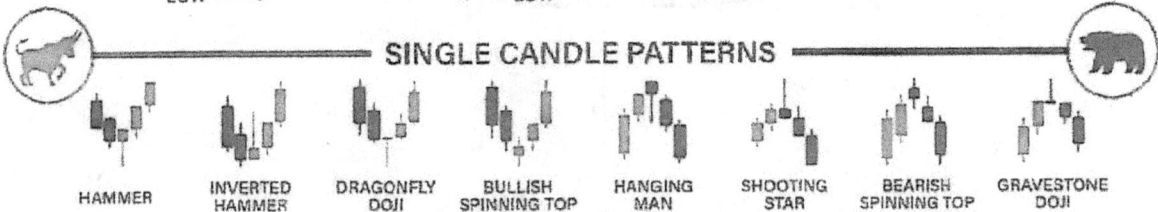

HAMMER   INVERTED   DRAGONFLY   BULLISH   HANGING   SHOOTING   BEARISH   GRAVESTONE
          HAMMER   DOJI   SPINNING TOP   MAN   STAR   SPINNING TOP   DOJI

DOUBLE CANDLE PATTERNS

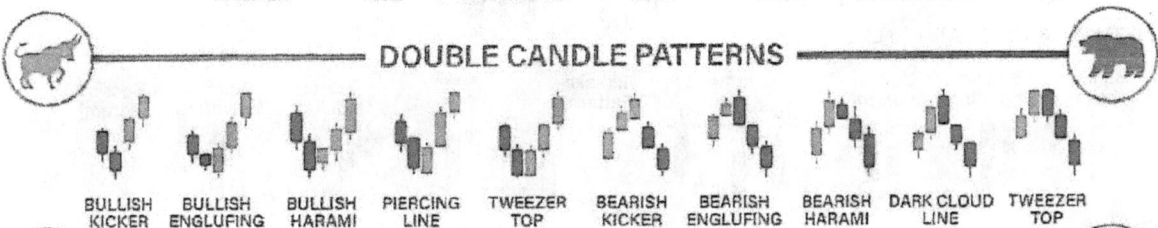

BULLISH   BULLISH   BULLISH   PIERCING   TWEEZER   BEARISH   BEARISH   BEARISH   DARK CLOUD   TWEEZER
KICKER   ENGLUFING HARAMI   LINE   TOP   KICKER   ENGLUFING HARAMI   LINE   TOP

TRIPLE CANDLE PATTERNS

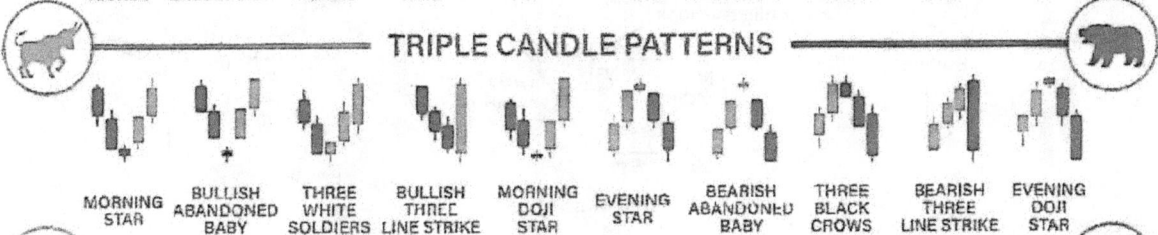

MORNING   BULLISH   THREE   BULLISH   MORNING   EVENING   BEARISH   THREE   BEARISH   EVENING
STAR   ABANDONED   WHITE   THREE   DOJI   STAR   ABANDONED   BLACK   THREE   DOJI
           BABY   SOLDIERS   LINE STRIKE   STAR   BABY   CROWS   LINE STRIKE   STAR

CONFIRMATIONS

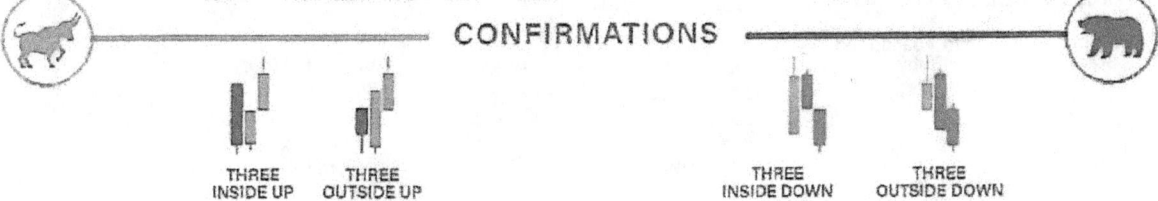

THREE   THREE   THREE   THREE
INSIDE UP   OUTSIDE UP   INSIDE DOWN   OUTSIDE DOWN

CANDLESTICK CHEAT SHEET

BULLISH CANDLESTICK PATTERNS

SINGLE CANDLE PATTERNS

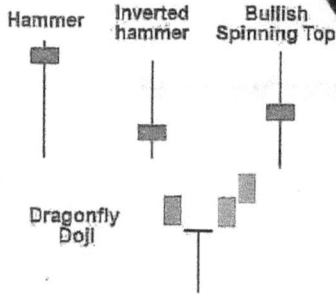

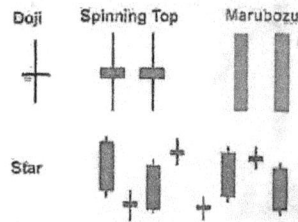

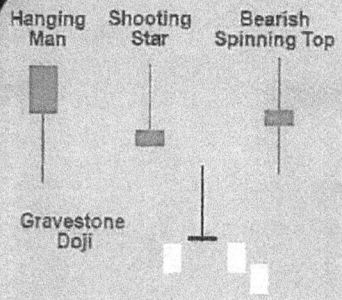

Hammer
Inverted hammer
Bullish Spinning Top

Dragonfly Doji

TWO CANDLE PATTERNS

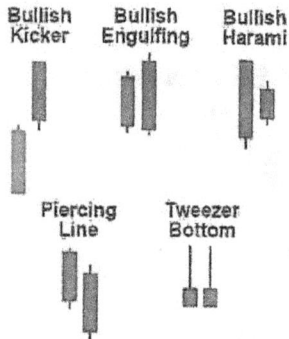

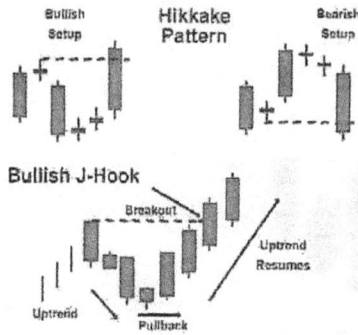

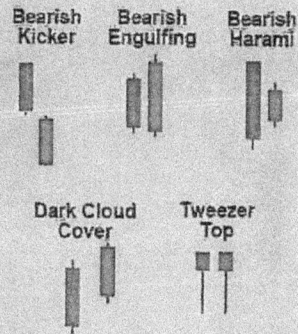

Bullish Kicker
Bullish Engulfing
Bullish Harami

Piercing Line
Tweezer Bottom

THREE CANDLE PATTERNS

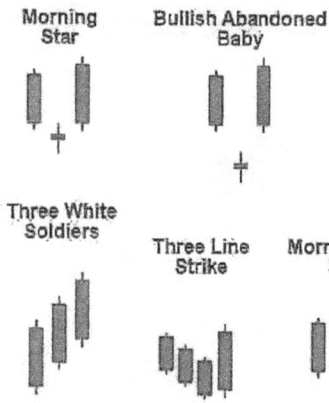

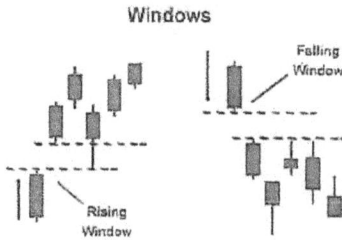

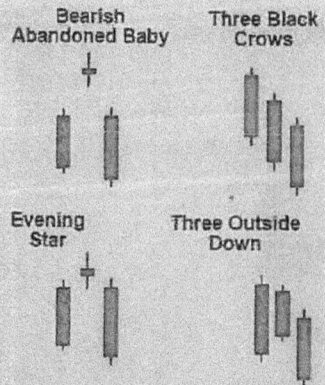

Morning Star
Bullish Abandoned Baby

Three White Soldiers

Three Line Strike
Morning Doji Star
Three Outside Up
Three Inside Up

NEUTRAL/BASIC PATTERN

CLOSE
UPPER SHADOW
HIGH
OPEN
OPEN
REAL BODY
LOWER SHADOW
CLOSE
LOW

CANDLESTICK BASICS

Doji
Spinning Top
Marubozu

Star

Bullish Setup
Hikkake Pattern
Bearish Setup

Bullish J-Hook

Breakout
Uptrend Resumes
Uptrend
Pullback

Windows

Falling Window
Rising Window

BEARISH CANDLESTICK PATTERNS

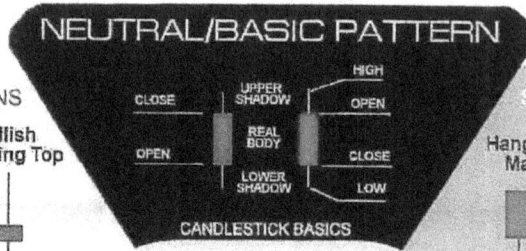

SINGLE CANDLE PATTERNS

Hanging Man
Shooting Star
Bearish Spinning Top

Gravestone Doji

TWO CANDLE PATTERNS

Bearish Kicker
Bearish Engulfing
Bearish Harami

Dark Cloud Cover
Tweezer Top

THREE CANDLE PATTERNS

Bearish Abandoned Baby
Three Black Crows

Evening Star
Three Outside Down

CANDLESTICKS WITH SIGNALS

HAMMER

BUY

HANGING MAN

SELL

SHOOTING STAR

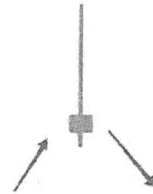

SELL

MORNING STAR

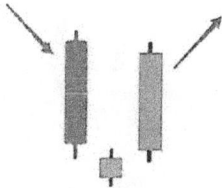

BUY

THREE INSIDE UP

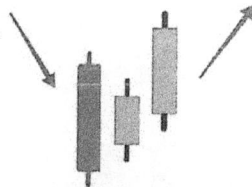

BUY

BEARISH BREAKAWAY

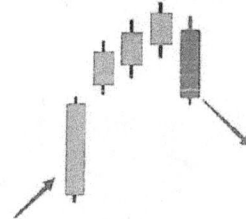

SELL

BULLISH BREAKAWAY

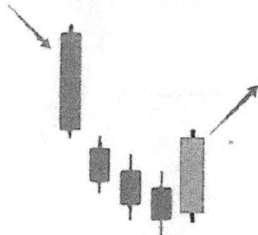

BUY

EVENING STAR

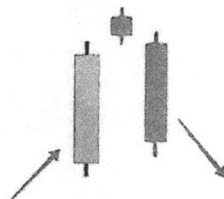

SELL

THREE OUTSIDE DOWN

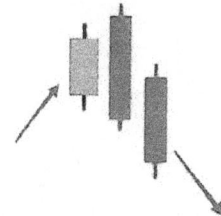

SELL

BULLISH

BULLISH ENGULFING

HAMMER

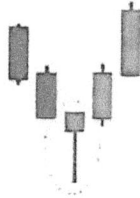

INVERTED HAMMER

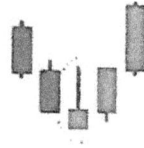

MORNING STAR

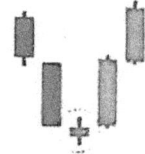

DRAGONFLY DOJI

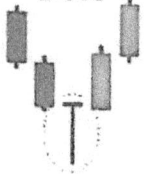

PIERCING LINE

TWEEZER BOTTOM

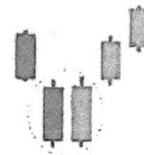

THREE WHITE SOLDIERS

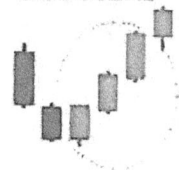

BEARISH

BEARISH ENGULFING

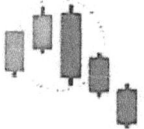

HANGING MAN

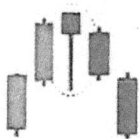

SHOOTING STAR

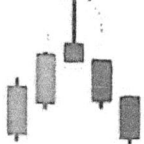

EVENING STAR

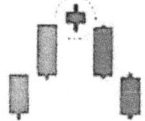

GRAVESTONE DOJI

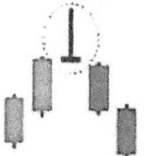

DARK CLOUD COVER

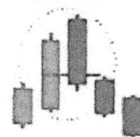

TWEEZER TOP

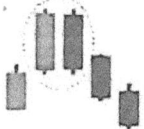

THREE BLACK CROWS

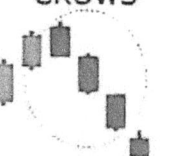

BULLISH CANDLESTICK PATTERNS

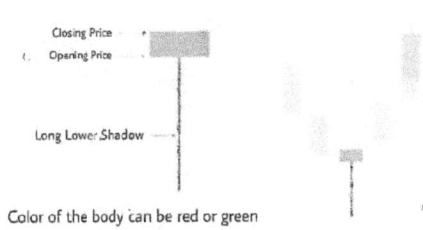

Closing Price •
Opening Price •
Long Lower Shadow —
Color of the body can be red or green

HAMMER PATTERN

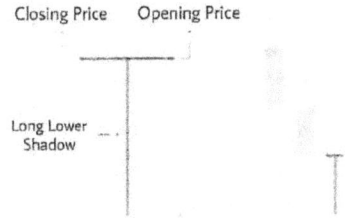

Closing Price   Opening Price

Long Lower
Shadow

DRAGONFLY DOJI

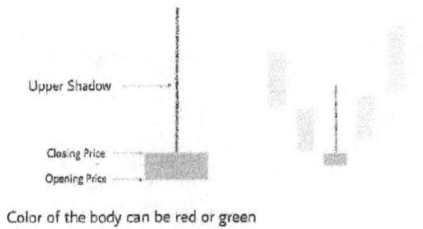

Upper Shadow —
Closing Price —
Opening Price —
Color of the body can be red or green

INVERTED HAMMER

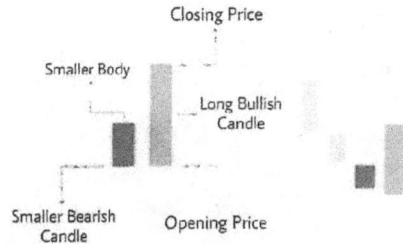

Closing Price

Smaller Body

Long Bullish
Candle

Smaller Bearish
Candle   Opening Price

BULLISH ENGULFING

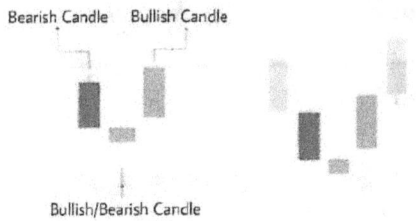

Bearish Candle   Bullish Candle

Bullish/Bearish Candle

MORNING STAR

Bearish Candle   Bullish Candle

Doji

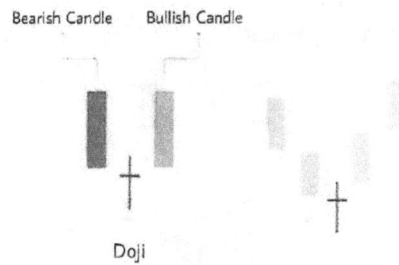

MORNING DOJI STAR

BULLISH CANDLESTICK PATTERNS

PIERCING LINE

MORNING STAR

MORNING DOJI STAR

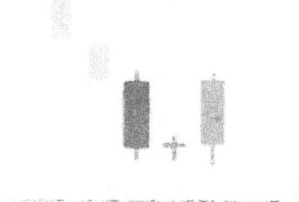

HAMMER

BULLISH SEPARATING LINES

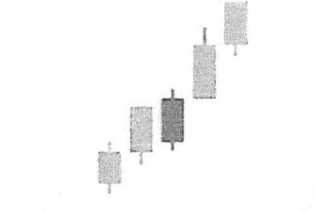

THREE WHITE SOLDIERS

INVERTED HAMMER

BULLISH ENGULFING

DRAGONFLY DOJI

BULLISH REVERSAL PATTERNS

ABANDONDED BABY

MORNING DOJI STAR

THREE INSIDE UP

THREE OUTSIDE UP

BREAKAWAY

DOJI STAR

DRAGONFLY DOJI

ENGULFING

HAMMER

LADDER BOTTOM

MORNING STAR

PIERCING LINE

CANDLESTICKS FORMATION

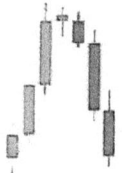
EVENING STAR

BULLISH HARAMI

TWEEZER BOTTOM

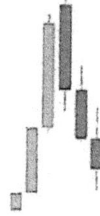
DARK CLOUD COVER

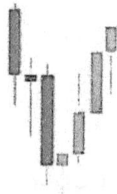
HAMMER

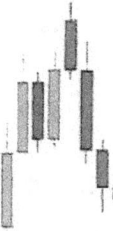
THREE BLACK CROWS

THREE WHITE SOLDIERS

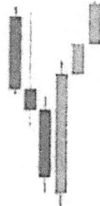
BULLISH ENGULFING

BEARISH ENGULFING

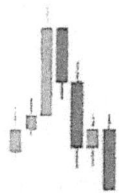
BEARISH HARAMI

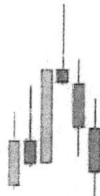
SHOOTING STAR

GRAVESTONE DOJI

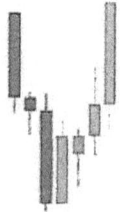
PIERCING LINE

TWEEZER TOP

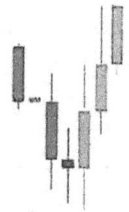
MORNING STAR

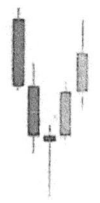
DRAGONFLY DOJI

HIGH PROBABILITY CANDLESTICK PATTERNS

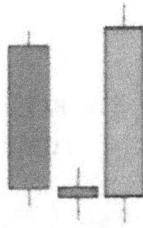

BULLISH ENGULFING	MORNING STAR	BULLISH PIN BAR	BULLISH HARAMI

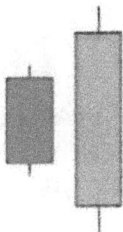

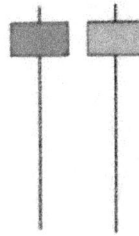

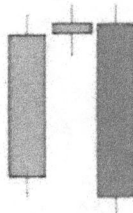

BEARISH ENGULFING	EVENING STAR	BEARISH PIN BAR	BEARISH HARAMI

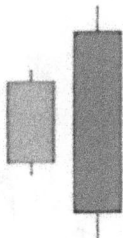

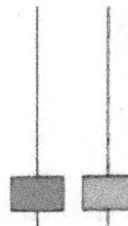

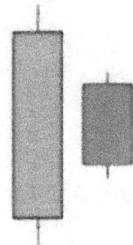

CANDLESTICK PATTERNS

BULLISH ENGULFIN G

THREE BLACK CROWS

TWEEZER BOTTOMS

BEARISH ENGULFIN G

BEARISH MARUBOZU

TWEEZER TOPS

THREE WHITE CROWS

GRAVESTONE DOJI

DRAGONFLY DOJI

MORNING STAR

BULLISH MARUBOZU

BULLISH DOJI

TECHNICAL ANALYSIS

ENGULFING CANDLESTICKS

THE BODY LENGTH OF THE ENGULFING CANDLE OVERLAPS THE BODY OF THE PREVIOUS CANDLE

BULLISH ENGULFING

BULLISH CANDLE OPENS LOWER
THAN THE PREVIOUS CANDLE
CLOSE, AND CLOSES ABOVE
PREVIOUS CANDLE OPEN

BEARISH ENGULFING

BEARISH CANDLE OPENS
ABOVE PREVIOUS CANDLE
CLOSE, AND CLOSES BELOW
PREVIOUS CANDLE OPEN

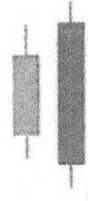

EXAMPLES

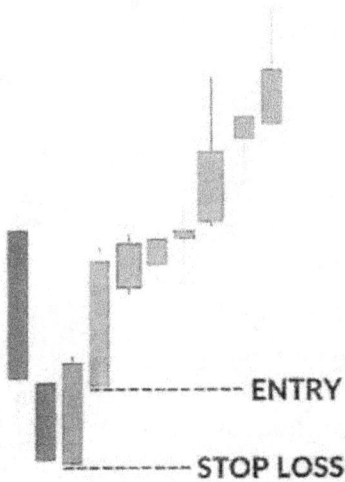

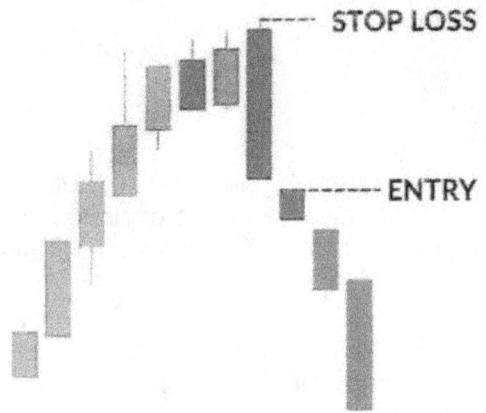

Option Trading

In its simplest form, option trading is when you buy or sell an underlying asset at a pre-negotiated price by a certain future date. Considered a contract, options offer the buyer and seller different contracts depending on the type of contract they hold, along with the underlying asset.

Each option contract will always have to exercise your option. The price associated with any option is known as the "strike price." Buyers pay premiums for the rights granted by the contract. Calls and Puts are different. Call options allow you to buy the asset at a stated price, while Put options allow the holder to sell the asset at a stated price within a specific timeframe.

One way you can use options to generate income is when you buy call options or become an option writer. There are American and other foreign option contracts, but our focus here is on

---

Pro se Tip: (!)

Options are the most direct way to invest in oil!

American Options can be simpler than others; our reason is that American options can be exercised any time before the option's expiration date.

Types of Options

CALL

Call options give you the right, but not the obligation, to purchase the underlying security at the "strike price" on or before the expiration date. These types of options become valuable when the underlying security rises in price (calls have a positive delta).

PUTS

Put options give you the right, not the obligation, to sell the underlying stock at the "strike price" on or before expiration. Going long on a put is a short position in the underlying security since the put would gain value as the underlying price falls (Puts have negative deltas). Other Puts, such as "Protective Puts," (are a risk and management strategy that uses option contracts that investors employ to guard against the loss of owning a stock or asset.

Typically, option contracts represent 100 shares of the underlying security. You pay a premium fee for each contract (Ex. When an option premium is 35 cents per contract. Buying one contract costs $35 ($0.35 x 100 = $35) because, as not previously, each option contract represents 100 shares. The premium of #0.35 is partially based on the strike price, while sometimes, it is even based on the price for buying or selling the security until the expiration date.

One of the best advantages of options is that they help limit your downside risk by just a (min.) premium in relation to what 100 shares of stock would cost you on the open market.

Option Strategies

Covered Call Strategy: simply means to buy a naked call option [which is an options strategy in which an investor writes (sells) call options on the open market without owning the underlying security]. You can structure a basic covered call [which refers to a financial transaction in which the investor selling call options owns an equivalent amount of the underlying security] or buy-write [which is when an investor buys a security with options available on it and simultaneously writes (sells) a call option on that security]. These strategies work because they generate income while reducing the risk of investing in stock alone.

Married Put Strategy: When you purchase an asset and simultaneously purchase put options for an equivalent number of shares, you can sell the stock at the strike price. Each contract is worth 100 shares.

Bull Call Spread: is when you simultaneously buy calls at a certain strike price [a set price at which a derivative contract can be bought or sold when exercised] while also selling the same number of calls at a higher strike price. Both call options will have the same expiration date and asset. This is a good strategy if you are bullish on the underlying asset.

Bear Put Spread Strategy: this strategy entails simultaneously purchasing put options at a specific strike price and selling the same number of puts at a lower price. If you are bearish about an underlying asset, use this strategy.

Protective Collar: Performed mainly by purchasing an out-of-the-money (OTM) [is an expression used to describe an option contract that only contains extrinsic value\ put option while simultaneously writing an ("OTM") call option, when you also already own the underlying asset.

Options Greek Terminology

Delta: represents the charge rate between the option price and a $1 charge in the underlying assets price. Delta of a call option has a potential range between [0 and 1], while the delta of a put option ranges between [0 and -1]. If the delta is 0.50, on a long call option and the asset increases by $1.00, the option will increase in price by $0.50; on a long call option and the asset increases by $1.00, the option would increase in price by $0.50. Delta also represents the hedge ratio [compares the value of a position protected through the use of a hedge with the size of the entire position itself] for creating a delta neutral position for options. Suppose you purchase an American call option with a [0.40] delta. You will also need to sell 40 shares of stock to fully hedge.

Theta is the rate of change between the option price and time or time sensitivity, also known as option time decay. It indicates the amount an option price decreases as the time to expiration decreases, all else being equal.

Gamma: the rate of change between an options delta and the underlying asset price.

Vega: the rate of change between an option's value and the underlying asset's implied volatility.

Options Brokers / Platforms for Investing

While several option brokers, platforms, and Apps allow you to buy options, here are some of the best. Remember, setting these accounts up will have to be done by your outside support system because they will need to use their information and ID card to set up most accounts; not all require it.

- Tastyworks.com

  Min $0

  Fees: $1 to open option contract, $0 to close option contract

- E*TRADE (us.etrade.com)

  Min $0

  Fees: $0.50-$0.65 per contract

- Webull.com (also has an app)

  Min: $0

  Fees: listed options no commission (on the website)

- TDAmeritrade.com

  Min: $0

  Fees: $0.65 per option contract

- Ally Financial (ally.com)

  Fees: $0 - $0.50 per contract

- Robinhood (robinhood.com) also Robinhood App

  Fees: $0.00

- Moomoo App

  Fees: $0.00

  Easy set up

- Fidelity (www.Fidelity.com)

  Min: $0

  Fees: $0 fees per trade

Option Charts and Strategies

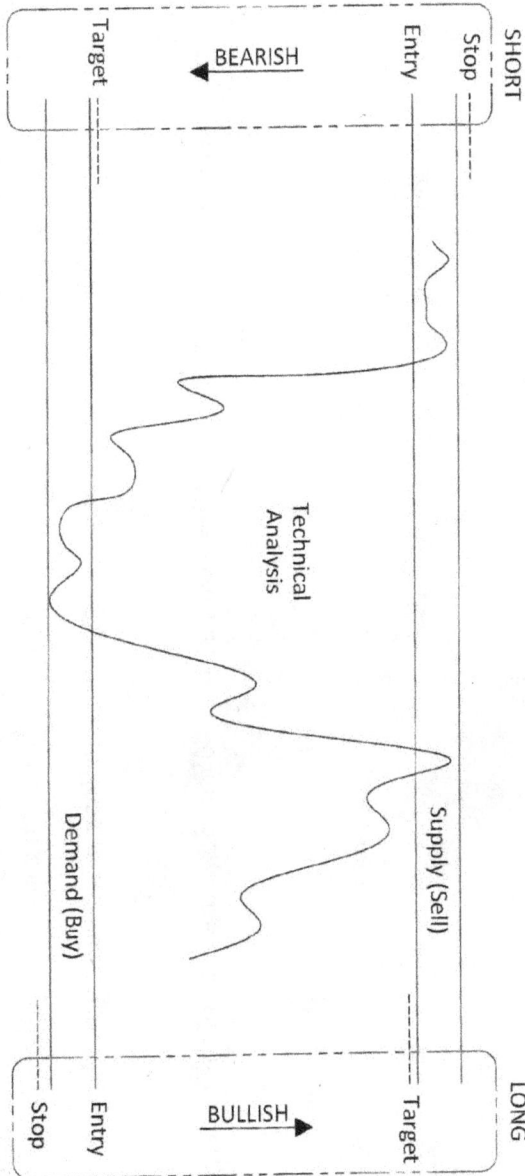

AOA (At or Above)

Supply - Institutional Sell Orders

Bear / Call		IV High	Credit	OTM
Bearish	Short Call*	IV High	Credit	OTM
	Long Put	IV Low	Debit	ITM
Bear / Put		IV Low	Debit	ITM

*Sell Call = Naked Call

AOB (At or Below)

Demand - Institutional Buy Orders

Bull / Call		IV Low	Debit	ITM
Bullish	Long Call	IV Low	Debit	ITM
	Short Put	IV High	Credit	OTM
Bull / Put		IV High	Credit	OTM

SHORT

◄ BEARISH

Stop — Entry — Target

Technical Analysis

Supply (Sell) — Demand (Buy)

BULLISH ►

LONG

Target — Entry — Stop

LONG (BUY)

When Buying, you buy rights

This gives you the option to buy if you want.

Buy when....
- Volatility is Deflated
- ITM (In the money) Strike
- Over 90 days expiration date
- Delta .5 - 1.0

SHORT (SELL)

When Selling, you take on an obligations

This obligates you to sell if the option is exercised.

Sell when....
- Volatility is Inflated
- OTM (Out the money) Strike
- Less than 30 days expiration date
- Delta .5 - 0.0

LEARN ABOUT THE GREEKS

DELTA
- Delta measures how much an options price is expected to change per $1.00 change in the price of the underlying stock or security.
- This affects the Option price.
- A Long Call with a .30 Delta should theoretically move $0.30 for every $1.00 move in the underlying stock or security.
- Delta can also be used to help estimate the likelihood that an option will expire In The Money (ITM)

Example: A Long Call with a .50 delta = about a 50% chance expiring In The Money (ITM)

GAMMA
- Gamma measures the rate Delta may change with each $1.00 change in the price of the underlying stock or security.
- This affects the Delta

THETA
- Theta measures the change in price of the option for a one-day decrease in time to expiration.
- Time decay works for Short Options
- Time decay works against Long Options
- This affects the Option price.

VEGA
- Vega measures how sensitive an option is to changes in volatility of the underlying asset.
- This affects the Option price.

RHO
- Rho measures the change in value based on a 1% change in the interest rate.
- Rho is often the least used Options Greek.
- This affects the Option price.

OPTIONS FLOWCHART

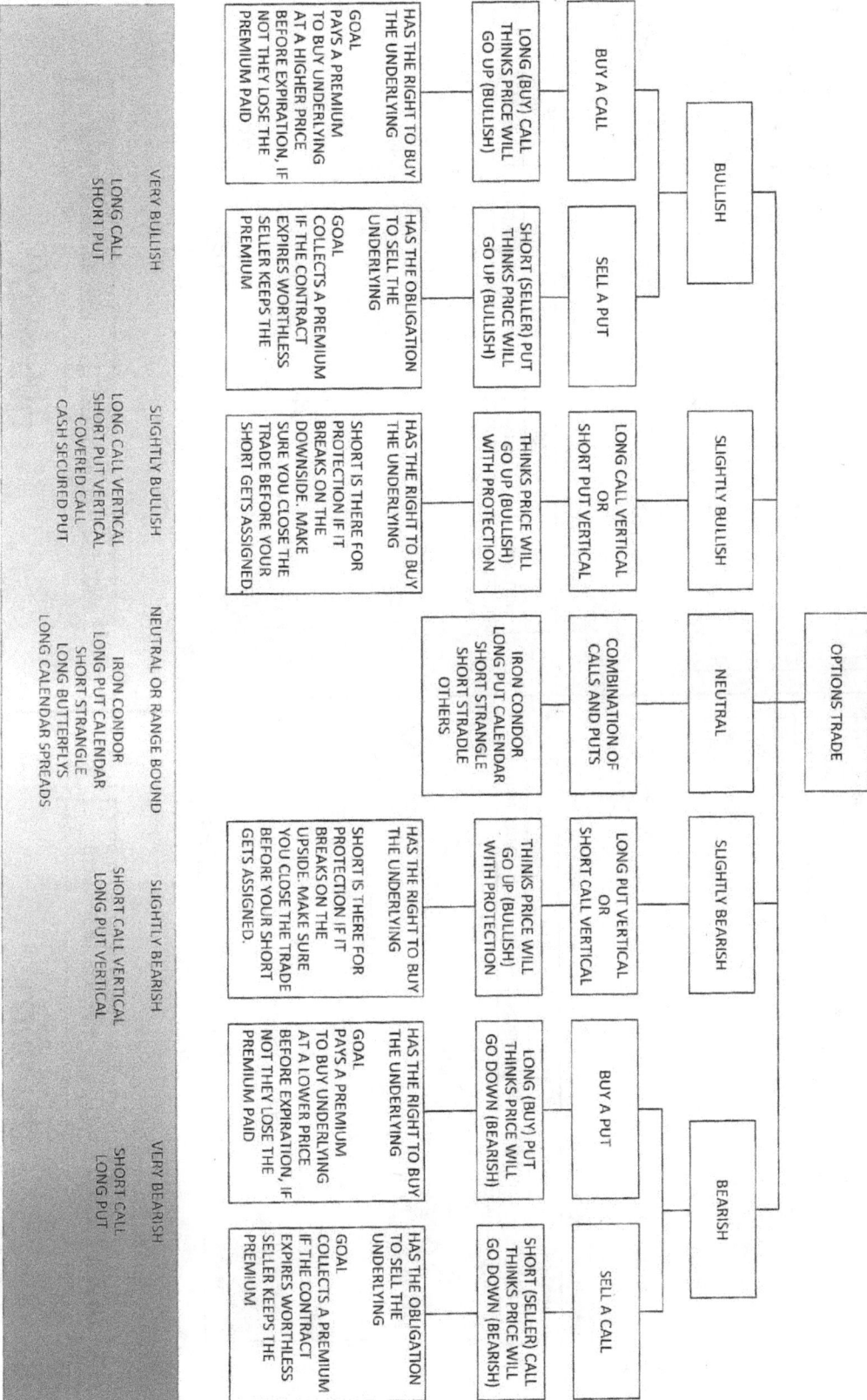

OPTIONS TRADE

BULLISH

BUY A CALL
- LONG (BUY) CALL THINKS PRICE WILL GO UP (BULLISH)
- HAS THE RIGHT TO BUY THE UNDERLYING
- GOAL PAYS A PREMIUM TO BUY UNDERLYING AT A HIGHER PRICE BEFORE EXPIRATION, IF NOT THEY LOSE THE PREMIUM PAID

SELL A PUT
- SHORT (SELLER) PUT THINKS PRICE WILL GO UP (BULLISH)
- HAS THE OBLIGATION TO SELL THE UNDERLYING
- GOAL COLLECTS A PREMIUM IF THE CONTRACT EXPIRES WORTHLESS SELLER KEEPS THE PREMIUM

SLIGHTLY BULLISH

LONG CALL VERTICAL OR SHORT PUT VERTICAL
- THINKS PRICE WILL GO UP (BULLISH) WITH PROTECTION
- HAS THE RIGHT TO BUY THE UNDERLYING
- SHORT IS THERE FOR PROTECTION IF IT BREAKS ON THE DOWNSIDE. MAKE SURE YOU CLOSE THE TRADE BEFORE YOUR SHORT GETS ASSIGNED.

NEUTRAL

COMBINATION OF CALLS AND PUTS
- IRON CONDOR LONG PUT CALENDAR SHORT STRANGLE SHORT STRADDLE OTHERS

SLIGHTLY BEARISH

LONG PUT VERTICAL OR SHORT CALL VERTICAL
- THINKS PRICE WILL GO UP (BULLISH) WITH PROTECTION
- HAS THE RIGHT TO BUY THE UNDERLYING
- SHORT IS THERE FOR PROTECTION IF IT BREAKS ON THE UPSIDE. MAKE SURE YOU CLOSE THE TRADE BEFORE YOUR SHORT GETS ASSIGNED.

BEARISH

BUY A PUT
- LONG (BUY) PUT THINKS PRICE WILL GO DOWN (BEARISH)
- HAS THE RIGHT TO BUY THE UNDERLYING
- GOAL PAYS A PREMIUM TO BUY UNDERLYING AT A LOWER PRICE BEFORE EXPIRATION, IF NOT THEY LOSE THE PREMIUM PAID

SELL A CALL
- SHORT (SELLER) CALL THINKS PRICE WILL GO DOWN (BEARISH)
- HAS THE OBLIGATION TO SELL THE UNDERLYING
- GOAL COLLECTS A PREMIUM IF THE CONTRACT EXPIRES WORTHLESS SELLER KEEPS THE PREMIUM

VERY BULLISH
- LONG CALL
- SHORT PUT

SLIGHTLY BULLISH
- LONG CALL VERTICAL
- SHORT PUT VERTICAL
- COVERED CALL
- CASH SECURED PUT

NEUTRAL OR RANGE BOUND
- IRON CONDOR
- LONG PUT CALENDAR
- SHORT STRANGLE
- LONG BUTTERFLYS
- LONG CALENDAR SPREADS

SLIGHTLY BEARISH
- SHORT CALL VERTICAL
- LONG PUT VERTICAL

VERY BEARISH
- SHORT CALL
- LONG PUT

LONG CALL

BIAS - VERY BULLISH	DEBIT (BUY)	IV LOW

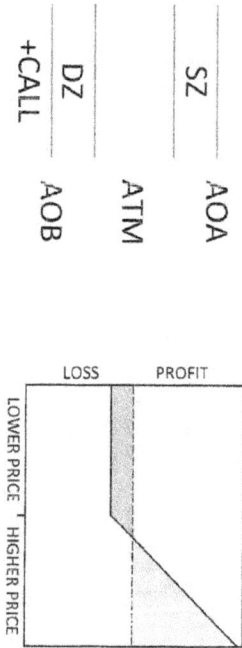

SZ _____ AOA

DZ _____ ATM

+CALL _____ AOB

		RECCOMENDATIONS		
BUY / SELL	OPTION TYPE	STRIKE PRICE	DELTA	EXPIRATION
BUY	CALL	ITM	0.5 - 1.0	> 90 DAYS

.50 - 1.0 Delta means an estimated 50% - 100% chance of expiring ITM, which you want.

Goal of the trade:
For the price to Increase in value

Maximum Potential Profit:
Unlimited profit potential

Break Even Point:
Strike price + Cost of the Call

Maximum Potential Loss:
Premium paid for the Call option

Time Decay:
This is against you. This will negatively impact your trade

Implied Volatility:
An increase in Volatility will increase the value of your trade

Consider closing the trade when:
- You hit 75% - 80% of its max gain
- The trade is going the wrong way
- Close a 5-10 days prior to expiration

AOA = AT OR ABOVE SUPPLY ZONE
ATM = AT THE MONEY
AOB = AT OR BELOW DEMAND ZONE
ITM = IN THE MONEY
OTM = OUT OF THE MONEY

LONG PUT

BIAS - VERY BULLISH	DEBIT (BUY)	IV LOW

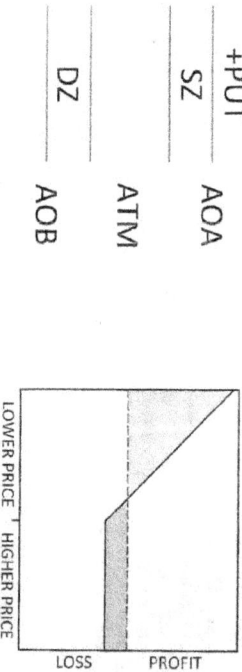

+PUT _____ AOA

SZ _____ ATM

DZ _____ AOB

		RECCOMENDATIONS		
BUY / SELL	OPTION TYPE	STRIKE PRICE	DELTA	EXPIRATION
BUY	PUT	ITM	0.5 - 1.0	> 90 DAYS

.50 - 1.0 Delta means an estimated 50% - 100% chance of expiring ITM, which you want.

Goal of the trade:
For the price to Decrease in value

Maximum Potential Profit:
Substantial profit potential

Break Even Point:
Strike price - Cost of the Put

Maximum Potential Loss:
Premium paid for the Put option

Time Decay:
This is against you. This will negatively impact your trade

Implied Volatility:
An increase in Volatility will increase the value of your trade

Consider closing the trade when:
- You hit 75% - 80% of its max gain
- The trade is going the wrong way
- Close a 5-10 days prior to expiration

AOA = AT OR ABOVE SUPPLY ZONE
ATM = AT THE MONEY
AOB = AT OR BELOW DEMAND ZONE
ITM = IN THE MONEY
OTM = OUT OF THE MONEY

COVERED CALL

BIAS - SLIGHTLY BULLISH	CREDIT (SELL)	IV HIGH

-CALL _____ AOA

SZ _____ ATM

DZ _____ AOB

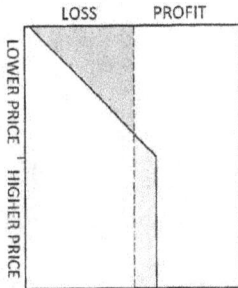

LOSS / PROFIT

LOWER PRICE / HIGHER PRICE

YOU MUST HAVE THE SHARES OF STOCK TO COVER IF YOU GET ASSIGNED

.20 - .30 Delta means an estimated 20% - 30% chance of expiring ITM, which you want.

RECCOMENDATIONS

BUY / SELL	OPTION TYPE	STRIKE PRICE	DELTA	EXPIRATION
SELL	CALL	OTM	.20 - .30	20 - 50 DAYS

Goal of the trade:
To generate income by selling OTM calls on stock you already own

Maximum Potential Profit:
Premium + Gains in underlying up to the strike price

Break Even Point:
Purchase price of the stock - the Premium

Maximum Potential Loss:
Amount lost if underlying stock falls to zero

Time Decay:
This is on your side. The more days that pass, the cheaper it will be to buy back.

Implied Volatility:
An decrease in Volatility will increase the value of your trade

Consider closing the trade when:
- You are close to being assigned
- The trade is going the wrong way
- Close a 5-10 days prior to expiration

AOA = AT OR ABOVE SUPPLY ZONE
ATM = AT THE MONEY
AOB = AT OR BELOW DEMAND ZONE
ITM = IN THE MONEY
OTM = OUT OF THE MONEY

CASH-SECURED PUT

BIAS - SLIGHTLY BULLISH	CREDIT (SELL)	IV HIGH

-CALL _____ AOA

SZ _____ ATM

DZ _____ AOB

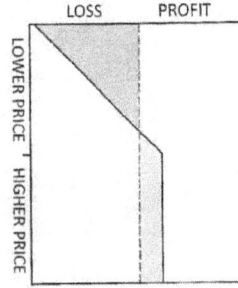

LOSS / PROFIT

LOWER PRICE / HIGHER PRICE

YOU MUST HAVE THE CASH TO BUY THE STOCK TO COVER IF YOU GET ASSIGNED

.20 - .30 Delta means an estimated 20% - 30% chance of expiring ITM, which you want.

RECCOMENDATIONS

BUY / SELL	OPTION TYPE	STRIKE PRICE	DELTA	EXPIRATION
SELL	PUT	OTM	.20 - .30	20 - 50 DAYS

Goal of the trade:
For the price to Decrease in value or expire worthless. You have the cash to buy the stock if the contract is put to you.

Maximum Potential Profit:
Premium received from sel ing the Put

Break Even Point:
Strike price - Premium

Maximum Potential Loss:
Losses in the underlying if assigned and the stock falls to zero

Time Decay:
This is on your side. The more days that pass, the cheaper it will be to buy back.

Implied Volatility:
An decrease in Volatility will increase the value of your trade

Consider closing the trade when:
- You are close to being assigned
- The trade is going the wrong way
- Close a 5-10 days prior to expiration

AOA = AT OR ABOVE SUPPLY ZONE
ATM = AT THE MONEY
AOB = AT OR BELOW DEMAND ZONE
ITM = IN THE MONEY
OTM = OUT OF THE MONEY

LONG CALL VERTICAL

BIAS - SLIGHTLY BULLISH	DEBIT (BUY)	IV LOW

-CALL	SZ	AOA
	DZ	ATM
+CALL		AOB

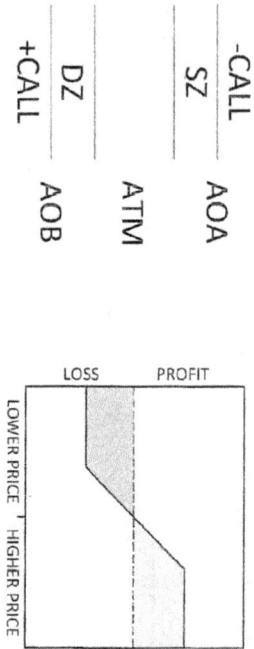

LOSS / PROFIT

LOWER PRICE | HIGHER PRICE

RECCOMENDATIONS

BUY / SELL	OPTION TYPE	STRIKE PRICE	DELTA	EXPIRATION
SELL	CALL	OTM	---	20 - 30 DAYS
BUY	CALL	ITM	.60 - .80	20 - 30 DAYS

.60 - .80 Delta means an estimated 60% - 80% chance of expiring ITM, which you want.

Goal of the trade:
To capture potential increases in the stock price while attempting to reduce the time in the trade due to time decay when using a limited-risk strategy.

Maximum Potential Profit:
At Short Strike or difference between both Strikes - Net Premium

Break Even Point:
The Long Call Strike price + Net Premium

Maximum Potential Loss:
Total Debit paid

Time Decay:
Slightly Neutral. It will help your short, but hurt your long strike

Implied Volatility:
Depends on the strike price locations

Consider closing the trade when:
- You hit 75% - 80% of its max gain
- The trade is going the wrong way
- Close a 5-10 days prior to expiration

AOA = AT OR ABOVE SUPPLY ZONE
ATM = AT THE MONEY
AOB = AT OR BELOW DEMAND ZONE
ITM = IN THE MONEY
OTM = OUT OF THE MONEY

LONG PUT VERTICAL

BIAS - SLIGHTLY BEARISH	DEBIT (BUY)	IV LOW

+PUT	SZ	AOA
	DZ	ATM
-PUT		AOB

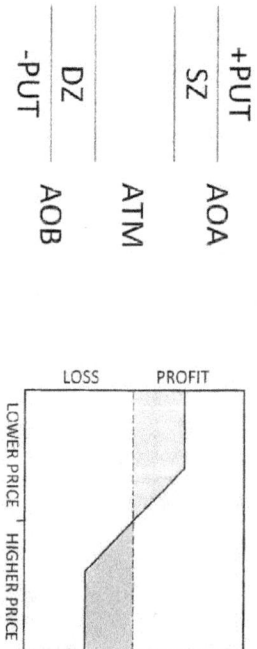

LOSS / PROFIT

LOWER PRICE | HIGHER PRICE

RECCOMENDATIONS

BUY / SELL	OPTION TYPE	STRIKE PRICE	DELTA	EXPIRATION
BUY	PUT	ITM	---	20 - 30 DAYS
SELL	PUT	OTM	0.6 - 0.8	20 - 30 DAYS

.60 - .80 Delta means an estimated 60% - 80% chance of expiring ITM, which you want.

Goal of the trade:
To capture potential decreases in the stock price while attempting to reduce the time in the trade due to time decay when using a limited-risk strategy.

Maximum Potential Profit:
At Short Strike or difference between both Strikes - Net Premium

Break Even Point:
The Long Put Strike price + Net Debit

Maximum Potential Loss:
Total Debit Paid

Time Decay:
Slightly Neutral. It will help your short, but hurt your long strike

Implied Volatility:
Depends on the strike price locations

Consider closing the trade when:
- You hit 75% - 80% of its max gain
- The trade is going the wrong way
- Close a 5-10 days prior to expiration

AOA = AT OR ABOVE SUPPLY ZONE
ATM = AT THE MONEY
AOB = AT OR BELOW DEMAND ZONE
ITM = IN THE MONEY
OTM = OUT OF THE MONEY

SHORT CALL VERTICAL

BIAS - SLIGHTLY BEARISH	CREDIT (SELL)	IV HIGH

SZ ———— AOA
+CALL
-CALL
DZ ———— AOB
ATM

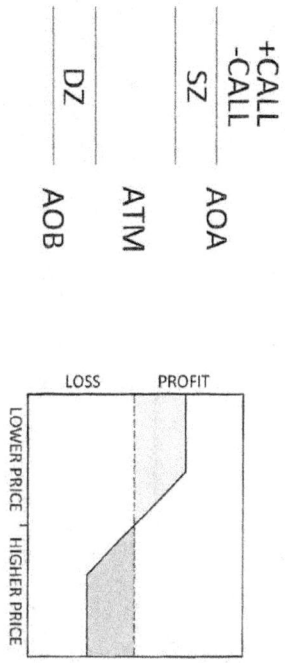

LOSS   PROFIT
LOWER PRICE   HIGHER PRICE

RECCOMENDATIONS

BUY / SELL	OPTION TYPE	STRIKE PRICE	DELTA	EXPIRATION
BUY	CALL	OTM	---	20 - 50 DAYS
SELL	CALL	OTM	.20 - .30	20 - 50 DAYS

.20 - .30 Delta means an estimated 20% - 30% chance of expiring ITM, which you want.

YOU MUST HAVE THE SHARES OF STOCK TO COVER IF YOU GET ASSIGNED

Goal of the trade:
To potentially profit from sideways trending and down-trending movement

Maximum Potential Profit:
Net credit (difference between the two premiums)

Break Even Point:
Short Strike + Net Credit

Maximum Potential Loss:
(Short Strike - Long Strike) - Net Credit

Time Decay:
Slightly Positive. It will help your short, but hurt your long strike

Implied Volatility:
Depends on the strike price locations

Consider closing the trade when:
- You are close to being assigned
- The trade is going the wrong way
- Close a 5-10 days prior to expiration

AOA = AT OR ABOVE SUPPLY ZONE
ATM = AT THE MONEY
AOB = AT OR BELOW DEMAND ZONE
ITM = IN THE MONEY
OTM = OUT OF THE MONEY

SHORT PUT VERTICAL

BIAS - SLIGHTLY BULLISH	CREDIT (SELL)	IV HIGH

SZ ———— AOA
DZ ———— AOB
-PUT
+PUT
ATM

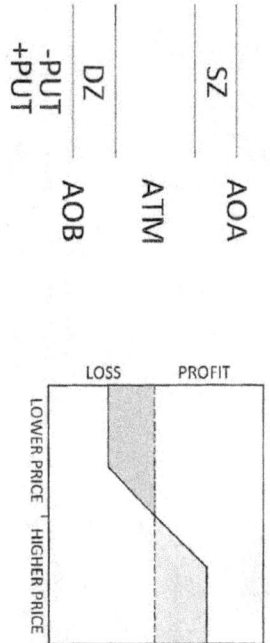

LOSS   PROFIT
LOWER PRICE   HIGHER PRICE

RECCOMENDATIONS

BUY / SELL	OPTION TYPE	STRIKE PRICE	DELTA	EXPIRATION
SELL	PUT	OTM	.20 - .30	20 - 50 DAYS
BUY	PUT	OTM	---	20 - 50 DAYS

.20 - .30 Delta means an estimated 20% - 30% chance of expiring ITM, which you want.

YOU MUST HAVE THE SHARES OF STOCK TO COVER IF YOU GET ASSIGNED

Goal of the trade:
To potentially profit from sideways trending and up-trending movement

Maximum Potential Profit:
Net credit (difference between two premiums)

Break Even Point:
Short Strike - Net Credit

Maximum Potential Loss:
(Short Strike - Long Strike) - Net Credit

Time Decay:
Slightly Positive. It will help your short, but hurt your long strike

Implied Volatility:
Depends on the strike price locations

Consider closing the trade when:
- You are close to being assigned
- The trade is going the wrong way
- Close a 5-10 days prior to expiration

AOA = AT OR ABOVE SUPPLY ZONE
ATM = AT THE MONEY
AOB = AT OR BELOW DEMAND ZONE
ITM = IN THE MONEY
OTM = OUT OF THE MONEY

IRON CONDOR

BIAS - RANGE BOUND	VARIES	IV HIGH

```
+CALL ─── SZ ─── AOA
-CALL

       DZ ─── ATM
       AOB

-PUT ─── 
+PUT
```

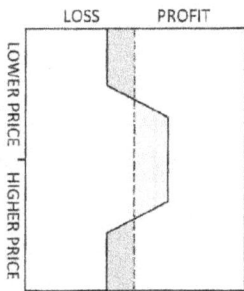

PROFIT / LOSS

LOWER PRICE   HIGHER PRICE

RECCOMENDATIONS

BUY / SELL		OPTION TYPE	STRIKE PRICE	DELTA	EXPIRATION
SZ	BUY	CALL	OTM	---	20 - 50 DAYS
	SELL	CALL	OTM	.20 - .30	20 - 50 DAYS
DZ	SELL	PUT	ITM	.20 - .30	20 - 50 DAYS
	BUY	PUT	ITM	---	20 - 50 DAYS

.20 - .30 Delta means an estimated 20% - 30% chance of expiring ITM, which you want.

Goal of the trade:
To capture potential sideways stock movement with the price staying between the to short strikes. (.20 - .30 Deltas for the Short Strikes / 20 - 50 days out)

Maximum Potential Profit:
Premium received from closing the trade

Break Even Point:
Short Put Strike price - Premium or Short Call Strike price + Premium

Maximum Potential Loss:
The difference between the Long and Short Strikes - Premium

Time Decay:
Slightly Neutral. It will help your short, but hurt your long strike

Implied Volatility:
An decrease in Volatility will increase the value of your trade

Consider closing the trade when:
- You hit 75% - 80% of its max gain
- The trade is going the wrong way
- Close a 5-10 days prior to expiration

AOA	=	AT OR ABOVE SUPPLY ZONE
ATM	=	AT THE MONEY
AOB	=	AT OR BELOW DEMAND ZONE
ITM	=	IN THE MONEY
OTM	=	OUT OF THE MONEY

SHORT IRON BUTTERFLY

BIAS - RANGE BOUND	VARIES	IV HIGH

```
+CALL ─── SZ ─── AOA
-CALL

-PUT ─── DZ ─── ATM
       AOB

+PUT ─── 
```

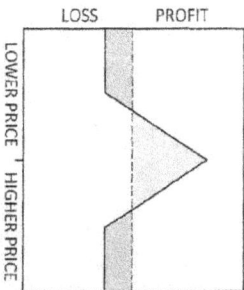

PROFIT / LOSS

LOWER PRICE   HIGHER PRICE

RECCOMENDATIONS

BUY / SELL		OPTION TYPE	STRIKE PRICE	DELTA	EXPIRATION
SZ	BUY	CALL	OTM	---	20 - 50 DAYS
	SELL	CALL	ATM	.20 - .30	20 - 50 DAYS
DZ	SELL	PUT	ATM	.20 - .30	20 - 50 DAYS
	BUY	PUT	ITM	---	20 - 50 DAYS

.20 - .30 Delta means an estimated 20% - 30% chance of expiring ITM, which you want.

Goal of the trade:
To have minimal to no movement on the stock within a specific time frame. This is an advanced trade used by seasoned Veterans.

Maximum Potential Profit:
The Net Premium recieved

Break Even Point:
ATM Strike + Premium, or ATM Strike - Premium

Maximum Potential Loss:
High Strike - Middle Strike - Net Premium recieved

Time Decay:
This is on your side. You want all of the options to expire worthless with minimal price change

Implied Volatility:
An increase in Volatility would decrease the value of your trade

Consider closing the trade when:
- You are close to being assigned
- The trade is going the wrong way
- Close a 5-10 days prior to expiration

AOA	=	AT OR ABOVE SUPPLY ZONE
ATM	=	AT THE MONEY
AOB	=	AT OR BELOW DEMAND ZONE
ITM	=	IN THE MONEY
OTM	=	OUT OF THE MONEY

LONG STRANGLE

BIG MOVE EITHER WAY	DEBIT (BUY)	IV LOW

```
+CALL —— AOA
 SZ  —— ATM
 DZ  —— AOB
+PUT —— AOB
```

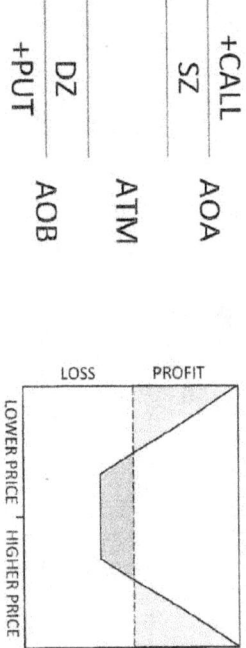

LOSS / PROFIT — LOWER PRICE / HIGHER PRICE

RECCOMENDATIONS

BUY / SELL	OPTION TYPE	STRIKE PRICE	DELTA	EXPIRATION
BUY	CALL	OTM	0.5 - 1.0	> 90 DAYS
BUY	CALL	OTM	0.5 - 1.0	> 90 DAYS

Goal of the trade:
To capture a quick and significant move in the stock price while attempting to reduce the time in the trade due to time decay.

Maximum Potential Profit:
If price goes up, it could be unlimited. If price goes down it could be The Strike price - Net Debit

Break Even Point:
The Strike price + Net Debit, or The Strike price - Net Debit

Maximum Potential Loss:
Total Premium Paid

Time Decay:
This is against you. This will negatively impact your trade

Implied Volatility:
An increase in Volatility will increase the value of your trade

Consider closing the trade when:
- You hit 75% - 80% of its max gain
- The trade is going the wrong way
- Close a 5-10 days prior to expiration

```
AOA = AT OR ABOVE SUPPLY ZONE
ATM = AT THE MONEY
AOB = AT OR BELOW DEMAND ZONE
ITM = IN THE MONEY
OTM = OUT OF THE MONEY
```

SHORT STRANGLE

LITTLE TO NO MOVEMENT	CREDIT (SELL)	IV HIGH

```
-CALL —— AOA
 SZ  —— ATM
 DZ  —— AOB
-PUT —— AOB
```

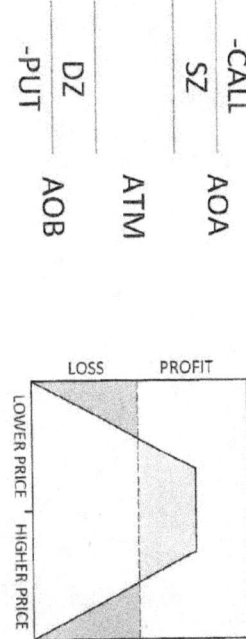

LOSS / PROFIT — LOWER PRICE / HIGHER PRICE

RECCOMENDATIONS

BUY / SELL	OPTION TYPE	STRIKE PRICE	DELTA	EXPIRATION
SELL	CALL	OTM	.20 - .30	20 - 50 DAYS
SELL	CALL	OTM	.20 - .30	20 - 50 DAYS

Goal of the trade:
To have minimal to no movement on the stock within a specific time frame. This is an advanced trade used by seasoned Veterans.

Maximum Potential Profit:
Premium received from selling the Call and Put

Break Even Point:
The Short Call Strike price + Premium, or the Short Put Strike price - Premium

Maximum Potential loss:
If price goes up, it could be unlimited. If price goes down it could be The Strike price - Net Credit

Time Decay:
This is on your side. The more days that pass, the cheaper it will be to buy back.

Implied Volatility:
A Decrease in Volatility will increase the value of your trade

Consider closing the trade when:
- You are close to being assigned
- The trade is going the wrong way
- Close a 5-10 days prior to expiration

```
AOA = AT OR ABOVE SUPPLY ZONE
ATM = AT THE MONEY
AOB = AT OR BELOW DEMAND ZONE
ITM = IN THE MONEY
OTM = OUT OF THE MONEY
```

LONG STRADDLE

BIG MOVE EITHER WAY	DEBIT (BUY)	IV LOW

```
SZ _____        AOA
+CALL
+PUT             ATM
DZ _____        AOB
```

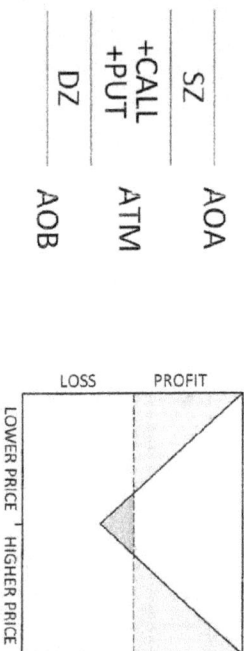

LOSS / PROFIT — LOWER PRICE / HIGHER PRICE

RECCOMENDATIONS

BUY / SELL	OPTION TYPE	STRIKE PRICE	DELTA	EXPIRATION
BUY	CALL	ATM	N/A	20 - 50 DAYS
BUY	PUT	ATM	N/A	20 - 50 DAYS

Goal of the trade:
To capture a quick and large move in the stock price while attempting to reduce the time in the trade due to time decay.

Maximum Potential Profit:
If price goes up, it could be unlimited. If price goes down it could be The Strike price - Net Debit

Break Even Point:
The Strike price + Net Debit, or The Strike price - Net Debit

Maximum Potential Loss:
Total Premium Paid

Time Decay:
This is against you. This will negatively impact your trade

Implied Volatility:
An increase in Volatility will increase the value of your trade

Consider closing the trade when:
- You hit 75% - 80% of its max gain
- The trade is going the wrong way
- Close a 5-10 days prior to expiration

AOA = AT OR ABOVE SUPPLY ZONE
ATM = AT THE MONEY
AOB = AT OR BELOW DEMAND ZONE
ITM = IN THE MONEY
OTM = OUT OF THE MONEY

SHORT STRADDLE

LITTLE TO NO MOVEMENT	CREDIT (SELL)	IV HIGH

FYI - A SHORT STRANGLE IS SIMILAR WITH A LARGER PROFIT AREA

```
SZ _____        AOA
-CALL
-PUT             ATM
DZ _____        AOB
```

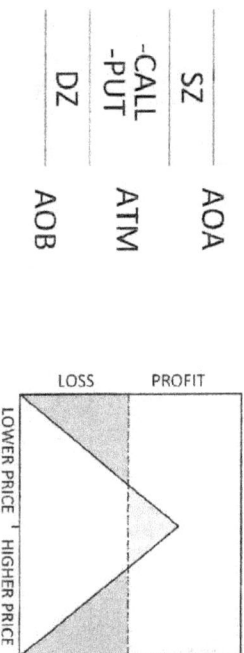

LOSS / PROFIT — LOWER PRICE / HIGHER PRICE

RECCOMENDATIONS

BUY / SELL	OPTION TYPE	STRIKE PRICE	DELTA	EXPIRATION
SELL	CALL	ATM	N/A	20 - 50 DAYS
SELL	PUT	ATM	N/A	20 - 50 DAYS

Goal of the trade:
To have minimal to no movement on the stock within a specific time frame.
This is an advanced trade used by seasoned Veterans.

Maximum Potential Profit:
Premium received from selling the Call and Put

Break Even Point:
The Short Call Strike price + Premium, or the Short Put Strike price - Premium

Maximum Potential Loss:
If price goes up, it could be unlimited. If price goes down it could be The Strike price - Net Credit

Time Decay:
This is on your side. The more days that pass, the cheaper it will be to buy back.

Implied Volatility:
A Decrease in Volatility will increase the value of your trade

Consider closing the trade when:
- You are close to being assigned
- The trade is going the wrong way
- Close a 5-10 days prior to expiration

AOA = AT OR ABOVE SUPPLY ZONE
ATM = AT THE MONEY
AOB = AT OR BELOW DEMAND ZONE
ITM = IN THE MONEY
OTM = OUT OF THE MONEY

STRIKE PRICE DEFINITIONS

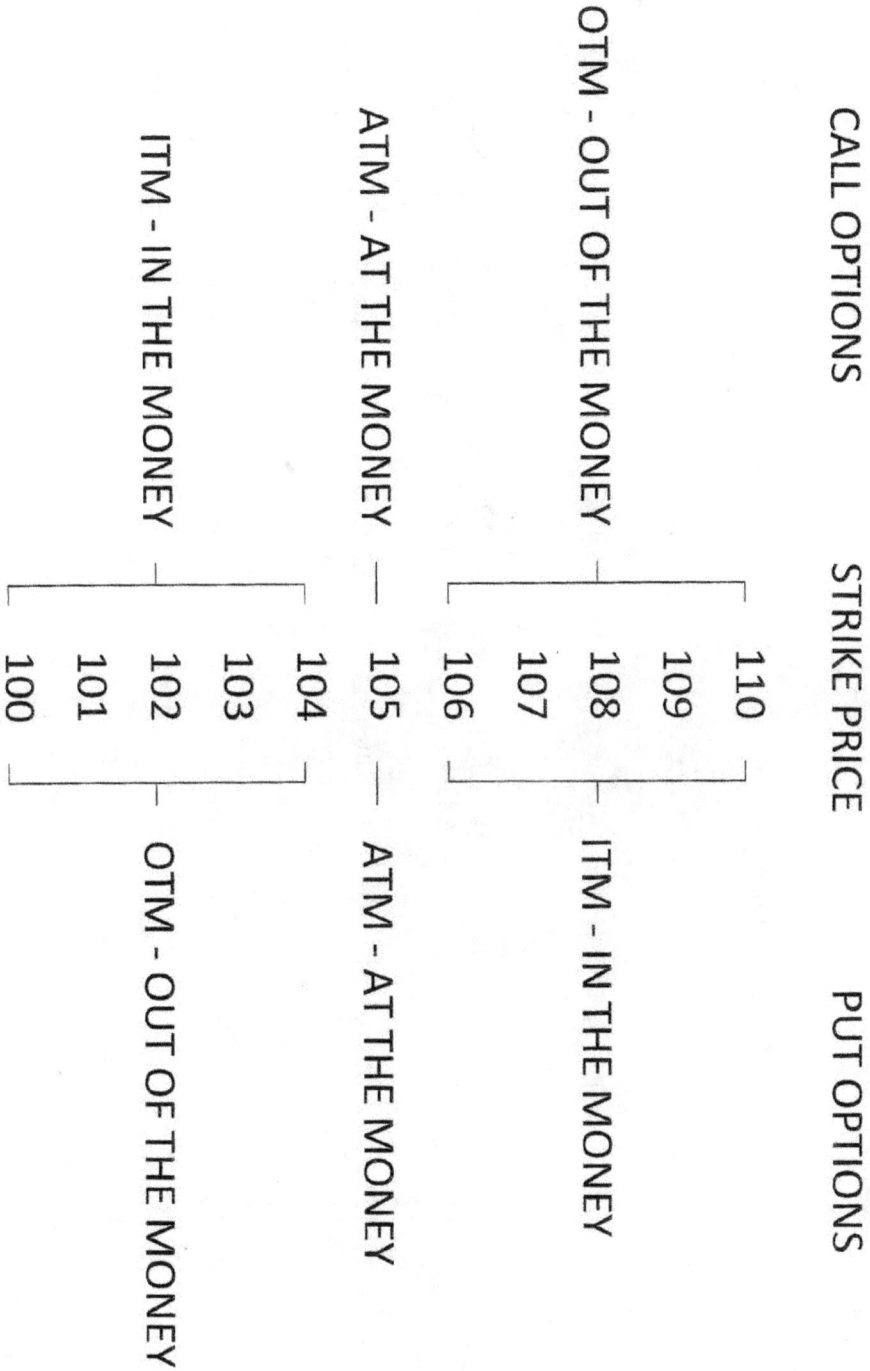

CALL OPTIONS	STRIKE PRICE	PUT OPTIONS
OTM - OUT OF THE MONEY	110	
	109	
	108	ITM - IN THE MONEY
	107	
	106	
ATM - AT THE MONEY	105	ATM - AT THE MONEY
	104	
	103	
ITM - IN THE MONEY	102	OTM - OUT OF THE MONEY
	101	
	100	

The diagram above helps explain when you would consider your strike At The Money (ATM), In The Money (ITM), and Out of The Money (OTM). This is based off the strike price in relation to the actual price, and if you are doing a Call or Put.

SINGLE LEG GREEK INFLUENCE OPTIONS CHART

	DELTA	VEGA	THETA	GAMMA	RHO
LONG CALL	WORKS FOR YOU	WORKS FOR YOU	WORKS AGAINST YOU	WORKS FOR YOU	WORKS FOR YOU
LONG PUT	WORKS AGAINST YOU	WORKS FOR YOU	WORKS AGAINST YOU	WORKS FOR YOU	WORKS AGAINST YOU
SHORT CALL (COVERED CALL)	WORKS AGAINST YOU	WORKS AGAINST YOU	WORKS FOR YOU	WORKS AGAINST YOU	WORKS FOR YOU
SHORT PUT (CASH SECURED PUT)	WORKS FOR YOU	WORKS AGAINST YOU	WORKS FOR YOU	WORKS AGAINST YOU	WORKS FOR YOU

The chart above shows how the Options Greeks affect a single leg Options trade.

- What happens when Delta increases?
- What happens when Vega increases?
- What happens as each day passes (Theta)?
- What happens when Gamma increases?
- What happens when Rho increases?

174

THETA TIME DECAY

PERCENT OF PREMIUM REMAINING

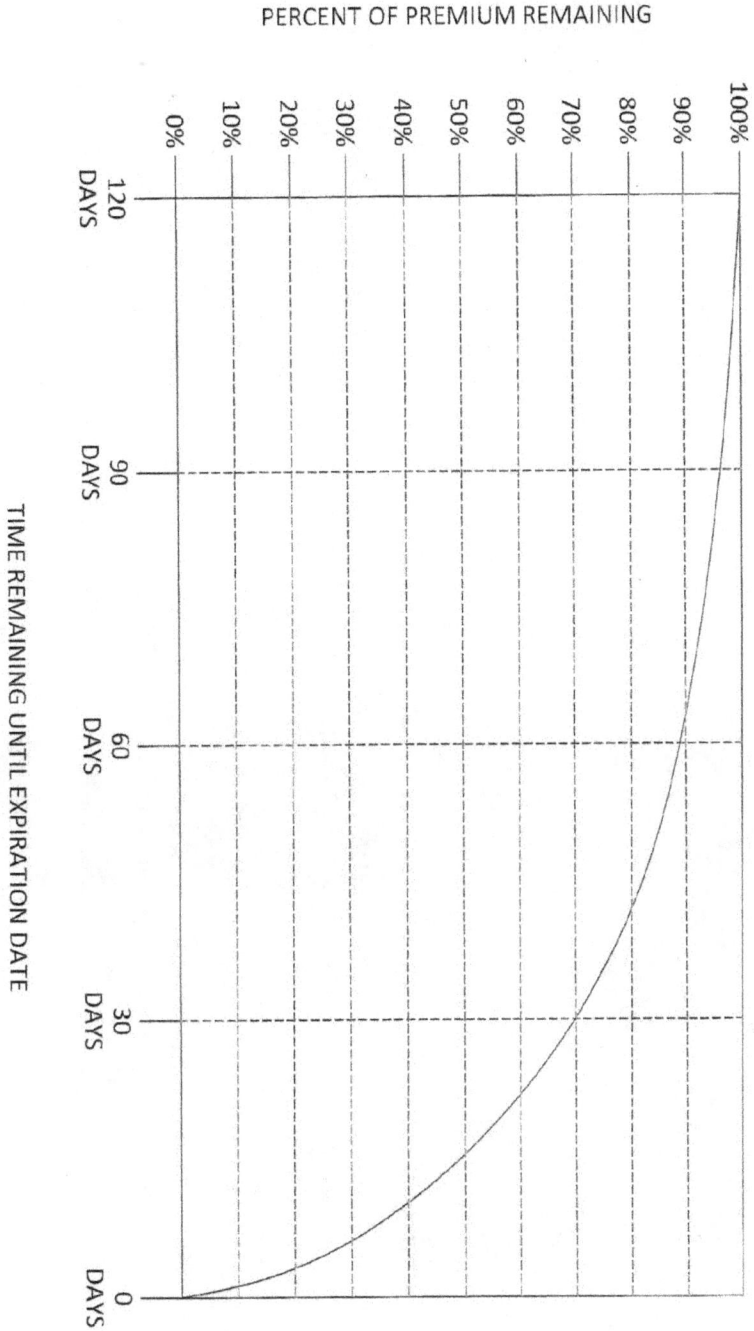

TIME REMAINING UNTIL EXPIRATION DATE

This chart shows you the typical affect that Theta has on Price as time goes on.

The percent of Premium (profit) decreases exponentially as you get closer to expiration.

This is why when you buy options, it is general practice to go further out in time to avoid Theta decay.

This is also why when you sell options, it is general practice to go closer to expiration to have Theta decay work in your favor.

This chart is for reference only, Please check your trading software for specifics based on your trade.

PLEASE READ

1. Any trading involves risk. Make sure you understand the risks involved, as you can lose all your money and more.

2. Keep in mind that Options trading is a leveraged trading style, where you can win or lose large amounts.

3. With Options, you need to be mindful of expiration dates, and make sure you close out of your trades if you are losing or happy with your profit, or roll your trades if you are still making money a few days prior to expiration.

4. Watch your obligation to be assigned, if you do not want to be assigned, you want to be mindful of where the price is once it gets close to assignment and have an exit strategy.

5. Always try out new trade ideas in a paper money account that doesn't involve real money to test it out to avoid big loses while learning the strategy. Once you prove you can be profitable, then you move the strategy to your money account.

TOP METAVERSE STOCKS

The newest craze in the technology world is the Metaverse. One of the biggest companies in the world, Facebook, changed its parent company name to "Meta" to shift the companies they own to the Metaverse. Everybody is on board with the future of technology, but some are taking different steps to get there. Some make the games, while others build the electronics for this space. The Metaverse is a whole ecosystem/world. It's a collective online space where physical and virtual realities merge. Metaverse stock is the capital raised by Metaverse–related businesses and corporations through the issuing and subscription of shares. I just wanted to give you some top stocks and ETFs in this space now so you don't miss out on anything; in my next book, I will break this industry down more, with more investment opportunities available.

Metaverse Stocks

- Roblox [RBLX] – online entertainment platform
- Match Group [MTCH]
- Take-Two Interactive [TTWO] video game publisher
- Nvidia [NVDA] produces graphic and video processing chips
- Unity Software [U] owns the most popular 3D video game engines
- Autodesk [ADSK] publishing ubiquitous industrial and architectural 3D design software.
- Microsoft [MSFT] Tech and software company. Owns several video game platforms.

Metaverse ETFs

- Roundhill ball Metaverse ETF
- The Simplify Volt Fintech Disruption EFT
- Subversive Metaverse ETF
- ProShares Metaverse ETF
- eToro Metaverse Life Smart Portfolio
- Evolve Metaverse ETF

- Horizons Global Metaverse Index ETF
- Defiance ETF
- Fount Metaverse ETF

SELF-DIRECTED IRAs

These IRAs allow asset protection while letting you invest, and did I mention they're tax-free? Welcome to the world of the wealthy. Billionaires hold billions of dollars in these tax-free accounts while you use 401(k)s to prepare for retirement. Maybe not you, but ask someone in your family if they have a 401(k). SDIRAs allow you to invest in real estate, private mortgages, private company stock, oil and gas limited partnerships, precious metals, digital assets, horses, livestock, and intellectual property. These accounts are only administered by a custodian or trustee, but you, the account holder, directly manage them. These are available either as a [Traditional IRA] to which you take tax-free distributions. Both are tax-advantaged accounts.

Opening one of these accounts is as simple as finding a qualified IRA custodian specializing in these types of SDIRA accounts. Some include:

- Equity Trust (www.trustetc.com)
- IRA Financial (www.irafinancialgroup.com)
- uDirect IRA (www.udirectira.com)
- The Entrust Group (www.theentrustgroup.com)
- Alto IRA (www.altoria.com)
- Rocket Dollar (www.rocketdollar.com)

Each one offers different types of investment options to you, but you choose what to invest in, not them. The key difference between a traditional and a Roth IRA is when you pay the taxes. Traditional IRAs allow you an up-front tax break, but you pay taxes on your contributions and earnings as you withdraw them during retirement. However, when you contribute to a Roth IRA, you don't get a tax break, but your contributions and earnings grow tax-free, and qualify distributions are tax-free.

SDIRAs open several potential investment pools to invest in, but one big thing is investment real estate being held in your SDIRA account. Even more special is that these accounts are so diverse that you can hold partnerships, tax liens, and franchise businesses. But as with all things that are good for you, some things can't be held in these accounts, such as life insurance, stocks from s-corporations, no self-dealing transactions, and no collectibles [antiques, toys, coins, comic books, and stamps]. If you don't follow the rules, the entire account could be considered distributed to you, which means you will be on the hook for all the taxes plus the penalty.

Using your SDIRA to purchase real estate investment property will require you to get a custodian, an entity specializing in self-directed accounts. That will manage the transition and associated paperwork. What will happen is that your IRA and you are separate entities. The IRA will own the property, not you. The property title will be in the IRA name, such as "ABC Trust Company Custodian (FBO [Your Name] IRA." FBO stats for "for the benefit of." Must stay as an investment, no vacations there, or second home, must be to flip, sell, or rent out to someone else. You can't buy any investment real estate from family members [self-dealing], nor can you/IRA purchase property you already own. Don't be stupid; build wealth; you don't have to cheat to win. Make sure it's done the right way. Build/start your business, hire yourself as an employee, and start to build wealth through an SDIRA. One of the highest-profile billionaires to use this strategy is Peter Thiel, founder of Pay-Pal with Elon Musk, who had $5 billion in a Roth IRA since 2019. What he did, so can you, because it all follows the same laws you would have to follow. Because the Roth IRA allows you to hold alternative assets, i.e., private company shares or real estate, Thiel was able to shelter his investments while getting tax-free growth and untaxed distributions. SDIRAs can be used as Peter Thiel did without breaking laws, but other investments can be put in an SDIRA, such as:

- Real Estate Syndications
- LLCs
- Farm Animals
- Partnerships
- Cryptocurrency
- Movie Projects
- Oil/Gas
- Precious Metals
- Private Stock [Think of Peter Thiel]
- Equipment Leasing
- Forex Accounts

It is easy to do these types of investments above; remember, just pick a custodian from the list above or another you like, fund it via cash contribution, or if you already have a 401(k) or regular IRA, you can transfer funds from these existing accounts. Pick your investment from the approved list above and start building wealth directed by you, not some pension fund manager on Wall Street, who gets paid whether he/she loses your money or makes you money. Another thing is that there are no limits to the number of IRA accounts you can own. You should only know that the IRS limits annual contribution maximums across all your accounts. If you want to read about how to set up an LLC with your IRA, see the checklist and operating agreement enclosed to study. It is provided by www.irallcchecklist.com, a leading company with over 2,500+ clients and 17 years in business doing this.

American IRA
Self-Directed IRAs and 401Ks

NEW VISION TRUST COMPANY
Custodian,
A South Dakota Trust Company

New Account Checklist

Step 1:

To open your IRA with American IRA, LLC we will need:

- **Account Application** (Complete all pages)
- **Photo ID** (submit a copy of your driver's license, passport, or valid government-issued photo ID)

Once you've completed all required forms, send to:

By Mail: American IRA, LLC -135 Broad Street, Asheville NC 28801
Overnight: American IRA, LLC -135 Broad Street, Asheville NC 28801
By Fax: (828) 257-4948
By Email: NewAccounts@AmericanIRA.com

Step 2:

Fund your account

- **Transfer Form:** Use this form to transfer funds from your existing IRA to your new IRA.
  Please note that your existing IRA custodian may require a Medallion Guarantee Stamp, which is much like a notary seal. Check with your bank to obtain this stamp.
- **Rollover/Direct Rollover Form:** This form documents the rollover of your cash or asset to your new IRA. You will need to contact your current provider to initiate the rollover.
  - A rollover contribution occurs when you take receipt of assets or cash for up to 60 days before reinvesting in a new retirement plan.
  - A direct rollover contribution occurs when you move assets or cash directly from your qualified retirement plan to a new retirement plan.

Step 3:

Read and keep the following forms for your files:

- 5305 Custodial Agreement – is available online
- Copy of Application

Need Help? Call 1-866-7500-IRA(472) and a client services representative will assist you in opening your account today!

American IRA, LLC
Processing Office-135 Broad Street | Asheville, NC 28801 | (828) 257-4949
AmericanIRA.com

New Vision Trust Company
401 E. 8th Street, Suite 200 R
Sioux Falls, SD 57103

American IRA
Self-Directed IRAs and 401Ks

135 Broad Street, Asheville, NC 28801
Phone: (828) 257-4949, Fax (828)257-4948
Email: NewAccounts@AmericanIRA.com

NEW VISION TRUST COMPANY

Custodian,
A South Dakota Trust Company
401 E. 8th Street, Suite 200 R
Sioux Falls, SD 57103

New Account Application

To initiate the account, please complete, sign and return:
- ☐ IRA Account Application
- ☐ Photocopy of your Government Issued ID (Patriot Act requirement)

1 Personal Information

Legal Name:	Birthdate:(mm/dd/yyyy)	Social Security Number:
☐ Mr. ☐ Ms. ☐ Mrs. ☐ Dr. _____		

Physical Address: (Required)	City, State, Zip:

Mailing Address: (Optional)	City, State, Zip:

Primary Phone:	Mobile:	Would you like to receive text messages regarding your account? ☐ Yes ☐ No

Current/Most Recent Occupation: (Required)	Title:	Marital Status: ☐ Single ☐ Married ☐ Widowed or Divorced

Email Address:	Driver's License Number:

2 Account Type

☐ ROTH	☐ SEP IRA – Complete SEP5305	☐ SIMPLE IRA
☐ Traditional	Employer Name:	Employer Name: _____
☐ Coverdell –Complete Coverdell Supplement Page	☐ Inherited IRA	
☐ Health Savings Account Check one: ☐ Self-only coverage ☐ Family Coverage	Check one: ☐ Traditional ☐ Roth ☐ SEP ☐ SIMPLE Original IRA Holder Name: _____	

3 Account Funding

☐ Annual Contribution	☐ Transfer Contribution Transfer from existing IRA or Employer Sponsored Plan.	☐ Rollover Contribution Take receipt of the assets for up to 60 days before reinvesting in a new retirement plan.	☐ Direct Rollover Contribution Rollover from Employer Sponsored Plan. (401k, 403b, 457, TSP)

4 Notifications

- **MINIMUM ACCOUNT BALANCE $750**
- All emails are sent encrypted for your safety.
- Statements will be e-mailed all account holders on an annual basis.

- We, American IRA, LLC, will call you, the Account Holder, to verify and confirm any outbound movement of cash from your account when we receive instructions requesting to send funds from your account. We will call you at the telephone number on file for you.

How did you hear about us? ☐ Internet ☐ REIA Group ☐ CPA ☐ Attorney ☐ Advisor ☐ Other:_____

5 Interested Party Designation

I hereby authorize the following representative as interested party on my self-directed IRA. I understand this named representative will have access to my account details, balance, holdings and any other account related activity. Interested parties DO NOT have the ability to sign on your behalf or move funds in or out of your self-directed account. I also understand that this will remain in effect until revoked in writing.

Name: (Individuals only)	Phone:	Email:
Name: (Individuals only)	Phone:	Email:

Would you like the named interested party to be provided a login to view your account online? ☐ Yes ☐ No

6 — Beneficiary Information

Name (first, middle, last) Address (including country of residence)	Date of Birth (mm/dd/yyyy)	Social Security Number	Country of Citizenship	Relationship	Primary or Contingent?	Share %
1.						
2.						
3.						
4.						

Current Marital Status: ☐ **I am not married** – I understand that if I become in the future, I must complete a new Beneficiary Designation form.

☐ **I am married** – I understand that if I choose to designate a primary beneficiary other than my spouse, my spouse must sign below.

Spousal Consent (only required if your spouse is not the Primary Beneficiary – see note below)

The consent of spouse must be signed only if all of the following conditions are present:

    a. Your spouse is living;

    b. Your spouse is not the sole Primary Beneficiary name and;

    c. You and your spouse are residents of a community property state (such as AZ, CA, ID, NV, MN, TX, WA, LA, or NV)

I, the undersigned, am the spouse of the Custodial Account holder whose name is listed above. I hereby certify that I have reviewed the Designation of Beneficiary form and I understand that I have a property interest in the Custodial Account. I acknowledge that I have received a fair and reasonable disclosure of my spouse's property and financial obligations. I further acknowledge and consent to the above Designation of Beneficiary, other than myself, as the primary beneficiary. I also understand that, by signing this, I am giving up all, or part, of my rights to receive benefits under this plan in the event my spouse dies. I assume full responsibility for any adverse consequences that may result. I have been advised to seek the advice of an attorney and/or financial advisor prior to signing any documents and I have sought the advice of counsel and/or financial advisor or do hereby waive my right to do so. No tax or legal advice has been given to me by the Custodian and/or Administrator related to this matter.

Signature of Spouse: _____ **Date:** _____

Account Owner Signature

In the event of my death, the balance in the account shall be paid to the Primary Beneficiaries who survive me in equal shares (or in the specified shares, if indicated). If the Primary or Contingent Beneficiary box is not checked for a beneficiary, the beneficiary will be deemed to be a Primary Beneficiary. If none of the Primary Beneficiaries survive me, the balance in the account shall be paid to the Contingent Beneficiaries who survive me in equal shares (or in the specified shares, if indicated). If I name a beneficiary which is a Trust, I understand I must provide certain information concerning such Trust to the Custodian.

I understand that I may change or add beneficiaries at any time by completing and delivering the proper form to the Administrator.

Account Holder Signature: _____ **Date:** _____

LEFT BLANK INTENTIONALLY

8 Acknowledgement

Custodian and Administrator: The Custodian for my Account will be New Vision Trust Company, a State Chartered South Dakota Trust Company, and the Administrator for my Account will be American IRA, LLC, A North Carolina Limited Liability Company, as identified in the Custodial Account Agreement (IRS Form 5305A, 5305-RA, 5305-SA, 5305-SEP, 5305-C, and 5305-EA). I understand that the Custodian may resign by giving me written notice at least 30 days prior to the effective date of such resignation. I understand that if I fail to notify the Custodian and/or Administrator of the appointment of a successor trustee or custodian within such 30 day period, then the assets held by the Custodian in my Account (whether in cash or personal or real property wherever located, and regardless of value) will be distributed to me, outright and free of trust, and I will be wholly responsible for the tax consequences of such distribution.

My Account is "Self-Directed" What does "Self-Directed" mean? Self-Directed means I, as the Holder of the Account, am solely responsible for the investment of all assets within my Account and giving Custodian and/or Administrator the directives to take any action on behalf of the Account. That means I am responsible for the selection, management, monitoring and retention of all investments held within my Account. The investments I select may involve a high degree of risk, and neither Custodian nor the Administrator will provide investment advice nor make any investigation or determination as to the prudence, viability, suitability, legality, or safety of the investments that I select. The assets selected for investment are solely my responsibility. This requires that I assure myself of the financial soundness and appropriateness of the investment for my Account and retirement objectives and I should have all investments reviewed by a competent legal, tax, and/or financial advisor.

No Investment Advice: I acknowledge and agree that the Custodian does not provide or assume responsibility for any tax, legal or investment advice with respect to the investments and assets in the Custodial Account and shall not be liable for any loss which results from my exercise of control over the Custodial Account. I further understand and agree that the Custodian neither sells nor endorses any investment products. If the services of the Custodian were marketed, suggested or otherwise recommended by any person or entity, such as a financial representative or investment promoter, I understand that such promoters and/or marketers are not in any way agents, employees, representatives, affiliates, partners, independent contractors, consultants, or subsidiaries of the Custodian, and that the Custodian is not responsible for and are not bound by any statements, representations, warranties or agreements made by any such promoter, marketer or entity. I agree to consult with my own CPA, attorney, financial planner and/or any other professionals I deem necessary or advisable, prior to directing the Custodian to make any investment in my Account. I and my beneficiary(ies) release, indemnify and agree to hold the Custodian harmless in the event that any investment or sale of the assets in the Custodial Account, pursuant to a direction by me or my Investment Advisor, violates any federal or state law or regulation or otherwise results in a disqualification, penalty, tax or fine imposed upon the Custodian, the Administrator, me or the Custodial Account.

Account Fees I have agreed, by opening an Account with Custodian and/or Administrator, to pay all fees and charges that are made against my Account in accordance with the Fee Schedule provided and incorporated by reference herein. All fees are due upon presentment. If, after notice, my Account remains past due for 30 days and if no cash available in my Account, Custodian and/or Administrator may liquidate assets within the Account to satisfy these obligations. If my Account is unfunded with zero value, I understand my Account will continue to incur IRA fees until I provide written notice to Custodian and/or Administrator

Non-Endorsement Custodian and/or Administrator do not endorse any investment made by me, or provide any investment advice to me about my investments. Custodian and/or Administrator's review of investments is for the sole benefit of Custodian and/or Administrator for the purpose of determination of administrative and/or legal feasibility of the investment and should not be construed as an endorsement or opinion of any investment, investment company, or investment strategy. Custodian and/or Administrator do not endorse any broker, financial advisor, investment advisor, or other party involved with the investments chosen by me. Neither Custodian nor Administrator conducts any due diligence review of any investment, nor will Custodian and/or Administrator make any investigation with regards to any investment, any issuer or sponsor of any investment, or any officer, director, or other person or entity involved or affiliated with any investment. I understand and agree that Custodian and/or Administrator will not review or evaluate the prudence, viability, suitability, legality, or merits of any investment held in my Custodial Account. I understand that Custodian and/or Administrator permit my Account to invest in a wide variety of investments based on administrative factors only.

Indemnification: The Custodian shall have no duty other than to follow the written instructions of me, my agents, investment advisors and/or Designated Beneficiaries, and shall be under no duty to question said instructions and shall not be liable for any investment losses sustained by me under any circumstances. By performing services under this Agreement, the Custodian is acting as the agent of me, and nothing in this Agreement shall be construed as conferring fiduciary status on the Custodian. I agree to release, defend, indemnify and hold harmless the Custodian from any and all liability, claims, damages, actions, costs, expenses (including, without limitation, all reasonable attorneys' fees) arising from or related to the Custodial Agreement and/or Custodial Account, including but not limited to, losses to me and/or to my beneficiary(ies) as a result of any action taken (or omitted to be taken) pursuant to and/or in connection with any investment transaction directed by me, my agents, investment advisors and/or Designated Beneficiaries, including, without limitation, claims, damages, liability, actions and losses asserted by me or my beneficiary(ies). I agree to reimburse and/or advance to Custodian and/or Administrator, on demand, all legal fees, expenses, costs, fines, penalties and obligations incurred or to be incurred in connection with the defense, contest, prosecution or satisfaction of any claim made, threatened or asserted pertaining to any investment or action me, or my agent, directed through the Custodian, including, without limitation, claims asserted by me, any state or federal regulatory authority or self-regulatory organization. In the event of claims by others related to my Account and/or investment wherein the Custodian is named as a party, the Custodian shall have the full and unequivocal right, at their sole discretion, to select their own attorneys to represent them in such litigation and deduct from my Account any amounts to pay for any costs and expenses, including, but not limited to, all reasonable attorneys' fees, and costs and internal costs (collectively "Litigation Costs"), incurred by the Custodian in the defense of such claims and/or litigation.

Prohibited Transactions: I understand that my Account is subject to the provisions of Internal Revenue Code (IRC) Section 4975, which defines certain prohibited transactions. I acknowledge and agree that neither the Custodian nor the Administrator will make any determination as to whether any transaction or investment in my Account is prohibited under sections 4975, 408(e) or 408A, or under any other state or federal law. I accept full responsibility to ensure that none of the investments in my Account will constitute a prohibited transaction and that the investments in my Account comply with all applicable federal and state laws, regulations and requirements.

Responsibility for determining eligibility and tax consequences: I assume complete responsibility for 1) determining that I am eligible to make a contribution to my Account; 2) ensuring that all contributions I make are within the limits set forth by the relevant sections of the Internal Revenue Code; and 3) the tax consequences of any contribution (including a rollover contribution) and distributions.

Unrelated Business Income Tax: I understand that my Account is subject to the provisions of IRC Sections 511-514 relating to Unrelated Business Taxable Income (UBTI) of tax-exempt organizations. I agree that if I direct the Custodian and/or Administrator to make an investment in my Account which generates UBTI, I will be responsible for preparing or having prepared the required IRS Form 990-T tax return, an application for an Employer Identification Number (EIN) for my Account, and any other documents that may be required, and to submit them to the Custodian and/or Administrator for filing with the Internal Revenue Service at least ten (10) days prior to the date on which the return is due, along with an appropriate directive authorizing the Custodian and/or Administrator to execute the forms on behalf of my Account and to pay the applicable tax from the assets in my Account. I understand that the Custodian and the Administrator do not make any determination of whether or not investments in my Account generate UBTI; have no duty to and do not monitor whether or not my Account has incurred UBTI; and do not prepare Form 990-T on behalf of my Account.

Valuations: I understand that the assets in my Account are required to be valued annually at the end of each calendar year in accordance with IRC Section 408(i) or 223 (h) and other guidance provided by the IRS, and that the total value of my Account will be reported to the IRS on Form 5498 each year. I agree to provide the year end value of any illiquid and/or non-publicly traded investments, which may include without limitation limited partnerships, limited liability companies, privately held stock, real estate investment trusts, hedge funds, real estate, secured and unsecured promissory notes, and any other investments as the Custodian and/or Administrator shall designate, by no later than January 10th of each year, with substantiation attached to support the value provided. I agree to indemnify and hold harmless the Custodian and the Administrator from any and all losses, expenses, settlements, or claims with regard to investment decisions, distribution values, tax reporting or any other financial impact or consequence relating to or arising from the valuation of assets in my Account.

Payment Instructions I agree to furnish payment instructions to Custodian and/or Administrator regarding any invoice, assessment, fee or any other disbursement notification received by the Custodian and/or Administrator on behalf of my investments, and I understand that neither Custodian and/or Administrator has any duty or responsibility to disburse any payment until such instructions are received from me or my Designated Representative. Written direction shall include signature by facsimile or by electronic signature.

Non-FDIC-Insured Investments I acknowledge my investments are non-FDIC-insured and subject to loss in value. My investments may involve a substantial risk, may lack liquidity, and may result in a total loss of the investment my acknowledge and confirm that all risk and loss sustained in my Retirement Account will not affect my retirement income standard; and if a mandatory distribution arises, that I will meet any mandatory distribution requirements by utilizing my IRA and/or other retirement Accounts.

Electronic Communications, Signatures, and Records: Subject to any limitations contained in Treasury Regulation section 1.401(a)-21 and any other applicable federal or state law or regulation, I acknowledge and agree that the Custodial Account shall be subject to the provisions of the Uniform Electronic Transactions Act, as passed in the state where the Custodian is organized (South Dakota Codified Law Sections 53-12 et. seq.), and the federal Electronic Signature in Global and National Commerce Act (ESIGN Act, as contained in 15 U.S.C. 7001), as those laws pertain to electronic communication, electronic signatures, and electronic storage of Custodial Account records. In lieu of the retention of the original records, the Custodian may cause any, or all, of its records, and records at any time in its custody, to be photographed or otherwise reproduced to permanent form, and any such photograph or reproduction shall have the same force and effect as the original thereof and may be admitted in evidence equally with the original.

Affiliated Business Disclosure and Conflict of Interest Waiver: The Custodian, New Vision Trust Company, a State Chartered South Dakota Trust Company and American IRA, LLC, a North Carolina limited liability company (Administrator) are affiliated companies by reason of their common ownership and management. Because the two companies are under common ownership and management, the owners of American IRA, LLC, a North Carolina limited liability company will enjoy a direct and/or indirect financial benefit from the fees I pay to New Vision Trust Company, a State Chartered South Dakota Trust Company. By signing the Account Application, I acknowledge and understand that: 1) New Vision Trust Company, a State Chartered South Dakota Trust Company and American IRA, LLC, a North Carolina limited liability company are under common ownership and control. 2) by retaining New Vision Trust Company, a State Chartered South Dakota Trust Company, the Depositor is providing a financial benefit to the owners of American IRA, LLC, a North Carolina limited liability company 3) I am under no obligation to retain New Vision Trust Company, a State Chartered South Dakota Trust Company and that I am free to retain the services of another, unaffiliated Custodian, and 4) I, do acknowledge and confirm that I chose New Vision Trust Company, a State Chartered South Dakota Trust Company freely and with no influence from the Custodian and/or Administrator.

Investment Funding Requirements I understand and agree that I cannot make investments without having available liquid funds in my Account. In addition, if any investment contains provisions for future contractual payments or assessments, (including margin calls), I acknowledge and agree that such payments or assessments shall be borne solely by my Account to the extent such payment is authorized by me or my Designated Representative, and may reduce or exhaust the value of my Account. I further agree to indemnify Custodian and/or Administrator for any and all payments or assessments which may imposed as a result of holding the investment within my Account, and I agree that neither Custodian nor Administrator shall be under any obligation to extend credit to my Account or otherwise disburse payment beyond the cash balance of my Account for any payment or assessment related to the investment. I agree that I am solely responsible for verifying that any bills to be paid from my Account, and accompanying payment instructions, have been received by Custodian and/or Administrator. I further agree that neither Custodian nor Administrator shall be responsible for late fees assessed by any third party where I have not verified that payment instructions have been received, or where the receipt of instructions or documentations has been delayed. Any funds received into a Custodian and/or Administrator Account which is made by check may be subject to a seven (7) business day clearing period before funds are available to invest. ALL NEW ACCOUNTS are subject to a seven (7) calendar day waiting period before any funds can be invested.

9   Fee Schedule

One Time Account establishment: $50 (paid upon initial application)

Annual Fees

☐ Option One: $285 annually

- $95 transaction fee (Purchase/Sale of an Asset)
- Minimum Account Balance $750

☐ Option Two: $450 annually

- Unlimited transactions (Purchase/Sale of an Asset)
- Minimum Account Balance $750

Accounts under $7500 pay an Annual Fee of only $165 or $330 for unlimited transactions!

Processing Fees

- Wire Transfer (incoming/outgoing): $30
- Cashier's Check (includes overnight shipping): $50
- ACH/Trust/Voided Checks: $10
- Certified Mailing: $10
- Overnight Mailing: $20 plus shipping costs
- Notary: $5

Miscellaneous Fees

- Exchange, Re-registration, Re-characterization of an Asset/Liability or Leveraged Asset: $95
- Special services, such as but not limited to, research of closed accounts, processing foreclosures, and tax issues $75 per 1/2 hour. (Minimum charge in increments of half hour.)
- Federal or State Tax Withholding $10
- Expedited Investment Review: $95
- Partial or Full Account Termination - Includes transfer of assets from your account and lump-sum distributions: .005 of the termination value (plus applicable transaction fees): min$150 - max $500.
- Deposit Research (if deposit coupon is not included with deposit) $25
- Copy/Cleared/Canceled checks; Reproducing tax documents (5498/1099); Duplicate Statements $15
- Returned Items, Stop Payment Request, Credit Card Decline $30
- Regularly Scheduled Distribution Fee(Monthly/Quarterly/Annually)$25
- 990-T Processing, Reversal of Fees for Alternate Payment Method $50
- If fees are deducted from your account causing your cash balance to fall below the required minimum account balance $25 per month until account is brought back to the minimum balance.

*Annual Record keeping Fees are not prorated when an account closes.

A credit card convenience fee of 4% will be charged for all credit card transactions

Pay Fees By: ☐ Visa   ☐ MC   ☐ AMEX   ☐ Discover   ☐ Deduct fees from my undirected cash account

Card Number:_____   Exp. Date_____   Security Code:_____

Name on Card: _____   Billing Zip Code:_____

> A credit card is required with each account

Annual account fees are not prorated and are withdrawn from undirected funds (defined as any cash in the Custodial Account not invested pursuant to a specific investment direction by you, as the depositor, hereinafter referred to as "Depositor"), unless Depositor elects to pay by credit card or debit card as specified above. Transaction fees are due prior to funding the transaction. Fees paid from Depositor's account will be reflected on Depositor's statements, which are available online. If there are insufficient undirected funds in Depositor's account, or where any credit card payments are declined, Custodian may liquidate other assets in Depositor's account to pay for such fees after a 30-day notification, in accordance with the Custodial Agreement and Disclosure Statement. Late Payment Fees: Depositor will be charged $25 per month, or any portion of any month, an invoice remains past due, or the maximum allowable under applicable state law. Depositor agrees and directs Custodian that Depositor's un-directed cash be placed into a state and/or Federal banking institution, unless Custodian is otherwise directed by Depositor. Depositor understand that if fees are not paid within thirty (30) days after Custodian has provided a written past due notice, Custodian may begin the process of closing Depositor's account. Depositor understands that any asset distributed directly to Depositor as part of closing Depositor's account will be reported to the IRS on Form 1099 and may subject Depositor to possible taxes and penalties. Depositor agrees that accounts with past due fees, unfunded accounts, and accounts with zero value will continue to incur administrative fees until such time as Depositor notifies Custodian, of intent Depositor's to close the account or until Custodian resigns. In accordance with Depositor's Account Application, this Fee Disclosure is part of Depositor's Agreement with the Custodian and must accompany Depositor's Application. Custodian reserve the right to change its Fee Schedule at any time with a 30-day notice to Depositor.

10   Account Acceptance

By my signature below, I acknowledge and declare that I have examined this New Account Application, and to the best of my knowledge and belief, it is true, correct and complete. I further declare and acknowledge I have read the Custodial Agreement (Forms 5305A, 5305-RA, 5305-SA, 5305-SEP, 5305-C, and 5305-EA), Fee Schedule, Privacy Notice and Account Disclosure Statement and agree to abide by the terms as currently written, or as they may be amended from time to time. In the event of a conflict between this New Account Application, Fee Schedule, Privacy Notice and/or Account Disclosure Statement, the Custodial Agreement shall govern. This Agreement, which shall include the Custodial Agreement, Fee Schedule, Privacy Notice, New Account Application and Account Disclosure Statement, is the complete and exclusive agreement between the parties with respect to my Custodial Account and shall supersede any prior agreements and communications (both written and oral) related to my Custodial Account.

Account Holder Signature:_____

Account Holder Printed Name:_____ Date:_____

Custodian(or authorized representative) Signature:_____

Printed Name:_____ Date:_____

American IRA
Self-Directed IRA and 401Ks
135 Broad Street, Asheville, NC 28801
Phone: (828) 257-4949, Fax (828)257-4948
Email: NewAccounts@AmericanIRA.com

Transfer Form

NEW VISION TRUST
COMPANY
Custodian,
A South Dakota Trust Company
401 E. 8ᵗʰ Street, Suite 200 R
Sioux Falls, SD 57103

1	**Account Information**

Your Name:	Social Security Number:
Address:	City, State, Zip:
Phone Number:	American IRA Account Number:

2	**Current Custodian/Trustee Information**

Name of Custodian/Trustee:	Account Number:
Address:	City, State, Zip:
Phone Number: ☐ I have attached a copy of my current statement **(Required)**	Type of account: ☐ Traditional ☐ Roth ☐ SEP ☐ 401k ☐ HSA ☐ CESA ☐ SIMPLE ☐ Inherited

3	**Transfer Details**

☐ Option One: Cash Transfer

  ☐ Complete
  ☐ Partial – SEND ONLY $ _____
Please send cash via: ☐ Check ☐ Wire

☐ Option Two: In-Kind Transfer

  ☐ Complete
  ☐ Partial – Send ONLY the assets listed below
Please send cash via: ☐ Check ☐ Wire

Checks and In-Kind Transfers are to be titled as New Vision Trust Custodian FBO (Account Name) (Account Type)
Wired funds are available following business day. Check funds are available after 7 business days.

How would you like this request sent to your current custodian? ☐ Certified Mail ($10)   ☐ Overnight Mail ($20 plus shipping costs)

Asset Description	Amount

4	**Signature and Acknowledgement**

1. I hereby agree to the terms and conditions set forth in the Type of Asset to be Transferred section and acknowledge having established a self-directed account through the execution of the (type of plan) account application.
2. I understand the rules and conditions applicable to an Account Transfer.
3. I qualify for the account transfer of assets listed in the Type of Asset to be Transferred section above and authorize such transactions.
4. I understand that no one at the Custodian and/or Administrator has authority to agree to anything different than my foregoing understandings of Custodian and/or Administrator policy.
5. By my signature below, I confirm that I have read and consent to the terms of this document and I further acknowledge that I have read and consent to the terms of the New Account Application, Custodial Agreement (Form 5305, 5305-A, 5305-RA, 5305-SA, 5305-SEP, 5305-C or 5305-EA, as application, "collectively referred to as "5305" or 401K Plan Agreement ("Sponsored Plan") as applicable, Fee Schedule, Account Disclosure Statement and any other documents that govern my Custodial Account or Sponsored Plan, as such documents are currently written, or as they may be amended from time to time, (the "Documents"), which are incorporated by reference herein. (In the event of a conflict between the Documents and the 5305 and/or Sponsored Plan applicable to my Custodial Account, the 5305 or Sponsored Plan shall govern).

Your Signature: _____

Date: _____

(Medallion Guarantee Stamp)

Acceptance of Receiving Custodian

By signing this form the Custodian accepts of the transfer, rollover or direct rollover described above and agrees to apply the proceeds upon receipt to the Account established by the Custodian, on your behalf. The Custodian ASSUMES NO TRUST OR FIDUCIARY OBLIGATIONS TO YOU AS IT HAS NO INVESTMENT CONTROL OVER YOUR FUNDS AND ACTS ONLY AS PASSIVE CUSTODIAN OF YOUR FUNDS.

New Vision Trust Company, A State Chartered South Dakota Trust Company

By: _____

Date: _____

Account Number: _____

Type of Account
☐ Traditional   ☐ Roth   ☐ SEP   ☐ 401k   ☐ HSA   ☐ CESA
☐ Inherited   ☐ SIMPLE

Corporate Headquarters: New Vision Trust Company, 401 E. 8th Street, Suite 200R, Sioux Falls, South Dakota 57103

Rev. 04/18

Page 1 of 1

American IRA
Self Directed IRAs and 401Ks
135 Broad Street, Asheville, NC 28801
Phone: (828) 257-4949, Fax (828)257-4948
Email: NewAccounts@AmericanIRA.com

Rollover/Direct Rollover
Form

NEW VISION TRUST COMPANY
Custodian,
A South Dakota Trust Company
401 E. 8ᵗʰ Street, Suite 200 R
Sioux Falls, SD 57103

1	**Account Information**		
Your Name:		Your SSN:	
Address:		City, State, Zip:	
Phone Number:		American IRA Account Number:	

2	**Current Custodian/Trustee Information**
Name of Custodian/Trustee:	Account Number:
Address:	City, State, Zip:
Phone Number:	Is this an Inherited Account?	Type of account: ☐ Traditional ☐ Roth ☐ SEP ☐ Qualified Plan ☐ HSA ☐ ESA ☐ SIMPLE

3	**Rollover Details**

The total amount I am rolling over is: $ _____   ☐ Indirect Rollover   ☐ Direct Rollover

I am an eligible person to perform this transaction: (select one)

☐ Plan Participant   ☐ Spouse Beneficiary of Account   ☐ Non-spouse Beneficiary of Account   ☐ Responsible Individual
☐ Ex-spouse of account due to divorce/legal separation or court order

Rollover Instructions to Resigning Custodian

To roll over CASH, please follow the instruction below. Contact our office for wire instructions.
To roll over INVESTMENTS (Private Stock, Real Estate, LLCs, Notes, etc.), please complete the asset description below and contact us regarding the re-registration of your investment.
Cash and Assets are to be made payable/assigned to: New Vision Trust Custodian FBO (Account Name) (Account Type)

Asset Description:	Amount:

4	**Signature and Acknowledgement**

By my signature below, I confirm that I have read and consent to the terms of this document and I further acknowledge that I have read and consent to the terms of the New Account Application, Custodial Agreement (Form 5305, 5305-A, 5305-RA, 5305-SA, 5305-SEP, 5305-C or 5305-EA, as application, "collectively referred to as "5305" or 401K Plan Agreement ("Sponsored Plan") as applicable, Fee Schedule, Account Disclosure Statement and any other documents that govern my Custodial Account or Sponsored Plan as such documents are currently written, or as they may be amended from time to time, (the "Documents"), which are incorporated by reference herein. (In the event of a conflict between the Documents and the 5305 and/or Sponsored Plan applicable to my Custodial Account, the 5305 or Sponsored Plan shall govern).

I hereby agree to the terms and conditions set forth in this rollover form and acknowledge having established a Self-Directed Account through execution of the (Type of Account) Account Application. I understand the rules and conditions applicable to a **Rollover or Direct Rollover**. I qualify for the ☐ Rollover or ☐ Direct Rollover of assets listed in the Asset Liquidation above and authorizes such transactions. If this is a Rollover or Direct Rollover, I have been advised to see a tax advisor due to the important tax consequences of rolling assets into a self-direct account. If this is a Rollover or Direct Rollover, I assume full responsibility for this Rollover or Direct Rollover transaction and will not hold the Plan Administrator, Custodian, as disclosed in the Custodial Agreement, or Issuer of either the distributing or receiving plan liable for any adverse consequences that may result. I understand that no one at Custodian and/or Administrator has authority to agree to anything different than my foregoing understandings of Custodian and/or Administrator policy. If this is a Rollover or Direct Rollover, I irrevocably designate this contribution of assets with a value of $ _____ as a rollover contribution. *By signing this form, I certify that I am completing this rollover within:*

A. 60 calendar days following the day I received the assets, I have not performed a rollover from an IRA within the last 12 months and the rollover DOES NOT contain my

Required Minimum Distribution

B. If I am a non-spouse beneficiary, this is a direct roll over from an employer plan and the rollover contribution DOES NOT contain my Required Minimum Distribution.

Print Name: _____

Your Signature: _____   Date: _____

Corporate Headquarters: New Vision Trust Company, 401 E. 8th Street, Suite 200R, Sioux Falls, South Dakota 57103

Rev. 04/18

Page **1** of **1**

187

COMMODITIES INVESTING

Commodity investing pre-dates stock and bond exchanges. Starting with spices and silk, now on exchanges spanning the globe. There are many ways to invest in commodities, either directly or indirectly by buying shares in companies or exchange traded funds [ETF].

Inflation is higher than it has been in 40 years. However, commodities are a sector that has been proven to protect your investment from them. Commodities demand goes up during inflation. Compared to the U.S. Dollar, commodity prices rise while the dollar declines. Oil is a commodity that's not just used for fuel like gasoline but also is refined to include other products such as plastics, medicines, linoleum, shingles, ink, cosmetics, synthetic fibers, solvents, fertilizer, asphalt, etc. Supply and demand control oil prices generally; when demand exceeds supply, prices tend to rise. When demand falls, prices fall. Although OPEC used to control the global crude oil markets, which means the Middle East, the U.S. is now the world's largest net producer of crude oil and also leads in natural gas.

Making investments in this commodity isn't easy because they don't sell oil at the store. The most direct path to owning oil outright is "Futures" [This will be discussed in detail in my next book], but that is a volatile, capital-intense sector that I won't go into detail about until my next book. So, let's focus on other practical investments to make money. Purchasing stock in oil companies, crude oil mutual funds [I prefer not using mutual funds], but I will supply the info, and you take the action. ETFs that focus on oil commodities and trade on the stock market are easy investments.

Some examples of these top stocks are:

- Occidental Petroleum [OXY]
- Hess [HES]
- Coterra Energy [CTRA]
- Devon Energy [DVN]
- Marathon Petroleum [MPC]
- Exxon Mobil [XOM]
- Valero Energy [VLO]
- Marathon Oil [MRO]
- Conoco Philips [COP]

You can also invest in Energy Sector ETFs such as:

- Van Eck Low Carbon Energy ETF [SMOG]
- First Trust Global Wind EFT [FAN]
- First Trust Nasdaq Clean Edge Green Energy ETF [QCLN]
- iShares Global Clean Energy ETF [CNRG]

GOLD

This market is diverse and has the potential to grow. Gold is used in jewelry, technology, and by central banks, which gives it its global appeal. Precious metals such as gold have always been a good hedge against inflation. As the dollar goes down, the price of gold goes up. Another thing that affects the price of gold that's more important than any other factor is that Central Banks [i.e., Federal Reserve Bank], which hold gold, massive amounts of it, one day might decide to diversity [as they say] their monetary reserves by buying more gold, affects the price of gold. But as you have read the "What is Money?" part in the intro of this book, you know that because central banks have all this gold, they dump cheap gold in the reserves onto the open market to suppress the rise of gold prices around the world, so fiat currency would rise. Pushing gold prices down is a monetary system scheme by Central Banks to continue controlling gold prices. Gold moves up in value based on other factors. Such as right now, "high inflation." Investing in gold can be done directly or indirectly, like crude oil. You can buy physical gold bullion bars or coins.

Some of these Physical gold purchasing companies are:

- Money Metals Exchange [www.moneymetals.com]
- APMEX (American Precious Metals Exchange) [www.apmex.com]
- JM Bullion [www.jmbullion.com]
- SD Bullion [www.sdbullion.com]
- BGASC [www.bgasc.com]
- Golden Eagle Coin [www.goldeneaglecoins.com]

Another way is through futures contracts when you must deposit an "initial margin." The thing about buying gold futures is that if the price rises, you will profit; if the price drops, you can lose your investment. A more in-depth look at futures will be in my next book, but you can check out these websites and Apps if you want to purchase future contracts for gold.

Best Future Brokers

- Ninjatrader.com
- Tickmill.com
- Tradovate.com
- Discounttrading.com

- OptimusFutures.com

- GenericTrade.com

- Tradestation.com

- TD Ameritrade [start.tdameritrade.com]

- Charles Schwab [schwab.com]

Gold can also be purchased by buying stocks in companies that deal with gold, or you can buy gold ETFs from off of stock exchanges. Here are some of the top precious metal companies and ETFs in this space:

- Southern Copper Corp. [SCCO]

- Franco Nevada Corp [FNV]

- Royal Gold, Inc. [RGLD]

- Newmount Corp [NEM]

- Agnico Eagle Mines, LTD [AEM]

- Barrick Gold [GOLD]

- Kinross Gold [KGC]

- Sibanye Stillwater [SBBW]

- Gold Resource [GORO]

- Osisko Gold Royalties [OR]

Commodities ETFs

- SPDR Gold Trust [GLD]

- iShares Silver Trust [SLV]

- Aberdeen Standard Physical Silver Shares ETF [SIVR]

- Aberdeen Standard Physical Palladium Share ETF [PALL]

- United States 12-Month Oil Fund [UN]

- United States 12-Month Natural Fund [UNL]

- Teucrium Corn Fund [CORN]

- Teucrium Soybean Fund [SOBY]

- Invesco DB Commodity Index Tracking Fund [DBC]

Other forms of commodities that are good investments include base metals, which are common metals used in commercial product industries such as construction and manufacturing. While relatively inexpensive, supply chains are stable because they can be found worldwide. You can invest by buying directly, but the best way is by holding stocks in companies that provide these base metals. Some of these base metal companies are:

- PolyMet Mining [PLM]
- Genesis Energy, LP [GEL]
- Solitario Exploration and Royalty Corp. [XPL]
- StoneX Group, Inc. [SNEX]
- Materion Corp. [MTRN]
- Hecla Mining Company [HL]

Commodity Investing is a great hedge against inflation, plus a perfect way to diversify your portfolio. All these stocks and ETFs can be purchased using traditional trading websites and apps, which were talked about at the top of this part. Keep in mind that there are other commodities like:

LITHIUM:
- Albemarle [ALB]
- Ganfeng Lithium [GNEN.F]
- Sociedad Quimica y Minera de Chile [SQM]
- Livent [LTHM]
- Lithium Americas [LAC]

Metal/Steel:
- Newmount Corp [NEM]
- Nucor [NUE]
- Rio Tinto [RIO]
- Freeport McMoran [FCX]
- Cleveland-Cliffs [CLF]
- Alcoa [AA]
- BHP Group [BHP]
- Sun Coke Energy, Inc. [SXC]
- Southern Copper Corp. [SCCO]
- Vale SA [VALE]

Energy EFTs:
- Energy Select Sector SPDR Fund [XLE]
- Vanguard Energy ETF [VDE]
- SPDR S&P
- Fidelity MSCI Energy Index ETF [FENY]
- iShares vs Energy ETF [IYE]

- SPDR S&P Oil and Gas Equipment and Services [XES]

Explore the commodity market to make big investments in this sector, which is poised to explode over the next few years. Also, a little news: Russia cut off the Natural Gas pipeline to Europe over the war in Ukraine. Right now, the Euro is under $1.00. The natural gas crisis is hurting all of Europe. The U.S.A. is the biggest natural gas producer in the world, so look at companies that develop natural gas and shipping companies that would have to ship natural gas on ships to Europe. It's about to be a big move in this market. There aren't many shipping companies in America that move natural gas around the world, so do your research because America is about to start shipping natural gas to Europe.

As this part on investing has shown you, investing in multiple areas allows you to have ownership across multiple sectors that put income into your pockets. Dividend Investing, MLPs, ETFs, Forex, options, the Metaverse, and Self-Directed IRAs are all some of the vehicles you must be involved in to position yourself for building wealth, now and once you are released. This shows you that nothing should be in your way to financial freedom. Align your objectives, make a plan, and execute!

CREDIT INDEX

- Inquiry Letter #1
- Inquiry Letter #2
- Inquiry Letter #3
- Inquiry Letter #4
- Credit Rebuilding Letters
- Annual Credit Report Request Form
- Sample Debt Validation Letter
- Sample Debt Validation Letter When No Response

Inquiry Letter #1

[Date]

Credit Reporting Agency/Bureau
City, State, Zip

RE: REQUEST FOR CREDIT REPORT

To Whom It May Concern:

Please send me a copy of my credit report. My identifying information is as follows:

Name:

SS#:

Address:

City, State, Zip:

Birthdates:

Past residences (last five years):

Former Name(s)

Enclosed is $_____ as payment for the credit report.

If you have any questions, please contact me at (XXX) XXX-XXXX.

Thank you.

Sincerely,

Bruce Smith

[Letter #1]

Inquiry Letter #2

[Date]

Credit Reporting Agency/Bureau
City, State, Zip

RE: REQUEST FOR FREE CREDIT REPORT

To Whom It May Concern:

My credit application was recently denied, and according to the attached letter that I received less than sixty days ago from the company that denied credit to me, your credit bureau issued the report that was used to determine my credit evaluation.

Section 609 [15 USC 1681g] of the Fair Credit Reporting Act of 1970 provides that your credit bureau should send me all information on file that led to my credit application being denied. According to the provisions of Section 612 (b) [15 USC 1681j (b)], there should be no charge for this information.

Please send my credit report to the address below. The attached letter details additional information identifying my account.

If you have any questions or need additional information, please contact me at address noted below.

Thank you.

Sincerely,

Bruce Smith
Address
City, State, Zip
Social Security #

[Letter #2]

Inquiry Letter #3

[Date]

Credit Reporting Agency/Bureau
City, State, Zip

RE: DELETIONS TO CREDIT REPORT

To Whom It May Concern:

I received a copy of my credit report and am disputing some items that need to be deleted. I have highlighted and numbered these disputed items on the attached copy. The reasons why these items should be deleted are indicated below:

Item #   Reason for Deletion

According to the provisions of the Fair Credit Reporting Act § 611(a) [15 USC 1681i(a)], these disputed items must be reinvestigated or deleted from my credit record within 30 days. During the investigation period, these items must be removed from my credit report as the mere reporting of items prior to debt validation constitutes collection activity. I am also requesting the names, addresses and telephone numbers of individuals you contacted during your investigation.

Please notify me that the above items have been deleted pursuant to § 611 (a)(6) [15 USC § 1681j (a) (6)]. I am also requesting an updated copy of my credit report, which should be sent to the address listed below. According to the provisions of § 612 [15 USC § 1681j], there should be no charge for this report.

If you have any questions or need additional information, please contact me at address noted below.

Thank you.

Sincerely,

Bruce Smith
Address
City, State, Zip
Social Security #

[Letter #3]

Inquiry Letter #4

[Date]

Credit Reporting Agency/Bureau
City, State, Zip

RE: CORRECTIONS TO CREDIT REPORT

To Whom It May Concern:

I received a copy of my credit report and am disputing some items that need to be corrected. I have highlighted and numbered these disputed items on the attached copy. The reasons why these items should be corrected are indicated below:

Item #   Reason for Correction

According to the provisions of the Fair Credit Reporting Act § 611(a) [15 USC 1681i(a)], these disputed items must be reinvestigated or deleted from my credit record within 30 days. In the interim, these items should be noted on my credit record as "in dispute." I am also requesting the names, addresses and telephone numbers of individuals you contacted so that I may follow up.

If it is determined through your investigation that the disputed items are inaccurate, please correct my file and send me notification that the information has been updated or deleted. I am requesting an updated copy of my credit report, which should be sent to the address listed below. According to the provisions of § 612 [15 USC § 1681j], there should be no charge for this report.

If you have any questions or need additional information, please contact me at address noted below.

Thank you.

Sincerely,

Bruce Smith
Address
City, State, Zip
Social Security #

[Letter #4]

Credit Rebuilding Letters

[Date]

Credit Reporting Agency/Bureau
City, State, Zip

RE: FAILURE TO RESPOND TO DELTETION/CORRECTION LETTER

To Whom It May Concern:

On [insert date of first letter], I sent a letter requesting that you reinvestigate or delete disputed items from my credit report as well as place temporarily remove these items from my report during the investigation period. As of this date, you have failed to respond to my request. A copy of my original letter is attached for your review.

The law stipulates that you must investigate within 30 days of receiving my letter and respond within 5 days of completing your investigation. You have not followed the stipulations of the law.

I may suffer damages because I need to rely on an accurate and complete statement of my credit record and demand that you remove the disputed items from my report immediately as you failed to comply with the law. Otherwise, I will contact the Federal Trade Commission and advise them of your apparent disregard for consumer protection laws.

If you have any questions or need additional information, please contact me at the address noted below.

Thank you.

Sincerely,

Bruce Smith
Address
City, State, Zip
Social Security #

[Letter #5]

[Date]

CRA
City, State, Zip

RE: ADDITIONS TO CREDIT REPORT

To Whom It May Concern:

While reviewing a copy my credit report, I discovered that some of my credit references are not included but have been reported. Please add the following accounts along with my credit history as evidenced by the attached letter from the merchant to my credit report.

Merchant Name   Merchant #   Account #

I am requesting an updated copy of my credit report, which should be sent to the address listed below. According to the provisions of § 612 [15 USC § 1681j] of the Fair Credit Reporting Act, there should be no charge for this report because it currently is incomplete.

If you have any questions or need additional information, please contact me at the address listed below.

Thank you for your prompt attention to this matter.

Sincerely,

Bruce Smith
Address
City, State, Zip
Social Security #

[Letter #6]

[Date]

Credit Reporting Agency/Bureau
City, State, Zip

RE: UNAUTHORIZED INQUIRY

To Whom It May Concern:

I reviewed a copy of my credit report and [company name] ran an unauthorized credit inquiry on me on [date].

I never authorized such action and this constitutes a violation of my rights under the Fair Credit Reporting Act §604 as well as a violation of my rights to privacy. Please contact [company name] and investigate such occurrence.

I am requesting an updated copy of my credit report, which should be sent to the address listed below. According to the provisions of § 612 [15 USC § 1681j], there should be no charge for this report. In addition, as part of your investigation, please send the names, business address and phone numbers of those who made unauthorized credit inquiries so I may contact them directly.

If you have any questions or need additional information, please contact me at address listed below.

Thank you.

Sincerely,

Bruce Smith
Address
City, State, Zip
Social Security #

[Letter #7]

[Date]

Credit Reporting Agency/Bureau
City, State, Zip

RE: FRIVOLOUS LETTER REJECTION

To Whom It May Concern:

I am in receipt of your letter stating that my dispute of items in my credit report was "irrelevant and frivolous." I am upset that your credit reporting agency would try such a blatant stall tactic. I am demanding that you reinvestigate my credit file under the Fair Credit Reporting Act Section 611 [15 USC 1681I]. You have no way to ascertain the legitimacy of my action without investigating the items in question.

Enclosed is a copy of my original letter and credit report with the disputed items highlighted. Additional stall tactics on the part of your organization will be reported to the Federal Trade Commission.

If you have any questions, please contact me at the address listed below.

Thank you.

Sincerely,

Bruce Smith
Address
City, State, Zip
Social Security #

[Letter #8]

[Date]

CRA
City, State, Zip

RE: CONSUMER STATEMENT FOR DISPUTED ITEMS FOLLOWING
INVESTIGATION

To Whom It May Concern:

Your reinvestigation has not resolved my dispute regarding the accuracy and completeness of the
highlighted items on my attached credit report. According to the Fair Credit Reporting Act, §
611(b) [USC 15 1681i(b)], I am entitled to "file a statement setting forth the nature of the
dispute." I would like potential future creditors to be aware of the dispute, and want the
following statement included in my credit report:

[Consumer statement---100 words or less]

I am requesting an updated copy of my credit report which should be sent to the address listed
below. According to the provisions of § 612 [15 USC § 1681j], there should be no charge for
this report.

If you have any questions or need additional information, please contact me at the address listed
below.

Thank you.

Sincerely,

Bruce Smith
Address
City, State, Zip
Social Security #

[Letter #9]

[Date]

Credit Reporting Agency/Bureau
City, State, Zip

RE: CONSUMER STATEMENT FOR DISPUTED ITEMS

To Whom It May Concern:

According to the Fair Credit Reporting Act, § 611(b) [USC 15 1681i(b)], I am entitled to "file a statement setting forth the nature of the dispute." I would like potential future creditors to be aware of the dispute, and want the following statement included in my credit report.

[Consumer statement---100 words or less]

I am requesting an updated copy of my credit report, which should be sent to the address listed below. According to the provisions of § 612 [15 USC § 1681j], there should be no charge for this report.

If you have any questions or need additional information, please contact me at (XXX) XXX-XXXX.

Thank you.

Sincerely,

Bruce Smith
Address
City, State, Zip
Social Security #

[Letter #10]

[Date]

Credit Reporting Agency/Bureau
City, State, Zip

RE: CONSUMER STATEMENT TO MAKE CREDIT FILE COMPLETE

To Whom It May Concern:

According to the Fair Credit Reporting Act, § 611(b) [USC 15 1681i(b)], I am entitled to enter a consumer statement in my credit report so that the information is complete and the credit reporting process is fair and equitable to me. I would like the following statement to be made a part of my permanent record so that potential future creditors will be aware of certain circumstances that caused negative credit information.

[Consumer statement-100 words or less]

If you have any questions or need additional information, please contact me at the address listed below.

Thank you.

Sincerely,

Bruce Smith
Address
City, State, Zip
Social Security #

[Letter #11]

[Date]

Credit Reporting Agency/Bureau
City, State, Zip

RE: BANKRUPTCY ACCOUNTS NOT IDENTIFIED

To Whom It May Concern:

I received a copy of my credit report and the items listed below were included in my bankruptcy but are not identified as such on my credit report. Please see the attached copy of the credit report with these item numbers written next to the problem entries as well as a copy of my court documents which lists the creditors included in my bankruptcy.

According to the provisions of the Fair Credit Reporting Act § 611(a) [15 USC 1681i(a)], these disputed items must updated to reflect discharge in bankruptcy.

I am requesting an updated copy of my credit report, which should be sent to the address listed below. According to the provisions of § 612 [15 USC § 1681j], there should be no charge for this report.

If you have any questions or need additional information, please contact me at the address listed below.

Thank you.

Sincerely,

Bruce Smith
Address
City, State, Zip
Social Security #

[Letter #12]

[Date]

Credit Reporting Agency/Bureau
City, State, Zip

RE: REQUEST TO UPDATE FOR COMPLETENESS OF ACCOUNT HISTORY

To Whom It May Concern:

I received a copy of my credit report and am disputing information concerning my payment history. Accordingly, I am requesting that you investigate my dispute and add the attached history of payments to my credit file under the Fair Credit Reporting Act, § 611(a) [15 USC 1681i (a)].

I am requesting an updated copy of my credit report, which should be sent to the address listed below. According to the provisions of § 612 [15 USC § 1681j], there should be no charge for this report. Additionally, if you contact any entity (person or company) in order to make the necessary updates, please provide the names, business address and telephone numbers so that I may follow up directly if needed.

If you have any questions or need additional information, please contact me at the address listed below.

Thank you.

Sincerely,

Bruce Smith
Address
City, State, Zip
Social Security #

[Letter #13]

[Date]

Credit Reporting Agency/Bureau
City, State, Zip

RE: MAILING-LIST RESTRICTIONS

To Whom It May Concern:

I do not wish to have my name, address, telephone number, credit file or other information sold or traded with any marketers. In addition, please do not allow credit issuers to prescreen my credit file for credit offers.

I am requesting that all information about me and my accounts remain private. I want my name, address and credit data excluded from your marketing lists.

Thank you for your assistance with this matter.

Sincerely,

Bruce Smith
Address
City, State, Zip
Social Security #

[Letter #14]

[Date]

Creditor   *****SENT VIA CERTIFIED MAIL*****
City, State, Zip

RE: **REPAYMENT AGREEMENT FOR ACCOUNT**

Dear [name]:

Thank you for speaking with me on [date] regarding my account. As discussed, I have been prompt in paying in the past, but have recently been late due to the following circumstance(s):

I am requesting an amended repayment agreement until my financial situation improves. I would like to pay $[amount] for the next [number] payment periods. After that time, I agree to resume making my full monthly payments.

I understand that during this time I will not be using any credit with [company name].

If my situation changes, I will contact you immediately.

Thank you for your understanding and assistance with this matter. If you have any questions or need additional information, please contact me at the address listed below.

Sincerely,

Bruce Smith
Address
City, State, Zip

[Letter #15]

[Date]

Creditor   *****SENT VIA CERTIFIED MAIL*****
City, State, Zip

RE: NOTICE OF OVERDUE ACCOUNT

Dear [name]:

I am aware that my account (#) is overdue, but I have been unable to make payments in a timely manner due to the following circumstances:

My financial difficulties are temporary. I can make a payment by [date]. I will be able to resume my regular payments as of [date]. During this modification period, I respectfully ask that you do not report my payments as late to the credit reporting repositories.

I appreciate you working with me during this difficult time. Your cooperation and understanding is greatly appreciated.

If you have any questions or need additional information, please contact me at the address listed below.

Sincerely,

Bruce Smith
Address
City, State, Zip

[Letter #16]

[Date]

Creditor   *****SENT VIA CERTIFIED MAIL*****
City, State, Zip

RE: REDUCED-PAYMENT REQUEST FOR ACCOUNT

Dear [name]:

I am currently experiencing financial difficulties because [reason].

I have examined my finances and developed a careful budget that includes payment to each creditor.

In order to provide for my necessary expenses, I am requesting that each creditor accept a reduced payment until my situation improves with the full understanding that the reduced payment is temporary. In place of my regular payment of [amount], I am requesting that you accept payment of [amount] each month.

I am making every effort to correct my financial situation and expect things to be resolved as of [date]. Until I resume my regular repayments, I will not incur any new debt obligation.

Upon your approval, I will immediately remit my first reduced payment.

Thank you for your understanding and cooperation during this difficult time.

If you have any questions or need additional information, please contact me at address listed below.

Sincerely,

Bruce Smith
Address
City, State, Zip

[Letter #17]

[Date]

Creditor   *****SENT VIA CERTIFIED MAIL*****
City, State, Zip

RE: REQUEST FOR CEASING PHONE CALLS

Dear [name]:

I have been receiving telephone calls from you concerning my account #. As you have been informed repeatedly, I cannot pay the bill at this time.

Under 15 USCA 1692 c of the Fair Debt Collection Practices Act, this is my formal notice for you to cease all telephone calls except for those permitted by federal law. I am not cutting off communication with your company but rather reduce all communication to writing.

Sincerely,

Bruce Smith
Address
City, State, Zip

[Letter #18]

[Date]

Creditor   *****SENT VIA CERTIFIED MAIL*****
City, State, Zip

RE: PROPOSAL TO SETTLE ACCOUNT

Dear [name]:

Based on our recent discussions, you are aware that I am in financial difficulties because of [reason] and am not currently able to make payments on my account.

My income barely covers my living expenses, and I have no assets to sell in order to pay you or my other creditors.

I am committed to paying this debt and am willing to offer a settlement of $_____ as payment in full.

Additionally, I ask that you report this account as "paid in full" and "paid as agreed" all major credit reporting agencies. I know you have discretion to report as you deem appropriate so long as consistent with federal law. If you agree to these conditions, please notify me in writing and I will immediately facilitate payment.

If you have any questions, please contact me at the address listed below.

Thank you.

Sincerely,

Bruce Smith
Address
City, State, Zip

[Letter #19]

[Date]

President
Company
City, State, Zip

RE: UNAUTHORIZED CREDIT INQUIRY

Dear [President's name]

I recently discovered that your company ran an unauthorized report on me on [date]. I did not authorize such an inquiry and demand that you contact [name of credit reporting agency] immediately and have your inquiry deleted from my credit file. You do not have a permissible purpose to pull my credit report hence invaded my right to privacy and may subject to a fine.

If you have any questions, please contact me at the address listed below.

Thank you for your prompt attention to this matter.

Sincerely,

Bruce Smith
Address
City, State, Zip

[Letter #20]

[Date]

Federal Trade Commission
Consumer Response Center
600 Pennsylvania Ave., NW
Washington, DC 20580

RE: CREDIT COMPLAINT LETTER

To Whom It May Concern:

I am writing to file a complaint against [creditor or credit reporting agency].

[Explain situation including name and telephone numbers of people you have spoken to]

Over the past several months, I have tried to resolve this issue, but to no avail. Enclosed is documentation regarding my dealings with [company] to date.

I am requesting your assistance in putting an end to this matter. If you have any questions or need additional information, please contact me at the address listed below.

Thank you for your assistance.

Sincerely,

Bruce Smith
Address
City, State, Zip

[Letter #21]

[Date]

Federal Trade Commission
Consumer Response Center
600 Pennsylvania Ave., NW
Washington, DC 20580

RE: PREDATORY LENDING COMPLAINT

To Whom It May Concern:

I am writing to file a complaint against [Loan Company] because of their predatory lending practices.

[Explain situation including name and telephone numbers of people you have spoken to]

I am requesting that you investigate this company and take any appropriate regulatory action, including any necessary referrals to state agencies. It is important that we put an end to these types of deceptive and unethical business practices.

If you have any questions or need additional information, please contact me at the address listed below.

Thank you for your assistance.

Sincerely,

Bruce Smith
Address
City, State, Zip

[Letter 22]

[Date]

[Credit Repository Agency]
Security Freeze
[Address]

RE: CREDIT FREEZE

Dear [Repository]:

I respectfully request a credit freeze on my credit file. My name is [your name].

My former name was (if applicable).

My current address is listed below. My former address was [former address].

My social security number is [social security number].

My date of birth is [date of birth].

I have enclosed photocopies of my state issued identification along with proof of current residence. (Utility bill will suffice).

I have enclosed a fee of $_____ for this service (Please check your state credit freeze laws to determine fee).

Or

I am victim of identity theft and have attached a copy of the investigative report from my local law enforcement agency. Per the laws of the state of [state], I do not have to render a fee for the aforementioned freeze request.

Thank you for your assistance.

Sincerely,

Bruce Smith
Address
City, State, Zip

[Letter 23]

[Date]

[Debt Collector Name]   *****SENT VIA CERTIFIED MAIL*****
[Address]

RE: VALIDATION OF ACCOUNT
      Account #: [Acct #]

To Whom It May Concern,

I neither affirm, nor deny this purported debt. You claim I owe your company [$].

This letter is being sent to you in response to an entry made on my Credit Report dated [date]. Please be advised that this is not a refusal to pay the debt, but a notice sent pursuant to the Fair Debt Collection Practices Act, 1: USC 1692g Sec 809 (b) that your claim that I owe you money is disputed, and validation is requested.

Under the Fair Debt Collections Practices Act, I have the right to request validation of the debt you say I owe you. I am requesting proof that I am the correct party, and there is some contractual obligation which is binding on me to pay this debt. This is NOT a request for "verification" via E-Oscar or proof of my mailing address, but a request for VALIDATION made pursuant to the above named Title and Section of the Fair Debt Collection Practices Act.

Reporting inaccurate and unsubstantiated information to a credit reporting agency may constitute fraud under federal law. Compliance with this request is required under the laws of state and federal statutes.

Debt validation includes the following:

1. Who was the original creditor on this account, and what was the account number?
2. What was the original amount owed? Please provide a complete payment history, starting with the original creditor.
3. Please provide me documentation that indicates that I agreed to pay someone this sum of money.
4. What was the original date of delinquency for this account?
5. Agreement that grants you the authority to collect on this alleged debt, or proof of acquisition by assignment.
6. What did you pay for this account, and how did you calculate the current amount owed?

I require compliance with the terms and conditions of this letter within 30 days of your certified receipt, or a complete removal from my credit profile, in writing, of your claim. In the event of noncompliance, I reserve the right to file charges and/or complaints with the FTC, and appropriate county, state, and federal authorities. I also hereby reserve my right to take private civil action against your company to recover damages.

In addition, the Fair Credit Reporting Act states that while this item is being investigated you must indicate to the bureau that the account is under dispute and will remove/cease from reporting this information to the Credit Reporting Agency until full validation has been completed.

I have sent a copy of this request for validation to the three national Credit Reporting Agencies to begin their 30-day investigational process concurrent with your investigation.

Sincerely,

Bruce Smith
Address
City, State, Zip

CC: TransUnion, Equifax, Experian

[Letter 24]

In addition, the Fair Credit Reporting Act states that while this item is being investigated you must indicate to the bureau that the account is under dispute and will remove/cease from reporting this information to the Credit Reporting Agency until full validation has been completed.

I have sent a copy of this request for validation to the three national Credit Reporting Agencies to begin their 30-day investigational process concurrent with your investigation.

Sincerely,

Bruce Smith
Address
City, State, Zip

CC: TransUnion, Equifax, Experian

[Letter 24]

[Date]

Bruce Smith
Address
City, State, Zip

RE: TERMS AGREEMENT
        (Debt collector acct #/ reference original acct #)

Dear Mr. Smith:

In regards to our verbal agreement to accept settlement of the amount owing on the above
described account, please accept this letter as our acceptance of the terms listed below once we
have received your payment.

TERMS:

1.   [Debt collector name] agrees to accept [$xxx.xx] as payment in full for debt originally
     owned by [original collector] [original account #] listed under [debt collector
     name/account number].

2.   [Debt collector name] agrees to report this tradeline to the three main Credit
     Repositories/Bureaus as a "Zero Balance" and "Paid as Agreed" account.

3.   [Debt collector name] will not give this tradeline any new account number, resell this
     debt or any remaining balance to any other party, re-age the or change the original date of
     delinquency for this account, or change the reporting status after the terms of the
     agreement have been met other than the agreement listed in #2 above.

4.   *(Note to consumer, negotiate for this #4 if possible, however if successful, you will not
     need terms #2 and #3. Make sure you leave enough time for your delivery method)*

     [Debt collector name] will remove the account in its entirety as it was reported in error.

This payment must be received by [debt collector] within __ business days of this letter at the
address listed below.

Sincerely,

Debt Collector
(Name/title of individual making decision)
Address
City, State

[Letter #25]

[Your full name]
[Credit report number]
[Identifying information requested by credit bureau, typically including:
- Date of birth
- Address
- Telephone number]
[Return address, if different from your registered address on your credit report]
[Optional: Social Security number or driver's license number]

[Date]

[Credit bureau's address—one of the following:
    Equifax Information Services, LLC, P.O. Box 740256, Atlanta, GA 30374
    Experian, P.O. Box 4500, Allen, TX 75013
    TransUnion Consumer Solutions, P.O. Box 2000, Chester, PA 19016]

Re: Disputing a medical collection account on my credit report

Dear [Equifax, Experian, or TransUnion],

I am writing to request the investigation and correction of a medical bill that appears on my credit report. The credit report number is **[report number]**. The medical bill is listed under account number **[account number]**, and the account was opened on **[opening date]** by **[name of debt collection agency]**.

The original owner of this debt is **[name of healthcare provider]**. The account reflects an alleged debt of **[amount owed]** for charges incurred on **[billing date for medical services]**.

This medical collection is **[inaccurate/incomplete/obsolete]** because **[describe which information is inaccurate or incomplete or why it should be deleted (e.g., the medical bill was paid by insurance or is more than seven years old)]**. I am requesting that the item **[be removed or otherwise changed]** to correct the information.

I have enclosed copies of my credit report with the disputed information highlighted. I have also attached **[any other supporting documents, such as payment records and court documents]** to support my dispute.

Please reinvestigate this medical collection and **[delete/correct]** it as soon as possible. Thank you for your attention to this matter.

Sincerely,

[Your Name]

Enclosures: **[List documents you are enclosing (e.g., a copy of your credit report)]**

Annual Credit Report Request Form

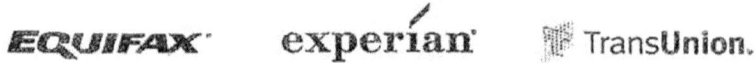

EQUIFAX   **experían**   **TransUnion.**

Annual Credit Report Request Form

You have the right to get a free copy of your credit file disclosure, commonly called a credit report, once every 12 months, from each of the nationwide consumer credit reporting companies - Equifax, Experian and TransUnion.

For instant access to your free credit report, visit www.annualcreditreport.com.

For more information on obtaining your free credit report, visit www.annualcreditreport.com or call 877-322-8228.

Use this form if you prefer to write to request your credit report from any, or all, of the nationwide consumer credit reporting companies. The following information is required to process your request. Omission of any information may delay your request.

Once complete, fold (do not staple or tape), place into a #10 envelope, affix required postage and mail to:

Annual Credit Report Request Service P.O. Box 105281 Atlanta, GA 30348-5281.

Please use a Black or Blue Pen and write your responses in PRINTED CAPITAL LETTERS without touching the sides of the boxes like the examples listed below:

A B C D E F G H I J K L M N O P Q R S T U V W X Y Z   0 1 2 3 4 5 6 7 8 9

Social Security Number:

Date of Birth: Month / Day / Year

— Fold Here —   Fold Here

First Name   M.I.

Last Name   JR, SR, III, etc.

Current Mailing Address:

House Number   Street Name

Apartment Number / Private Mailbox   For Puerto Rico Only: Print Urbanization Name

City   State   ZipCode

Previous Mailing Address (complete only if at current mailing address for less than two years):

House Number   Street Name

— Fold Here —   Fold Here

Apartment Number / Private Mailbox   For Puerto Rico Only: Print Urbanization Name

City   State   ZipCode

Shade Circle Like This → ●

Not Like This → ⊗ ⊘

I want a credit report from (shade each that you would like to receive):
○ Equifax
○ Experian
○ TransUnion

○ Shade here if, for security reasons, you want your credit report to include no more than the last four digits of your Social Security Number.

If additional information is needed to process your request, the consumer credit reporting company will contact you by mail.

Your request will be processed within 15 days of receipt and then mailed to you.

Copyright 2004, Central Source LLC

31238

G-1

Sample Debt Validation Letter

Sample Debt Validation Letter

(Send via certified mail, return receipt requested)

Date:

Your Name
Your Address
Your City, State, Zip

Collection Agency Name
Collection Agency Address
Collection Agency City, State, Zip

RE: Account # (Fill in Account Number)

To Whom It May Concern:

Be advised this is not a refusal to pay, but a notice that your claim is disputed and validation is requested. Under the *Fair Debt collection Practices Act (FDCPA)*, I have the right to request validation of the debt you say I owe you. I am requesting proof that I am indeed the party you are asking to pay this debt, and there is some contractual obligation that is binding on me to pay this debt.

This is NOT a request for "verification" or proof of my mailing address, but a request for VALIDATION made pursuant to 15 USC 1692g Sec. 809 (b) of the FDCPA. I respectfully request that your offices provide me with competent evidence that I have any legal obligation to pay you.

At this time I will also inform you that if your offices have or continue to report invalidated information to any of the three major credit bureaus (Equifax, Experian, Trans Union), this action might constitute fraud under both federal and state laws. Due to this fact, if any negative mark is found or continues to report on any of my credit reports by your company or the company you represent, I will not hesitate in bringing legal action against you and your client for the following: Violation of the Fair Debt Collection Practices Act *and* Defamation of Character.

I am sure your legal staff will agree that non-compliance with this request could put your company in serious legal trouble with the FTC and other state or federal agencies.

If your offices are able to provide the proper documentation as requested in the following declaration, I will require 30 days to investigate this information and during such time all collection activity must cease and desist. Also, during this validation period, if any action is taken which could be considered detrimental to any of my credit reports, I will consult with legal counsel for suit. This includes any listing of any information to a credit-reporting repository that could be inaccurate or invalidated. If your offices fail to respond to this validation request within 30 days from the date of your receipt, all references to this account must be deleted and completely removed from my credit file and a copy of such deletion request shall be sent to me immediately.

It would be advisable that you and your client assure that your records are in order before I am forced to take legal action.

CREDITOR/DEBT COLLECTOR DECLARATION

Please provide the following:

• Agreement with your client that grants you the authority to collect on this alleged debt.
• Agreement that bears the signature of the alleged debtor wherein he/she agreed to pay the creditor.
• Any insurance claims been made by any creditor regarding this account.
• Any Judgments obtained by any creditor regarding this account.
• Name and address of alleged creditor.
• Name on file of alleged debtor.
• Alleged account number.
• Address on file for alleged debtor.
• Amount of alleged debt.
• Date this alleged debt became payable.
• Date of original charge off or delinquency.
• Verification that this debt was assigned or sold to collector.
• Complete accounting of alleged debt.
• Commission for debt collector if collection efforts are successful.

Please provide the name and address of the bonding agent for «COLLECTIONAGENCY» in case legal action becomes necessary. Your claim cannot and WILL NOT be considered if any portion of the above is not completed and returned with copies of all requested documents. This is a request for validation made pursuant to the Fair Debt Collection Practices Act. Please allow 30 days for processing after I receive this information back.

Best Regards

[Your Signature]

cc Federal Trade Commission

[Your Letterhead]

Dear [name of infringer]

It has come to my attention that you have made an unauthorized use of my copyrighted work entitled [name of work] (the "Work") in the preparation of a work derived therefrom. I have reserved all rights in the Work, which was first published on [date] in [name of publication][, and I have registered the copyright].

Your work entitled [name of infringing work] and which appears [where infringing work has appeared] is essentially identical to the Work and clearly used the Work as its basis.

You neither asked for nor received permission to use the Work as the basis for [name of infringing work] nor to make or distribute copies of it. Therefore, I believe you have willfully infringed my rights under 17 U.S.C. Section 101 et seq. and could be liable for statutory damages as high as $150,000 as set forth in Section 504(c)(2) therein.

I demand that you immediately cease the use and distribution of all infringing works derived from the Work, and all copies, including electronic copies, of same, that you deliver to me, if applicable, all unused, undistributed copies of same, or destroy such copies immediately and that you desist from this or any other infringement of my rights in the future.

If I have not received an affirmative response from you by [date] indicating that you have fully complied with these requirements, I shall consider taking any and all legal remedies available to rectify this situation.

Sincerely,

(Your Name)

Important Notice: This is a sample form for illustrative purposes. This sample may not be suitable for your particular circumstances and different agreements or legal arrangements may be necessary depending on your jurisdiction. Therefore, you should not use this sample, or any part, without the advice of competent legal counsel.

Sample Debt Validation Letter When No Response

Debt Validation when there is no response from debt collector.

Your Name
Your Address
City, State 12345

Debt Collector
Address
Not My Town, NJ 08002

July 18, 2012

RE: Dispute Letter of 05/15/12

Dear Sir/Madame:

I have not heard back from you nor have I received validation from your company in over 30 days regarding my registered notice of dispute dated 05/15/12. You have also not supplied the demanded proof of the alleged debt.

For the record, I state again that as I have no account with you, nor am I your customer, nor have I entered into a contract with you, I must ask to attach copies for the following information in addition to the form provided at the end of this letter:

- Agreement with your company that grants you the authority to collect on this alleged debt
- Account history including beginning balance, every payment received and date it was posted to the account, any fees charged to the account, interest and interest rate charged to the account, along with any other account information you may have available.
- Agreement that bears my signature that supports I agreed to the creditor.
- Any insurance claims which have been made by any creditor regarding this account
- Any judgments which have been obtained by any creditor regarding this account

You have fifteen (15) days from receipt of this notice to respond. Your failure to respond in a timely manner, will work as a waiver to any and all of your claims in this matter, and will entitle me to presume that you sent your letter(s) in error. If in fact this error has been made, remove the trade line from my credit files and this matter is permanently closed.

Failure to respond within 15 days of receipt of this registered letter or failure of the removal of the incorrect information from my credit reports will force me to consider legal action in a small claims action against your company.

This Notice is an attempt to correct your records, and any information received from you will be collected as evidence should any further action be necessary. This is a request for information only, and is not a statement, election, or waiver of status.

I affirm under penalty of perjury under the Laws of United States of America, that the foregoing is true and correct, to the best of my knowledge and belief.

Sincerely,

Your Name

ABOUT THE AUTHOR

C.A. Knuckles is currently incarcerated in Maryland. He has built Pro Se Prisoner into the go-to financial literacy publishing brand. This new book series, Pro se Prisoner: Guide to Build Wealth, is the follow-up to his successful Pro se Prisoner: How to Buy Stocks and Bitcoin. Mr. Knuckles' goal is to help prisoners build wealth and learn about finances by giving them the knowledge to succeed while in prison. If you have questions or ideas or need advice about business-related matters, including investments, please contact him through his investment company.

The Attic Group, LLC

1 East Chase Street, Suite #1101

Baltimore, Maryland 21202

Mr. Knuckles would love to get your feedback about the book, make suggestions for the next one, or just let him know you liked it. Write to the above address. First, Becoming wealthy requires changing your mindset, obtaining knowledge, and taking action! Thanks for becoming a Pro se Prisoner!

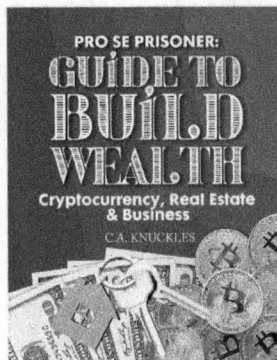

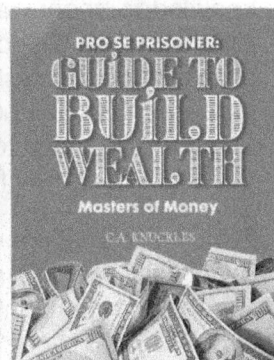

FREEBIRD PUBLISHERS

Thanks for your interest in Freebird Publishers!

We value our customers and would love to hear from you! Reviews are an important part in bringing you quality publications. We love hearing from our readers-rather it's good or bad (though we strive for the best)!

If you could take the time to review/rate any publication you've purchased with Freebird Publishers we would appreciate it!

If your loved one uses Amazon, have them post your review on the books you've read. This will help us tremendously, in providing future publications that are even more useful to our readers and growing our business.

Amazon works off of a 5 star rating system. When having your loved one rate us be sure to give them your chosen star number as well as a written review. Though written reviews aren't required, we truly appreciate hearing from you.

Sample Review Received on Inmate Shopper

poeticsunshine

☆☆☆☆☆ **Truly a guide**

Reviewed in the United States on June 29, 2023

Verified Purchase

This book is a powerhouse of information. My son had to calm/ground himself to prioritize where to start.

Freebird Publishers